Should Auld Acquaintance

SHOULD AULD ACQUAINTANCE

DISCOVERING *the* WOMAN BEHIND ROBERT BURNS

MELANIE MURRAY

NIGHTWOOD EDITIONS

2017

Nightwood Editions
P.O. Box 1779
Gibsons, BC von 1vo
Canada
www.nightwoodeditions.com

Cover design: TopShelf Creative
Typography: Carleton Wilson

Nightwood Editions acknowledges financial support from
the Government of Canada through the Canada Book Fund and
the Canada Council for the Arts, and from the Province of British Columbia
through the British Columbia Arts Council and the Book Publisher's Tax Credit.

This book has been produced on 100% post-consumer recycled,
ancient-forest-free paper, processed chlorine-free
and printed with vegetable-based dyes.

Printed and bound in Canada.

CIP data available from Library and Archives Canada.

ISBN 978-0-88971-328-4

for Damian and Gabriel

"Biography" meant a book about someone's life. Only, for me, it was to become a kind of pursuit, a tracking of the physical trail of someone's path through the past, a following of footsteps. You would never catch them; no, you would never quite catch them. But maybe, if you were lucky you might write about the pursuit of that fleeting figure in such a way as to bring it alive in the present.

—Richard Holmes, *Footsteps: Adventures of a Romantic Biographer*

…an act of redress on behalf of the millions and millions of women stuffed and crammed into graveyards who might well have never been born for all anyone knows about them.

—Nuala O'Faolain, *The Story of Chicago May*

TABLE OF CONTENTS

Prologue

May 2010

THE GRAVE LAY BEHIND THE PARISH CHURCH NOT FAR FROM the iron gateway to the street. A blue oval plaque identified it as *Burns' Four Children*. A square of off-white granite, mottled with moss and lichen, bore the inscription:

> *In memory of the infant children of the poet Robert Burns*
> *   and Jean Armour*
> *Jean, born 3rd Sept 1786, died at the age of 14 months*
> *Twin daughters, born 3rd March 1788, died a few days later*
> *Elizabeth Riddell Burns, born 21st Nov 1792, died Sept 1795*

Squatting on the grass, I gazed up to the second-storey window of the room in the red sandstone building my son and I had just visited—where Robert Burns and Jean Armour had lived for a short time after they married in 1788. It had a curtained box-bed covered in a grey-black patchwork quilt, a hooded cradle, and a couple of wooden armchairs. The narrow window looked out upon the graveyard. There were no other visitors, not even a curator about; it felt eerily quiet as I sat in the low armchair by the hearth, a cast-iron kettle hanging over the polished grate. I closed my eyes, felt suspended in time, as if the past was merging with the present. And for the first time, I thought about Jean Armour, born and raised here in Mauchline, a village in east Ayrshire where she met and married Robert Burns. I knew little about her. What would it have been like to be married to the philandering, dissolute, impoverished poet?

Our trip to Mauchline hadn't been planned. I'd been touring the Scottish Highlands with my twenty-seven-year-old son for a couple of weeks, researching our Murray ancestry for a memoir I was writing about my nephew who'd been killed three years earlier while serving with the Canadian military in Afghanistan. I wanted the book to create meaning out of his life and death, hoping it would help our family deal with his loss. With my research completed a couple of days before our flight home, we drove down to Ayrshire—Burns country. I wanted to see the cottage in Alloway where Scotland's most famous son was born in 1759.

That morning as we were leaving our B&B, carpeted throughout in red wool tartan, the proprietor suggested Mauchline as another Burns site of interest. It was a short drive, about ten miles from Alloway, so my son reluctantly indulged my desire to visit this one last place. He'd had enough of sightseeing. Alloway was crawling with tourists, and the authenticity of the experience was totally nullified with Burns's face plastered on street signs and on mugs, t-shirts, and napkins in the souvenir shops lining the main street.

But Mauchline was different. We had to search out the Burns House Museum on a narrow back street. Walking down the cobblestone close felt like stepping back through the centuries. The past still breathed in the red sandstone buildings and high stone walls, and in Jean and Robert's room with its plank floor and wood-beamed ceiling.

We viewed the rest of the museum with its display cases of Burns paraphernalia. One item caught my eye: a sepia-toned paper with the signature of Jean Armour near the ragged bottom edge. Though the ink was faded, her script was clear and even. I was pleased to discover this first important clue about her life: she may have been literate, not necessarily the norm for women in late eighteenth-century Scotland.

As we were about to exit the museum, a portly grey-haired man in a brown wool cardigan shuffled out of a small office. "Have ye been to the kirkyard yet?" he asked in a broad Ayrshire accent. "Their bairns are buried in the corner there, just after you climb the stairs." Pointing out the door, he handed me a pamphlet, *A Guide to Mauchline Kirkyard.* "A lot of Burns's friends are buried there too."

Kneeling at the two-century-old grave—identified in the guide as *The Armour Burial Ground*—I shook my head, unable to fathom what Jean Armour would have suffered with these deaths. Having witnessed the maternal grief that had crushed my sister in the past three years, I couldn't imagine how a mother could survive the anguish of losing four of her children.

As we drove out of the village, many questions swirled in my head. Who was Jean Armour? What kind of life did she have with Robert Burns? What happened to her daughters? What became of her and their five young sons after Burns died in poverty at age thirty-seven?

Those questions, along with that small second-floor room and the grave of the four baby girls, preoccupied me. Jean Armour seemed like so many of the faceless wives of famous men, never acknowledged for their roles in their great men's achievements.

And the central fact of her life, falling in love with a poet, resonated with me on a personal level. I wondered if this eighteenth-century woman's experience might illuminate my own.

So began my search for Jean Armour. Over the next two years, I read many biographies about Robert Burns as well as his extensive collections of letters, poems and songs. I attempted to piece together a picture of Jean from the snippets and fragments written about her; much of the information was speculative and some of the accounts conflicted. The few slim books dedicated to Jean Armour reiterated the same material; they failed to probe her inner life or capture the realism of her experiences. Her only surviving letters were written after her husband's death. There were many blank pages in her story. As Burns's poems and letters testify, though Jean was the woman he married, she was but one of many women in his life, and not the one most written about. Nancy McLehose, known as Clarinda, gets the most biographical ink since a whole volume of their correspondence remains. But Jean Armour emerged as a footnote in the life of the poet, a blurry image that wouldn't come into focus: *Bonnie Jean*, a stereotype of the long-suffering wife—utterly devoted and eternally forebearing.

All my reading verified the adage that real life is often more improbable than fiction. What I learned about the circumstances of Jean's eleven years with Robert Burns would be deemed too melodramatic, too improbable in a novel. Moreover, my research left me with more questions than answers: Why did she marry him? Or, as most biographers frame it, why did Burns marry Jean, an uncultured village lass? What was it like for her to be denounced in the church as a fornicator and be kicked out of her family home because of premarital relations with Burns? How did she cope with giving birth to two sets of twins out of wedlock? Why was she willing to take in the children Burns had with other women and raise them as her own? How much did she assist the poet in the central work of his life, collecting and amending the old Scots songs? What was it like for her to go into labour on the day of her husband's funeral? After Burns died in poverty, how did she raise six young children on her own? And after his death, how did living in the shadow of the famous poet impact Jean and her children?

The more I read and speculated about Jean Armour's life, the closer I felt to her as a woman whose experiences mirrored some of my own: meeting a poetry-man, falling in forbidden love, then watching your sedate, predictable life veer completely off-course. By probing Jean's fatal attachment, maybe I could understand my own, and exorcise the ghost that's haunted all my intimate relationships.

Jean Armour was a much more complex woman than the shadowy figure portrayed in literary history. I wanted to bring her to life, give her a voice, and let her walk into the light. But to reclaim her, I knew I would have to uncover the world in which she lived. Not only by reading books, but by travelling back to Scotland—to Mauchline, to Ellisland and to Dumfries—back to the landscapes, the towns and the houses she inhabited. I would walk in her footsteps. Maybe then, if I paid attention and listened closely, I would be able to hear her speak.

PART I

The Belle of Mauchline

1785–1789

In Mauchline there dwells six proper young belles.
The pride of the place and its neighborhood a',
Their carriage and dress, a stranger would guess,
In Lon'on or Paris they'd gotten it a'.
Miss Miller is fine, Miss Markland's divine,
Miss Smith she has wit, and Miss Betty is braw,
There's beauty and fortune to get wi' Miss Morton;
But Armour's the jewel for me o' them 'a.

MAY 8, 2013. CARS SWISH BY, WIPERS CLACKING, HORNS honking down the narrow street. Pedestrians bustle by on the slick sidewalk, chins tucked into their collars. This busy streetscape is not the village I've carried in my mind these past three years—the Mauchline of Jean Armour, a simplified eighteenth-century map I printed from the town's website. Jet-legged and sleep-deprived, I look around, trying to get my bearings, then walk uncertainly to the street corner. All the signposts seem to be missing—in the literal sense as well. I spot a small sign high on the side of a brick building—*Loudon Street*—and sigh with relief, the address of my B&B.

I turn left and check the numbers on the shops; I'm heading in the right direction. My small suitcase rumbles along behind me, bumping over the curbs. A gust of wind upturns my umbrella and sleety rain drenches my face. Welcome to Scotland. I remember reading somewhere that after the Scottish government spent £125,000 on a campaign for a new tourism slogan, they decided on just that: *Welcome to Scotland*.

During my previous trip up into the desolate, windswept northern Highlands—the home of our Murray forebears—my son had commented, "I can see why they left." It seems I'm destined to be back in this country; I'm connected, not only genetically to this land of my ancestors, but also through an eighteenth-century Scottish woman who has taken up residence in my imagination.

After napping for a few hours in my snug attic room at the Ardwell—the only bed and breakfast in town—I don my raincoat and head out into the murk and mist of late afternoon. I stroll back up Loudon Street to the Fairburn Hotel, recommended by my host as the best place to eat in Mauchline. Called the McClelland Inn in the eighteenth century, it was here that the Burns Reading Society met weekly. On the outside wall, water trickles from a small fountain recessed into the sandstone—the Loudon spout. Flowing from Ayrshire's oldest artesian well, the fountain has been running here since the village was founded in the twelfth century.

Inside, the modern dining room has lost any trace of its eighteenth-century origins; the interior and exterior seem completely at odds. When I ask the young server about the history of the building and its connection to Burns, she says she has no idea.

I order what I know to be the most reliable choice in a Scottish restaurant, and the fried haddock and chips do not disappoint.

Re-energized, I continue my stroll up Loudon, formerly the King's High Street. Most of the shops have refurbished frontages and large windows, but some retain the original red sandstone, their narrow upper windows bricked over. I'm almost at the Cross at the top of the street, a lively market area in Jean's time, when I see her. She stands on a sandstone pedestal in front of the library, golden daffodils and white narcissi blooming in boxes on either side—Jean Armour, bronzed, frozen in time. Her grey gown ripples in folds around her feet; shoulder-length wavy hair brushed off her forehead accentuates her wide eyes and high cheekbones. One arm is bent up, a finger touching the curve of her throat. The other arm reaches out with an open hand, a gesture that welcomes me like an auld acquaintance. Her full lips are turned up in a half-smile.

I reach up and take hold of her outstretched hand, cold and wet with rain. It feels a bit strange to be talking to a statue, but I look up into her sculpted face and whisper, "Show me. What do you want me to know?"

I follow her gaze out towards Castle Street, formerly the Back Causeway, where she and Robert Burns lived when they were first married.

The stone archway is a portal to an eighteenth-century cobbled street lined with red sandstone buildings and stone walls draped with dripping vines; no people, no vehicles, no signs—only discreet blue oval plaques identifying historical sites. The Burns House Museum is closed for the day, so I head towards the old castle. The light is fading fast, and I almost miss the plaque on the mossy stone wall: *Site of Hugh Morton's Black Horse Inn*.

I freeze in my tracks. This very site—according to one story—is where it all began. Here at the Black Horse Inn on an April evening in 1785. I can picture Jean—twenty years old, slender and long-legged, by all accounts, a mane of black hair set off with a scarlet ribbon. And Robert Burns, like a lapidary with a loupe, had his eye on her—*the jewel of them 'a*—long before they met.

"As lithe and spirited as a race horse that lass," Jean's father would say. For his eye is on Jean too, as he tries to rein her in and ensure his eldest daughter will make a match worthy of James Armour, a master stonemason and the major contractor in Mauchline. Chest puffed out, brass-tipped walking stick in hand, he struts though the village lanes. He built the Hawford Bridge as well as Loch Norris, the marquis of Bule's mansion at Cumnock. He employs many men and owns five cottages on their street in the Cowgate.

It's Race Week when men flock to Mauchline to race their horses from the Cross, up the steep road to Mossgiel and back. That night at Ronald's ballroom next to the Black Horse Inn, it may have been Ian MacLauchlan—the best fiddler in the west of Scotland—playing for a penny a reel. He has the place hopping. In red tartan trews, fiddle tucked under his whiskered chin, he glides his bow over the strings as feet stomp and hands clap.

> *My father was a fiddler fine*
> *My minnie she made manki-o,*
> *An I'm myself, a thumpin quean*
> *Wha danc'd the Reel o' Stumpie-o.*

On their toes, arms at their hips, across their chests, they skip and whirl. Even the stoutest matrons hop and spin around the room. Jean links arms with her partner, Robert Wilson. They've been walking out together for many months; though no promises have been made, she knows they're forthcoming. Robin—as they call him—is leaving the next day for his apprenticeship as a weaver in the town of Paisley, thirty miles north. Once he's shown that his prospects are sound, Jean is sure he'll win her father's approval.

A man, with a dog, prances into the middle of their set. A russet plaid draped over his white linen shirt in an unusual way; dark, wavy hair tied back at the nape of his neck with a black band of ribbon, two locks curling around his sideburns. He's the only man in the parish to wear his hair like that. And the way he dances is different too. He leaps to the measure of the reel, looping and flinging with high-stepping abandon, his face glowing, brown eyes snapping. All the while, the black-and-white collie follows close at his heels.

Jean knows he's the new tenant at Gavin Hamilton's farm. She's watched him swaggering down the village roads, a wide-brimmed hat edging his thick black eyebrows, always a book tucked under his arm. Poet Burns has already given the gossips plenty to wag their tongues about. They say he writes scandalous verses; that he fathered a bastard wean with Lizzie Paton, his family's servant girl, and was rebuked in the Tarbolton kirk as a fornicator. And, they say, he has no intentions of marrying Lizzie. His family thinks her too coarse, though they themselves are barely scratching out a living on their farm at Mossgiel.

A wide grin on his face, he twirls in front of Jean, arms waving above his head. But the collie trips up his fancy footwork. "Swith awa', Luath," he says, lightly booting the dog's curling tail. "Wish I could find a lass who'd love me as well as my dog," he chuckles.

"If you do," Jean says, "then I hope you'll be treating her better than your dog."

He laughs and grabs the next lass opening her arms to him.

* * *

Their first brief exchange stirs up my own deep well of memory, my uncannily similar chance encounter with a man—a poet as well—that would change the course of my life too; a meeting that also occurred in the middle of a dance floor.

Both young teachers, we transformed into our hedonistic shadow-selves every Friday night at Fredericton's Cosmo Club happy hour. Disco music blaring, red and blue strobe lights flashing, we were dancing the bump—that seventies dance fad—bumping hips and backsides with our partners to KC and the Sunshine Band: *That's the way I like it, uh-huh, uh-huh, That's the way I like it.* In the mayhem of rotating bodies, shaking booties and swinging arms, we veered into each other, laughing as our eyes locked and our hips hit together to the beat. He wore tight blue jeans, a striped green-blue rugby shirt and a denim jacket; his light brown hair curled around his ears. I knew who he was, but we hadn't met. I remembered his voice from the back of a Shakespeare class at UNB; he had dared to question Dr. Rowan's interpretations and make irreverent comments about the plays while I had sat in the front row dutifully scribbling notes. I had read some of his poems in the university literary journal, and recalled one in particular about his newborn daughter. I knew he was married. So was I.

The next morning Una, my B&B host, serves me a hearty Scottish breakfast—porridge, scrambled eggs, tattie scones and coffee—while apologizing for the miserable weather. "Ach, it's dreich oot," she says, in the same accent that Jean herself would have had.

"Pardon me?" We're speaking the same language, but have to listen closely to understand each other.

Rain pelting my umbrella, I set out, eager to discover the village sites I've read about, places that have taken on a near-mythical stature in my mind: the Mauchline burn, the bleaching green, the old castle, Poosie Nansie's, the Cowgate, St. Michael's Kirk.

The Mauchline burn still runs by the old castle, but it's not the stream that has been flowing through my imagination—the wide burn where village women once did their washing then spread it to dry on a spacious grassy area. Now only a narrow brook trickles between sunken cement dykes. A high wooden fence separates it from a swath of grass bordered by tangles of bushes. Although the plaque identifies it as the Bleaching Green, I can't reconcile this shrunken setting with my envisioning of what transpired on this patch of grass—about a week after the penny reel dance.

White mountain daisies dot the greening grass, and the first lime-green buds are sprouting on the hawthorns. The air is sweet with spring. Choruses of skylarks warble their nesting songs, and robins flit by with twigs dangling from their beaks. Jean sits cross-legged beneath a great yew in the middle of the green, its branches quivering with the cawing of rooks. Her sister Nelly lies stretched out, eyes closed to the sun warming her freckled face. They've just finished scrubbing their sheets in the burn, thumping them with the wooden beetle, dipping and wringing, then spreading them out to dry in the sun. Jean gazes at the pure white rectangles, anticipating the fragrance of sun and grass when she crawls into bed that night.

Loud barking erupts from behind her. She swivels around. A dog bounds up from the burn, racing straight for their patch of linens—a collie with an up-curling tail and shaggy black-white coat. "Away with you," Jean hollers, hurling a stone at the dog. It yelps then scuttles over the sheets, leaving a muddy trail of paw prints in its wake.

"Luath, Luath," a man calls.

Luath, Cuchullain's guard dog in an old highland song, Jean recalls. Then she remembers that deep voice.

Winded from running, he pauses to catch his breath. "Lassie," he says, removing his hat, "you shouldna be throwing stones at the poor creature. But at his master who's nae the wits to keep him at heel." He smiles, not just with his mouth that flashes an even row of white teeth, but with his eyes too. His entire face lights up with the warmth of his grin. "Robert Burns of Mossgiel," he says with a slight bow.

Jean is about to say he has no need of introducing himself, that all of Mauchline knows of Poet Burns. But she finds her normally quick tongue somehow tied, and her face flushes.

"Miss Armour, I believe?" He extends his hand down to where she kneels on the grass and pulls her onto her feet. She stands as tall as him, and their eyes meet; his deep brown like hers, and his hair as jet black as her own. Though his complexion is browned and roughened by the sun and the wind, it's as if she's meeting a long-lost fraternal twin.

He lifts her hand and presses his lips lightly against her wrist.

Gobsmacked by this bold display, Nelly jumps up. "We'd best be rinsing off the sheets," she says, snapping Jean out of her daze.

"To be sure," Jean says, unpinning her kilted gown from above her knees and straightening her bodice, "before the grime sets in."

"I'll see to that," he says, bundling the sheets into the willow basket. He heads for the stream, his collie scampering at his side. Jean smiles at Nelly, shrugs and turns to follow him.

"Jean," Nelly calls, "don't be glaikit." It's a word she uses whenever she thinks her sister is acting feather-headed. Though

Nelly is four years younger, she acts like the older sister, always disapproving of Jean's daffing with the lads. "I'll be seeing you back home then." Nelly frowns and stomps off across the green.

He's crouched on the bank, swirling the white cloth through the burn, high and rushing in the spring runoff. The sun beams through the clear water, gilding the brown stones on the rocky bottom. Jean grabs a sheet from the basket and—to keep her distance—squats beside Luath. The collie lies panting between them, pink tongue lolling out, black snout quivering with the myriad scents of spring, his breast and paws as white as the sheets they're dipping and churning.

"A bonnie creature, Mr. Burns," Jean says, "not much more than a puppy."

He strokes the dog's glossy black coat. "Ay, a gash and faithful tyke." Luath beams up at his master, utter devotion shining in his amber eyes.

"Have you found that lass yet to love you as well as your dog?"

"Nae," he grins, "but Luath's just led me to one that I wish would try."

His eyes on her, Jean feels her skin tingling, like warm goosebumps. She keeps sloshing the sheet, not lifting her head, though her hands are numb with cold.

"Jeanie, come try me," he chuckles, then breaks into the old song, with a slight variation:

> *Jeanie, come try me,*
> *Jeanie, come try me!*
> *If thou would win my love,*
> *Jeanie come try me!*

A melody Jean loves, and he's singing it so tunelessly that she can't help but join in to put him in the right key.

If thou should ask my love,
Could I deny thee?
If thou would win my love,
Jamie, come try me!

"Keep singing, Jean," he says. "You've the voice of a wood-note."

Her cheeks glow pink with the blood rushing to her face. "I love singing more than anything."

"Only one improvement's needed. You must change the last line to *Rabbie, come try me.*"

"I'd be playing you false if I did," she says, wringing hard on the sheet. "I'm good as promised to someone."

"The lad you were with at the penny reel?" He fixes her with his dark eyes. "Is your heart set on him?"

She looks away, suddenly unsure how to answer that question.

They spread the washing to dry in the late-afternoon sun, and he lays his plaid on the grass for Jean to sit upon. His hands are large and calloused, his fingernails split and broken. The hands of a farmer, she thinks, but the manners and speech of a gentleman. He switches easily between school English and the Scots dialect as he talks of his father's death the year before, and his family's move from their farm in Lochlea, three miles west of Mauchline. The eldest son, he's partnered with his brother Gilbert and leased the farm in Mossgiel to support their mother, two brothers and three sisters.

"So you're a farmer and a poet?"

"Ay, proud descendent of a long line of failed farmers," he grins. "My father was of the highlands, the son of a farmer. He battled the soil till it sent him to his grave."

He pauses, stares up into the sky streaked with wispy tails of clouds. "But when I'm plowing, verses fill my mind. I feel close to the earth, and to God." He shakes his head and adds, "Not the God of Daddie Auld at the kirk, mind you. But to creation: *To Him who walks on the wings of the wind.*"

He plucks a daisy from the grass. "This wee crimson-tipped flower, full in bloom, is often crushed beneath my plow." He twirls the flower between his fingers, and his face clouds over. "Is its fate any different from mine?"

Reaching over, he tucks the slender stem into Jean's hair. "A bonnie flower for a bonnie lass," he says, touching her hair. "Flowing locks… like the raven's wing."

In the saffron light of the setting sun, alone on the green, they fold the damp sheets. He insists on carrying the basket for her. Jean feels the watchful windows of the houses as they stroll along the Back Causeway to the Cross then down the High Street to the corner of the Cowgate. When he asks to step out with her again, Jean wavers. She sees a crossroad looming. Down one lane, Robert Wilson calls, promising a life that's safe and predictable. They've known each other since childhood, played games around the old castle, took dancing lessons together. He's kind and devoted, and has her father's approval. But another road has suddenly opened up, unfamiliar and intriguing, and another Robert summons her with his luminous eyes and silvery voice.

Her father's stern, grimacing face flashes in her mind. "I cannot say," she replies, stopping at the corner beside the Whitefoord Arms, her stone house just visible behind it. "I'll say guideen here, Mr. Burns."

"Rab," he says, smiling. "Rab the rhymer." He eyes the sign for the tavern. "Johnnie Doo's, my favourite howf. I'm here most evenings having a pint. The table by the back window." He gives her a knowing look. "Or I might be reading some verses to amuse the crowd."

He tips his broad-brimmed hat and heads for the door of the tavern, his collie gamboling close by his side.

* * *

I follow in their footsteps down the wet streets to the Cowgate. The sun glimmering through a break in the clouds has pedestrians looking up, nodding and meeting my eyes. They can tell I'm *from away*, my soggy Blue Plaque Guide clutched in my gloved hand and my camera dangling from my wrist. They assume I'm here because of Robert Burns, the village's only tourist draw. As the slogan on the front of the guide boasts, *Born in Alloway—Died in Dumfries—LIVED IN MAUCHLINE.*

Passing Jean at the Cross, I smile and wave before turning down Loudon Street towards Poosie Nansie's Hostelry. Immortalized in Burns's poem "The Jolly Beggars," the building looks much as it did in the 1700s, but for a tiled roof replacing the thatch and a freshly painted white exterior trimmed with black. In Jean's time, the inn's dissolute clientele—mostly vagrants, beggars and prostitutes—put it on the lowest rung of the village's thirteen hostelries. The innkeepers, Nanse and her husband, were charged with reselling stolen goods and called for rebuke before the kirk session. They ignored the petition. Nanse was summoned again for being constantly inebriated and bothersome to her neighbours. She showed up this time, but only to inform them she would damn well continue in the sin of drunkenness for as long as she lived.

On the corner, just down from Poosie Nansie's, a sign high on a soot-stained building reads *COWGATE.* I come to a standstill, suffused with the thrill of having reached the street where Jean Armour actually lived. And the smoke-grey building that is now a sports store was formerly the Whitefoord Arms, Burns's favorite tavern, Johnnie Doo's—the nickname of its proprietor John Dow.

> *Where Burns cam' wery frae the plough*
> *To hae a crack wi' Johnnie Dow*

On nights at e'en
An' whyles to taste the mountain dew
Wi' Bonnie Jean.

Behind Johnnie Doo's, just across the alley, stood the family home of Jean Armour.

Rounding the corner, I'm not expecting the Armour's stone cottage to still be here. But at the same time, I'm not ready for its absence, unprepared for only a cold blue plaque on a six-foot wall that reads *The Site of Jean Armour's Home*. Behind the brick wall, a modern two-storey house looks completely out of place, like an intruder.

I lean against the damp brick and try to conjure this site as it would have been in 1785, that evening after Rab and Jean's fateful meeting on the green. Recalling the portrait that literary history has painted of James Armour, I can well imagine what Jean would have encountered after she unlatched the heavy wooden door of the thatched-roof cottage and crossed the threshold.

Perhaps the aroma of mutton stew and the clamour of pots from the scullery remind Jean that she is late for supper. Squealing trickles down from the garret where her little brother and sisters are getting ready for bed. She tiptoes down the passage to the stairway leading up to her attic room. A voice booms from the parlour: "Jean?"

Her father sits in his brocade armchair, the large family Bible open on his lap. Jean cowers before him—head down, hands folded—her childhood posture for receiving a scolding. He peers up over the spectacles perched on the hook of his nose, his jowls wobbling: "You have missed the meal and prayers as well."

"I'm sorry, father. The sheets weren't dry and…"

"I've heard it all from Nelly." His eyes narrow to a steely point. "Is it that Mossgiel scoundrel you've been with all this time?"

"Oh, he's vera kind and gentlemanly, father. Not at all the way folks blether about him. And…" her voice quavers, "and he's asked to walk out with me again."

He springs from his chair, and the Bible thumps to the floor. "I'd rather see the deil himself coming to court my daughter," he shouts. His face glows as red as his silk cravat, and the roseate veins on his cheeks bulge. "You'll not set the village gabs a-steerin. I dinna pay ten and eight a year for the dearest pew in the kirk so the old wives can clatter about my daughter."

He paces before the hearth spewing a torrent of insults about the blasphemous, fornicating rake no decent lass would dare to be seen with. Then he halts in front of her, spittle drooling down his chin. "You will not be seeing that rhymer Mossgiel. You hear me, Jean?"

"Ay, father. Please forgive me."

"You will stay at home for the next week and reflect on God's fifth great commandment: *Honour thy father and mother*. Get to your knees now and say your prayers." Sinking back into his chair, he takes a sneeshin mill from his breast pocket, sniffs a pinch of snuff up each nostril then picks up the Bible.

But the right kind of prayers will not come. When Jean closes her eyes, the face of Rab Burns flares in the darkness inside her head; his eyes, his lips so quick to jest and grin; his voice, lilting with words in the mother tongue. By the time her father dismisses her, Jean's knees are burning as much as her desire to see that face and hear that voice again.

*   *   *

I recall that sensation so vividly—as if possessed by the spirit of another, obsessed with one thought only: to see him again. After that night on the dance floor, I poured my desire onto white paper, a stream of blue ink flowing into my journal as I tried to release my pent-up longing. Then I wrote the letter, not intending to mail it, just to feel I was speaking to him, sending thought waves into the air that he might somehow receive. But that was not enough.

I addressed an envelope to the school where he was teaching, and slipped the letter inside.

Then the week of waiting. I began to feel another part of myself emerging. On the surface, I appeared a happily married young woman, but lurking beneath was this daring persona, a secret trespasser in forbidden territory. I wonder if this is similar to the kind of split that Jean began to experience within herself—obedient young woman by day and furtive transgressor by night.

Over a bowl of steaming potato soup at the Fairburn Hotel, I watch rivulets of water trickling down the window pane and envisage Jean staring out her own rain-spattered window in the Cowgate, just a few hundred yards from here. Her reflection in the glass pulls me back to that life-changing week in May of 1785.

It's very likely that it rained every day. Not gentle spring showers, but downpours assaulting the windows and drumming on the roof. Jean's mother has plenty of chores for her. She must tend to her younger siblings and help them with their schoolwork. She cooks and cleans, spins yarn and darns socks. She fetches water from the pump-well at the Cross—her only breath of fresh air. Her mother has plenty of advice for her eldest daughter as well.

"Your father may be stern, but he's your best interests at heart," Mrs. Armour says, as they beat the oats on the knocking stone for a batch of oatcakes. "A woman's reputation is everything." It's been her mother's constant refrain since Jean started bleeding at age fifteen, around the same time her father began pointing above the front door to the Armour coat of arms with its Latin inscription—*Cassis tutissima virtus*: Virtue is the safest helmet.

"Dinna let a man touch you till you're wed," he warned. "He'll no be buyin' the coo if he can get the milk for naething."

Jean has always liked flirting with the lads, feeling the scorch of their eyes appraising her body. But Robin Wilson is the only one she's allowed to get close, holding hands as they walked home from the dances. She let him kiss her cheek the night before he left for Paisley. In truth, she was thinking of Rab Burns the whole time: *How would it feel to have his lips pressed against mine?*

The day after the penny reel, Jean met her friend at the Cross for the weekly market. Surveying bolts of colorful silk and stalls of leather shoes, they talked about the previous night and Burns's flashy dancing. Christina was a blonde beauty with a fortune of at least five hundred pounds, and her father—proprietor of the Black Horse Inn—was seeking a highly eligible match for his only daughter. She too had been warned: no respectable girl would be seen with that renegade—a plague on the parish! Giggling, Jean confessed her fantasy about the poet's sensuous lips. Christina's eyes widened then she leaned over and whispered in Jean's ear, "*Let him kiss me with the kisses of his mouth*. So sayeth Solomon the wise."

"I heard Lizzie Paton had her baby," Mrs. Armour says, mixing the ground oatmeal, water and goose fat into a smooth paste. "Her family's refused to take in her wean. So Lizzie's given her over to the father's family at Mossgiel."

"Mr. Burns is an honourable man then, owning up to his responsibility," Jean says, kneading the stiff ball of dough against the stone.

"He's a twenty-six-year-old man with a bastard wean to support along with a mother and half a dozen brothers and sisters." Mrs. Armour grabs the rolling pin and sprinkles a handful of meal on the baking board. "They say the only crop that farm can grow is thistles. Is that the kind of life you want, Jean? Cramped in a clay biggen, wondering how you'll feed your bawling brats?" With brisk strokes, she rolls out the dough into a thin sheet then cuts it into squares. "Your father did not allow you an education so you'd end up a farmer's wife."

Her father permitted Jean to attend the kirk school when most families in the village believe schooling is wasted on a girl. He encouraged her talent for singing and enrolled her in the Mauchline music school. Quick to learn her lessons and the Bible verses he set for his children to memorize, Jean earned the privileged place on his right side at the table. She sings his cherished hymns every evening after prayers. God the father watches over her from heaven, Jean was taught; just below him, her father governs her on earth: *Not my will but thine be done*.

Jean scoops the slices onto the round metal girdle and sets them onto the grate over the fire, thinking about that bitter edge in her mother's voice and the lines that have appeared in her face these past few years; fine wrinkles pinching her mouth, dark circles under her eyes, strands of grey streaking her black hair. She's a different mother than the one Jean knew as a child—so light-hearted, always crooning lullabies and ballads. Jean, her second child, learned to sing at her mother's breast: *Baloo, baloo, my wee, wee thing, O softly close thy blinkin' e'e*. After Jean, her mother bore nine more children. Three lie in the kirkyard beneath grey tablets of stone. Her first Robert lived but two weeks; her first Mary for twenty-one months; her second Robert died at nine months. Jean remembers how those lost babies changed her mother, as if another part of her fell into the grave with each one. Sadness dimmed her brown eyes, and her singing gradually ceased altogether.

Seeing her weep, her husband chided, "Submit to God's will. Do not repine at his dispensations. Praise the Lord for sparing the child the sorrow and trials of this vale of sin."

To mourn your dead children was a sin against God. Jean has never seen her father shed a tear. She sometimes wonders if his heart is encased in steel, moulded by the generations of Armours who were blacksmiths and stonemasons—a proud lineage of men transforming metal and rock, shaping it to their will. Just as her father has forged her, Jean realizes, into a dutiful daughter who has lived to please him.

"If you dinna fear your father," her mother reminds her, "you dinna fear God."

So until her episode with Rab Burns, Jean had not faced the brunt of her father's anger—nor the punishments her brothers suffered: whipped with the birch rod; shut up in the stable for a day with only bread and water. *He that spareth his rod hateth his son; but he that loveth him chasteneth him betimes*, her father intones from the Book of Proverbs. The only other book he's read to them—*A Token for Children: An Account of the Conversion, Holy and Exemplary Lives and Joyful Deaths of Several Young Children*—cautioned, "What will you do if you are sick and die with no grace in your heart, and be found naughty?"

Jean remembers the day, about a year earlier, when her father's tyranny was challenged for the first time. He'd objected to the lass his oldest son was courting. "A serving wench," he called her. When John said he'd court whomever he pleased, his father raised the rod to strike him. Taller than his father, and muscular from all the stone he'd been heaving as his father's apprentice, John seized the stick, waved it in front of his father's face as if challenging him to a duel. They eyed each other, wary and silent as circling cats. Then John cracked the rod over his knee and thrust it into the fire. A week later, he left home to work for a stonemason in Kilmarnock. Then James—two years younger than Jean—replaced him as apprentice; after a few months, he too fled to find work in the city.

Now her fourteen-year-old brother has quit school to work in the stonemasonry. Tall and slim and black-haired like Jean, Adam is more like her in temperament as well. He tells his sister, "I just try to please the old man and keep out of his way."

"I'm earning f-four pounds a year as an apprentice," Robin Wilson says, perched next to Jean on the settee. His eyes dart back and forth between her mother and father seated across the parlour. Back from Paisley to visit his family—and Jean—Robin describes the hand-loom skills he's learning from a journeyman weaver. His leg shakes, rattling the cup and saucer balanced on his knee, as his words sputter out with an uncharacteristic stammer. "B-but b-by next year I should be setting up my own shop." His mouth curves up in a hesitant half-smile. "P-Paisley's got the largest weaver's guild in Scotland."

"Rife wi' opportunity for a hard-working lad like yourself," Mr. Armour says. "Before long you'll hae the means to support a family."

Robin beams and glances over at Jean as her father talks on about the new Catrine Cotton Works recently built on the River Ayr outside the village. Robin nods and explains that their cotton yarn is replacing the silk and wool that's always been the staple of handloom weavers.

"Rain's f-finally let up," Robin says, peering out the window. "The sky's pink as a rose." He turns to Jean. "Would you care for a stroll along the burn?"

Jean looks into his earnest face, his fair skin aglow with anticipation. But before she can answer, her father interjects: "Ay, Jean, the fresh air would do you good."

She's desperate to get out after a week in the house, but she wavers, balking at what she now sees as her father's orchestration of her life. "Nae, I'm feeling rather poorly. Maybe a cold coming on," she says, her head bowed, face flushing.

At the door, Robin kisses her cheek and squeezes her hand. His touch stirs nothing in her but brotherly affection. Watching his lanky figure saunter down the cobbled street, she realizes it's a vastly different sensation from what Rab Burns has ignited in her, yearnings in her body and her mind for something she has yet to name.

The clock in the parlour chimes ten times. The house is quiet, only the soft breathing of Nelly asleep beside her. In the dim lamplight, Jean is reading from a book of Scottish ballads, trying to memorize "The Ballad of Sir Patrick Spens." She loves its rolling rhythm and the pictures it paints in her mind:

> *And I fear, I fear, my maister dear,*
> *That we will come to harm.*
> *I saw the new moon late yestreen,*
> *Wi' the auld moon in her arm*

She gets up to change into her nightdress and blow out the lamp, peeks out one last time between the criss-crossed cames of the glass down towards the tavern. Every evening that week she's peered down from her gable window and across the narrow lane to the Whitefoord Arms, hoping to catch a glimpse of him at the back table. Now, framed in a square of light, a man is leaning out the window, staring up at her. *Rab.* She turns the crank slowly so as not to make a squeak, and sticks her head out.

"What light through yonder window breaks?" he calls, a wide smile illuminating his face. "Jean, the fullest, brightest moon is blinkin' o'er the castle. Can you walk out a spell?"

She hesitates, but not for long. "I'll meet you at the kirk," she calls in a hushed voice, relieved her parents sleep on the other side of the house. Draping a shawl over her shoulders, Jean tiptoes down the stairs and through the dark passage to the front door. Drawing back the heavy brass bolt would awaken everyone, so she scuttles into the kitchen then out the through-gang. As she eases open the lock of the door into the stable, the horse whinnies and stamps her feet. Jean strokes the mare's chestnut mane then slips out into the night.

She runs like an escaping prisoner, expecting to be stopped any second by her father's commanding voice, or by a neighbour staggering out of Thomson's Tavern or the Whitefoord Arms. Around the corner, Poosie Nansie's thrums with fiddle music, singing, laughing and shouting. But the High Street, striated with moon beams, is deserted. She's never been out alone at night; her heart is beating double-time as she races across the street and through the iron gates to the stone steps of the kirk. Above its door, the leering faces of two gargoyles look even more sinister in the shadowy moonlight. Something darts out of the darkness; a flash of white and a snuffling breath circle her legs. A dog jumps up, then a hand reaches out and clutches her arm. "Jean, sae glad to see you," Rab says, his voice calming yet exciting her at the same time.

Arm in arm, they cross the kirkyard, manoeuvring through the tombstones. The yellow globe of the moon bathes the castle's sandstone tower and battlements in a glorious light. Jean tells him about her father's vehement reaction to their acquaintance, and Rab chuckles. "Och, he's pack an' thick with the elders," he says. "Three-mile prayers and hauf-mile graces. They're nae pleased with me. A few weeks ago, I read a not-so-flattering poem about Holy Willie at Johnnie Doo's. They've had several meetings since to look over their spiritual artillery. See if any of it might be pointed at profane rhymers." Willie Fisher—a bachelor farmer known for his religious bluster and his tippling—is the most vigilant of Reverend Auld's cronies, tracking sinners with the fervour of a bloodhound.

"Ay, tis surely that in father's craw," Jean says, then pauses, unsure of the right words.

"That and… well… your bairn with Lizzie Paton."

"Ah, my bonnie, wee Bess," he grins and hoists Jean up onto the ivy-smothered wall encircling the castle's courtyard. Clambering up beside her, he says, "She came a wee unsought-for, I'll admit. The righteous good clatter about me being a fornicator. But I'm proud to be a father. My mother and sisters dote on the wee lass."

"And Lizzie? Do you nae care for her?"

He gazes up at the moon, adrift in a memory. The only sound the squeaking of bats swooping around the belfry in Abbot Hunter's tower, its vaulted roof still bearing the coat of arms of the village's founder.

"We'd many a merry dint," Rab says, "but no promises were made. While I own a single crown Lizzie's welcome to share it." He slips his arm around Jean's shoulder and edges closer, his lips grazing her ear, his words a whisper. "Sometimes our bodies speak louder than our minds."

The sensations rippling through her own body are proof enough of that. But an inner voice rings out like an alarm going off in her head. "I must get back," she says, dropping to the ground, "in case Nelly wakens and sees I'm gone."

When they reach the corner of the Cowgate, the street is unlit, the public houses shuttered. Moon rays filter through wispy streaks of cloud. Drawing her into the shadow of the stone wall Rab says, "Tomorrow at nightfall?"

Her inner voice says, *No.* But meeting his eyes, Jean cannot utter the word. "Look up to my window around the same time. If I can get out, I'll signal with the lamp."

He smiles. "Like Romeo and Juliet." Then he leans in, his face not an inch from hers. "And my lips ready stand, to smooth your sweet ones with a tender kiss."

It is her first real kiss, full on the lips and full of longing. Their lips part slightly, and the tip of his tongue touches hers. She wants to taste more of him, to let go into her body's craving, an itch between her legs desperate to be scratched. But that badgering voice in her head intrudes again. She pulls away, tightens her shawl over her chest and hurries down the dark street.

*   *   *

Abbot Andrew Hunter's tower still stands, all that's left of the fifteenth-century monastery of the Monks of Melrose. In the eighteenth century, their castle morphed into the village's most popular trysting spot on summer nights, a lovely melding of divine and secular love. And now I see that the remaining tower of the old castle is attached to a large, two-storey L-shaped house, privately owned and occupied, so the grounds are inaccessible. As I stare at the crumbling turret, my first secret rendezvous slowly replays in my mind, a memory I didn't know I had.

It was a cold, clear February night. We met at the university library and hiked up the steep hill to the outskirts of the campus. Both still struggling to finish our MA theses in English, we talked about our progress—or lack thereof—and commiserated about how tough it was to find time for writing while teaching full-time.

"Why Hugh MacLennan?" he asked when I told him about my thesis topic. I prevaricated, not wanting to admit my unscholarly motivation for choosing this author: a crush on my advisor, a prof who'd written a book about MacLennan. He was focusing on Ethel Wilson's *Swamp Angel*, one of my favourite novels, about a woman who leaves a stifling marriage to discover a new life and herself.

We came to a wide empty field, white and clean as a blank sheet of paper, and tromped through the snow to a dark smudge in the middle—an old hay rake with rusty rungs and wheels. He climbed up onto the seat and drew me up onto his knee. Above us, every star in the cosmos seemed to be shining, and we looked for constellations. I was shivering in my leather coat, so he put his arms around me, a bear hug pulling me close. Too cold to linger, we trudged back across the crusty expanse and stopped at a huge grey boulder on the edge of the field. Leaning against it, he reached into the pocket of his duffel coat and brought out a joint. He lit it, sucked in the smoke then held it out to me. I had never smoked a cigarette, let alone pot. But not wanting to appear uncool, I smiled and tried to imitate his deep inhalation. The smoke seared the back of my throat, and I broke into a fit of uncontrollable coughing.

Laughing, he drew me in against him; his icy hands reached under my jacket beneath my sweater and caressed my back. "Skin like satin," he whispered.

We strolled back down the hill in a silence that was comfortable, only the squeak of our boots stepping in perfect time together. When we reached our cars, he said, "I'll call you." I wasn't sure that he would, but it didn't seem to matter. I drove home with a blissed-out smile on my face, humming "Que Sera, Sera." Back home, I pulled out my tattered copy of *Swamp Angel* and started reading: *Ten twenty fifty brown birds flew past the window and then a few stragglers, out of sight.*

A few days later a letter arrived in my mailbox at school, the address written in the powder blue ink of a fountain pen. I knew it was his handwriting though I'd never seen it before. On the single sheet of paper, words were typed in the middle of the white expanse:

Lady

of the rock

and rake

You are poems

Like Jean, I fell under the spell of a poetry man. *I'll be your Beatrice, if you'll be my Dante ... I'll be your Marianne, if you'll be my Leonard.* To be cast in the role of the muse was irresistible.

Thus Jean and I both began a life of clandestine meetings under the mantle of night. And from my reading of Burns's biographies, I can piece together fragments to make a picture of Jean's experience at that time, knowing all the manoeuvrings, the trepidation and the elation involved in maintaining a double persona.

On summer nights, they would meet in the silvery birch woods on the banks of the River Ayr. *And here by sweet endearing stealth, Meet the loving pair... And birks extend their fragrant arms to screen the dear embrace,* Burns writes in one of his poems. Their bodies are like magnets, and Jean can't resist the attraction. His hands are patient explorers, discovering a territory unknown to her as well. He slowly unfastens each button of her bodice. *Thy breasts are like two young roes, twins which feed among the lilies.* And so Jean learns the lovely psalms of David *Thy navel is like a round goblet which wanteth not liquor; thy belly is like a heap of wheat*—not a part of the Bible her father, nor Reverend Auld, ever reads.

"The kirk wants us to believe our flesh is sinful," Rab says, "but the Song of Solomon celebrates two bodies joining in pleasure and joy. Tis as close to heaven as you can get on earth. Ay, the wisest man the warl' e'er saw, he dearly loved the lasses." His hands move under her petticoat, caressing her thighs. His fingers slip into the throbbing moistness between her legs. She wants to let go, to fall back on the soft mossy bed. But for the price to be paid.

"Such pleasure can land a lass in hell," Jean says, wrenching herself out of his arms.

Many nights they can't meet. Jean sneaks out of her room, and the lamp is still glowing in the spence—her father up late, poring over his accounts or studying his Bible. So she makes a hasty retreat. But one evening, dying to get out, she peeks around the parlour door. Her father is slouched in his armchair asleep, his grey hair askew, the dregs of a whisky glass spilling onto the crotch of his breeches.

When she returns home a few hours later, the lamp is still burning and snoring sounds from the parlour. Her father, Jean realizes, has his own temptations to battle. Drunkenness is a venial sin, but isn't treated as an offence, Rab told her, or every gentleman and every elder—even Daddie Auld himself—would constantly be standing at the pillory.

* * *

From the sidewalk, I peer through iron gates at the big white house that's now connected to the old castle. Jean, I'm sure, would have spent many hours within the walls of this grand-looking home. Surrounded by tall trees and lush gardens, it was the former home of Gavin Hamilton, who encouraged Burns to publish his poems in 1786. The Burns brothers sublet their Mossgiel farm from Hamilton, who had stepped into his father's shoes as the village lawyer. Though from different classes, Burns and Hamilton were kindred souls from the outset, both liberal-minded and outspoken about the hypocritical ways of the Mauchline kirk. When the session publicly scolded Hamilton for allowing his servant to dig potatoes from his garden on the Sabbath, Burns wrote his satire about Holy Willy in Gavin's defence. Thereafter, the two men became close friends.

Many evenings Jean would have joined Rab and his best friends around a big oak table in Gavin's dining room, all well fortified with coggies of Manson's strong ale. Perhaps it was here that she first met Dr. John Mackenzie, who had tended Rab's father on his deathbed. And Davie Sillar, Rab's brother-poet and a fiddler, is there with his sweetheart Meg. Rab can pluck out melodies on the fiddle to accompany his verses, but he isn't a player like Davie, who has them singing and dancing to the lively tunes he steps with his bow. They are all sworn to secrecy about Jean's relationship with Rab.

At these soirées, Jean witnesses Rab's wit and intelligence, how he can talk circles around anyone about politics, religion or poetry. The authors and books he mentions are alien to her; the only books permitted in her home are the Bible and hymnals. Chameleon-like, he adapts his speech and manners to the company; one minute debating in the Queen's English with a doctor and a lawyer; the next minute chatting with Davie, Meg and Jean in the good Scots tongue. The lightning flashes in his eyes reveal his interest in everything and everyone—especially, Jean notices, Gavin's maid-servant. As she passes around trays of meal cakes and cheese, Rab's eyes linger on her honey-brown tresses and the décolletage of her gown.

"I can tell you're from the highlands, Mary Campbell," he grins. "The bonniest lasses in all of Scotland come from there."

"Ay, from Argyll on the Firth of Clyde," she says in a strong Gaelic accent, her long eyelashes fluttering.

"My father hailed from the high country. Tis in my blood too," Rab says as he stands, hand over his heart, and breaks into the old song—*My heart's in the Highlands, My heart is not here, My heart's in the Highlands a-chasing the deer*—while gazing at Highland Mary, as he comes to call her. Jean's ears and cheeks flame, the sting of jealousy piercing her for the first time, but by no means the last.

* * *

Dusk filters down into grey mist as I slowly retrace my steps along the Back Causeway. Although I've been here for just one day, the village feels strangely familiar; in that other life I'm inhabiting—1785—I've been wandering these streets for several months. Dragging my feet with the weariness of a time-traveller, I look forward to the hot shower and the warm bed awaiting me at Ardwell House. But near the end of the street, I spy another plaque on a building that backs onto the churchyard: *Nanse Tinnock's Tavern*. Bells ring in my mind, and I have to stop. Except for the tiled roof and enlarged windows, the old sandstone exterior looks just as it would have in Jean's time; most of the village houses were built from this same red stone carved out of the Ballochmyle cliffs just outside the village. It was at this inn that Burns recited poems that raised the kirk's alarm, most notoriously his satire about Mauchline's Holy Fair.

Every August, the second Sunday, hundreds of people flocked to the village for three days of prayer meetings in a huge wooden shelter set up in the kirkyard. Preachers from three parishes regaled sinners about the burning pits of hell awaiting them. In the refreshment tents, people ate, drank and gossiped. Mauchline's public houses did a brisk business as well, not to mention the village prostitutes. The preaching tent's back entrance led directly into the rear door of Nanse Tinnock's Tavern, which siphoned off a good portion of the congregation.

Now part of the Burns historical trust, the building is not open to the public. I try to peer through a window, but it's too dark inside to see anything. I can imagine, though, a low-ceilinged room dimly lit with fish oil lamps. It smells of smoke, spilled ale and the sweat of too many bodies crammed in a small space. The place is packed—standing room only—for news has spread that Poet Burns will be reciting his verses about the

Holy Fair tonight. Handwritten copies of the poem have already been circulating around the parish.

Jean sneaks in the pub's rear door and joins Rab and his friends at a table in the back corner. She's hedging her bets that neither her father nor his circle of elders would be seen in such an establishment. Nanse's daughter Jess sidles up to the patrons at the bar, her ample breasts spilling over her bodice, enticing men to follow her up the narrow staircase. The crowd is boisterous, fuelled by many drams of Kilbaigie, Nanse's house whisky. But when Rab moves into the middle of the floor and pulls a paper from his pocket, you can hear a penny drop.

Like a magician weaving a spell, he holds them with his voice lilting in the old Scots tongue:

> *My name is Fun—your cronie dear,*
> *The nearest friend ye hae;*
> *And this is Superstition here,*
> *An' that's Hypocrisy,*
> *I'm gaun to Mauchline Holy Fair,*
> *To spend an hour in daffin:*
> *Gin ye'll go there, yon runkle'd pair,*
> *We will get famous laughin*
>
> *At them this day.*

Hands clap and slap against knees, as men chortle at what they all know, but dare not utter.

The door of the tavern creaks open. Heads swivel around. A hush falls over the room. In a long blue overcoat, a three-cornered hat atop his grey wig, Reverend Auld enters. His narrowed eyes dart about the room. At his heels is Willie Fisher, his ruddy face glowering. Close behind him strides James Armour, clutching his pointed walking stick like a sword.

Jean lowers her face into her hands then slowly sinks beneath the table onto the dusty floor where Luath slathers her face with his sandpapery tongue. There's a shuffling of feet and some faint tittering, but Rab does not miss a beat. And he's still ranting on as Jean sneaks out the back door.

> *O happy is that man, an blest!*
> *Nae wonder that it pride him!*
> *Whose ain dear lass that he likes best,*
> *Comes clinkin down beside him!*
> *Wi' arms repos'd on the chair back,*
> *He sweetly does compose him!*
> *Which by degree, slips round her neck,*
> *An's loof upon her bosom,*
>
> *Unkend that day.*

The next morning her father stomps around the house in a foul temper. Jean stirs the pease brose while the wee ones chant their usual breakfast song in their sweet, high voices: *Once crowdie, twice crowdie, three times crowdie in a day.*

"Cease your bletherin' din," her father bellows and complains of a sick headache. He fumes about the blaspheming of that rhymer Burns last evening at Nanse Tinnock's and his evil influence on the younger generation. Even respectable men like Dr. John Mackenzie and Gavin Hamilton, he says, are under his sway.

"Surprised you'd be visiting such a doss-house," Jean says, ladling the steaming oats into the wooden cogs and passing them around the table.

Spoon suspended before his gaping mouth, his eyes contract to slits. "When Willie got wind of the entertainment, we'd no choice but to make an appearance," he says, pinning her with his steely eyes. "To remind everyone: the eyes of the Lord are always watching."

The October sun gilds the yellow leaves of the birches along the burn, and the rowan trees blaze with scarlet berries against an azure sky. As they meander along the leaf-strewn path, Robin is telling Jean about the cottage in Paisley he's hoping to lease. "Only two rooms," he says, "but such a view of the White Cart River."

"How lovely," Jean says, stopping beneath a rowan tree to pick berries for her little sisters to string into necklaces. Full of self-reproach for her duplicity, she's continued walking out with Robin during his monthly visits, so her father will assume nothing has changed. Rab knows all this, but she notices a spark of jealousy in his eyes whenever Robin's name comes up. "Ay, lang Robin Wilson, the Gallant Weaver," he says and drones the old song: *To the weaver's gin ye go, fair maid, To the weaver's gin ye go.*

Scuffing his feet through the rowan's spiky orange leaves. Robin asks, "Could you live in such a humble dwelling, Jean?"

She meets his blue eyes, glinting with expectation. He quickly adds, "I mean—just to start out, till I set up my own shop next year."

In the long seconds, a curlew whistles from the branches above them. Finally, Jean says, "You're a fine man, Robin. I want us always to be friends. But things have changed in the months you've been gone. I'm not the same." She shakes her head. "I'm not the lass for you."

"There's only ever been one lass for me. Ever since that first time we held hands at the dancing school." He pauses, his eyes squinting as he rummages through his mind. Then he says, "I still remember the reel."

Jean nods and smiles. "O'er the Muir Amang the Heather"?

"*She claimed my heart, and aye sin' syne,*" he sings softly. "*I canna think o' any ither.*"

"You were the best dancer in the class, always so quick to pick up the steps."

"I practised a lot—out in the byre," he chuckles, "hoping to impress you."

"And so you did."

The glow of memory fades from his eyes, and he says, "But whether I'm the lad for you is the question, isn't it? I don't put much store in the tattling of the rumour mongers, but..." A pained expression clouds his face, and he blurts out, "There's talk of you being seen with Burns of Mossgiel."

"Ay." She bites her lip as the blood rushes to her cheeks. "We fell acquainted a few months past."

"Is he the man for you then?"

"I'm not sure of that either," she says and tells him about her father's hostility towards Rab.

They walk back in silence, but for the crunching of their boots through the leaves swirling around their legs. Outside Jean's front door, Robin grasps both her hands and says, "I will wait until you are sure." She meets his gaze, as deep and unwavering as the declaration he utters. "Unless you marry another, Jean, I'll nae give up hope."

All Jean knows with any certainty is her yearning to be with Rab Burns. When the November nights turn frosty, and the corn stalks and barley rigs can no longer shelter them, she sneaks him into the stable adjoining her house. As the hard rains pelt the thatch roof, then the driving snows of December lash the narrow window, they snuggle in a bed of hay. But it takes more and more to satisfy their hunger for each other.

One night Rab says, "We can make our vows to each other and join our bodies as man and wife. An irregular marriage is recognized by the law, if not by the kirk."

Inhaling the sweet smell of straw, Jean feels a painful thrust as he moves inside her. Then ripples of pleasure draw him deep into the cave of her body. The waves swell, and swell to a peak, till she thinks her heart will surely burst. He shudders, stifles a cry in her ear.

Sealed together, a drug-like lassitude pulls them into sleep. Jean startles awake with Luath licking her hand, as if he—their guard dog—senses the risk in their sleeping.

The next morning, she notices the stain on her white petticoat, red as an apple. What it declares is just as startlingly clear: she has tasted the forbidden fruit. And, she thinks, it is good.

*　　*　　*

The occasional car swishes by in the dark, wet street below. I lie in my attic room sleepless, recalling those nights we stole out of our real lives. Listening to Van Morrison, we sailed together into the mystic. We read to each other from *The Spice Box of Earth*, and I wanted to believe in the gentle hedonism Leonard Cohen exalted.

> *As the mist leaves no scar*
> *On the dark green hill*
> *My body leaves no scar on you*
> *And never will*

This was the heart of our affair—no expectations, no pressure. He had a beautiful wife and two young children. And I had no illusions there would be anything more than those sustaining interludes. *We'd many a merry dint, though no promises were made.*

It's at this juncture, I realize, that Jean's and my parallel liaisons with our poets begin to diverge. I would eventually leave my marriage, not *for* this man, but *because* of him. It was as if I'd been bound in a cocoon and had suddenly discovered I could break out. Married at nineteen when I was reeling after my father's death, I had never lived on my own. I had dutifully followed the laid-out path: gone to university, married a tall, handsome man and obtained a teaching position—at the same high school I'd attended. But the narrowness and predictability of my life soon felt unbearable. My eyes had been opened to what a relationship might be. After five years, I knew such a meeting of minds could not be found with the older man I'd married, a PE teacher who lived for the game of basketball. If "a happy marriage is a long conversation," as the French writer Andre Maurois put it, I'd discovered we had little to say to each other.

So I packed my two cats and all that would fit into my Corolla, and moved into a dumpy little apartment too close to the highway. At the end of the term, I resigned from my teaching job, put on a backpack and flew solo to Europe.

Jean and I responded to the same impulses—to crack the mould we'd been cast in, to discover a buried part of ourselves, to satisfy our forbidden carnal desires. But she would suffer drastically different consequences.

The next day, it's pouring again, so hard that I decide to spend the morning in the library reading about the history of the village and local material about Burns's years here. Passing Jean's statue, glazed with water, I pause and look up into her face. Her sightless eyes, trickling with raindrops, seem to convey all the anguish I imagine she endured in this next chapter of her life. Lots has been written about this part of Jean Armour and Robert Burns's relationship, but only from the perspective of the poet, through his letters and his biographers.

Sitting in a back corner of the quiet room, books piled around me on the wooden table, I pull out my notebook. But Jean is too present in my mind, her predicament too demanding of my speculation. So I push aside *The History of Mauchline Village and Parish* and begin to write.

I suppose it would be in January 1786, soon after Hogmanay, that she has the first inklings of her condition. Her bleeding time, usually as regular as the phases of the moon, does not come. In the mornings she feels queasy, can't bear the smell of boiling oats or toasting bannock. The signs she recognizes well enough, having witnessed them many times in her mother. Perhaps she isn't alarmed at first, believing that she and Rab are as good as man and wife, and that her father will now be forced to accept him as her husband.

But before she tells Rab, she needs to be certain. So one night in mid-February, just before going to bed, she urinates into a bowl then sinks a needle into the cloudy yellow liquid. The next morning, the tiny red spots speckling the thin silver shaft flash the words she can no longer elude: *I am with child*. Words she will have to say to Rab that night, and soon have to utter to her father.

It's a bitterly cold evening with the north wind sweeping snow into high drifts around the byre. As soon as she bolts the door, Rab grabs her and smothers her with a long kiss that tastes of whisky. He bends her back until she loses her balance, and they tumble into the hay trying to stifle their laughter.

"Tis a glorious night," Rab says. "Winter's the best season of all. I had a rapturous walk today on the sheltered side of the wood. The wind was storming through the trees. It felt like the voice of God soothing me. I rushed home and took up my quill. *Old winter with his frosty beard...* Nae, I'll wait till I rewrite it, many times over I'm sure."

"Every day you've new verses spinning in your head. Is it winter that's inspiring your pen?"

"Tis a restful time on the farm. No plowing or sowing or harvesting to suck you dry. And..." he says rolling on top of her, "there's also a lass who deserves some credit. The verses seem to come so easy since I met you." In the pale light of the lantern, his dark eyes beam into hers. "My muse maun be thy bonnie sel'," he whispers, and kisses her forehead and her eyes; nibbles each ear, slathers her neck and breasts with kisses while lifting her petticoat and stroking her thighs. "And such a leg my bonnie Jean. Sae straight, sae taper, tight an' clean. None else come near it."

Her desire flares, and almost melts her resolve to speak. "Rab," she says, placing his wandering hand on her stomach, "creation is happening in here as well."

Her words are like water thrown on a fire. She can almost hear the fizzling as his entire body goes limp. The howling wind rattles the stable walls, and the mare snorts in her stall, filling the heavy silence.

"You're bairned?"

"Ay."

He bolts up and buries his head in his hands. It's then that Jean awakens from her romantic dream of marriage into the reality of their predicament. "How will we manage?" she sobs. "How can I tell my father?"

He pulls her into his arms. She hears the thumping in his chest. "I'll not forsake you, Jean. We're betrothed in our hearts and bodies. It's just the shock of it all. I've not the means to provide as you're accustomed."

From his waistcoat pocket, he pulls out a notebook and rips out a page. "I may be the last son-in-law James Armour wants, but he's no choice in the matter now." He yanks a quill from its holder and uncorks the inkhorn. Words flow onto the page. "This is a binding marriage contract in the courts of Scotland."

Jean takes the paper, so flimsy in her hands. But reading the words and his signature below them, she feels the heft of it.

> *Robert Burns, farmer of Mossgiel, and Jean Armour, spinster of Mauchline, do hereby acknowledge each other as husband and wife on this the 17th day of February 1786.*

She dries her eyes and signs her name next to his.

"Tomorrow we'll show it to your father."

Jean looks at him aghast. "Not the two of us. Bringing you home would be like dangling a red cape in front of a bull." She folds the paper and tucks it into her bodice. "I'll wait for just the right moment to deliver the news."

Days pass. The time will never be right, she realizes. Whenever she glimpses her father's dour face, the thought of passing him that paper leaves her quivering like a lamb before a lion. In the meantime, she and Rab sort through their options. The Mossgiel farm is a losing proposition, Rab says, scarcely supporting the nine of them: his mother, six siblings and wee daughter Bess. "I read books on farming. I calculated crops. I attended markets," he sighs. "But the first year, I bought bad seed. The second year we harvested too late. We lost a good half of both crops." But he's looking into a position that's come up in the Excise Service. He'd be one of those officers touring the country to sniff out the telltale smoke of illegal stills and to collect taxes on home-produced and imported goods, mainly liquor and tobacco. As a married man, he would meet one of the conditions for employment.

Jean suggests he could work for her father, cutting stone in his masonry or maintaining the several cottages he owns in the Cowgate. She envisions James Armour's heart softening once he embraces the prospect of a granbairn, the first child of the next generation of their family.

Many nights they can't meet. After abandoning suppers she can't stomach, Jean wants only to crawl into her bed. Every morning she retches into the chamber pot. Her mother, thinking her daughter has the grippe, tells her to rest. Then Jean's body starts to betray her. Her belly bulges with a little hump; her breasts swell, and her nipples turn dark and hard. By mid-March, when she can no longer fasten the buttons on her bodice, she knows the time has come.

The wheel whirrs from the corner of the spence where Mrs. Armour is spinning flax into linen yarn. A lump of coal glows and sizzles in the hearth. Legs stretched out on a footstool, his cravat hanging loose, Mr. Armour snoozes, wisps of air puffing between his lips. The Bible gapes open on his lap. He startles awake at the sound of Jean's footsteps and peers up over his pince-nez. "Well, lass, what is it? You're white as a sheet."

She clears her throat and swallows. "I have pledged myself in marriage."

"Marriage?" He slams the book shut. "Without my consent?"

"But Jean well knows your approval of young Robert Wilson." Her mother smiles, sidling over to pat her husband's arm.

"Nae, tis another Robert who has my heart." Jean unfolds the paper clutched in her sweaty palm and holds it out to her father.

His eyes flit over the words. His mouth falls open. "That rake-helly Burns," he bellows. "A thousand curses on him." He springs from his armchair as the Bible thuds onto the carpet.

"Jean," her mother gasps. "You don't mean…" She scans her daughter's body, and Jean knows she has guessed the rest.

Straightening her shoulders and cupping her hands over the small mound of her stomach, Jean draws a long breath and then another before she says, "I am with child."

Her father's eyes bulge. The colour drains from his face. His legs wobble and he collapses onto the floor.

"He's fainted away," her mother cries, running to the sideboard to fetch the cordial.

Jean crouches and tilts up her father's head as her mother puts the glass to his lips. His grey eyes blink several times before finding their focus and lighting upon his daughter. "Whore!" he hollers and spits into her face.

Jean lifts her hand to her cheek, as if she's been struck, then stands and turns to leave.

"Sit down," her father orders. Back on his feet, he gulps another glass of cordial and towers over her. "You… carrying the bastard of that fornicator. You have disgraced me. How can I hold my head up in this village?"

"Nae, not a bastard," Jean pleads and picks up the crumpled paper from the floor. "We are pledged as husband and wife."

He rips the paper from her hand, scrunches it into a ball and heaves it into the fire.

The white sheet curls at the edges, blackens, and dissolves into flakes of ash. Jean looks to her mother, hunched on the floor sniffling. And she is struck—like a kick to her belly—with the magnitude of what she's done. Falling on her knees at her father's feet, she sobs, "Forgive me."

"Seek your forgiveness from God." He shoves a pinch of snuff up each of his black-haired nostrils then strides across the room and slams the door behind him.

Jean inches open her bedroom door, praying that Nelly is already asleep. But she's sitting up in bed, the lamp casting a halo on the brown curls encircling her face. Nelly glares at her sister. "What did you expect? Disobeying father and carrying on with such a man? You've sinned against God and disgraced our family." She gathers the patchwork quilt around her shoulders and moves over to the farthest edge of the bed.

Jean blows out the lamp so Rab will know they can't meet tonight. Or maybe ever again. She dabs her eyes with her wet handkerchief. Kneeling beside the bed, she brings her hands together and tries to summon a prayer of contrition. When she shuts her eyes to call on God, an old man with a long white beard scowls at her.

A half-moon glints through the window illuminating the picture above the bed—the Madonna in her blue robe, embracing her infant son. Mary looks downs at her with such serenity that Jean knows she understands. She begins to think about the Holy Mother in a different way, about the scorn she must have suffered when she was found to be with child and unwed. Calmness washes over her, and resolve: *If Mary could endure it, so can I. She bore the Birth, freed us from care; Christ has my heart and eye.*

Sleepless, she tries to untangle her thoughts, muddled as a knotted ball of yarn. Choosing Rab means forsaking her family forever. But in denying him, she'll be breaking their vow. She imagines the vengeance her father could deliver upon him. Atop the clothes press sits her porcelain doll, her childhood companion, and the books her father gave her: a small leather-bound Bible, a worn copy of *The Pilgrim's Progress*, a book of hymns—*Divine Songs in the Easy Language for the Use of Children*. She's learned most of them by heart, and recalls the song her father always asked her to sing when one of his children disobeyed:

> *Have you not heard what dreadful plagues*
> *Are threatened by the Lord*
> *To him that breaks his father's law*
> *Or mocks his mother's word?*
> > *The ravens shall pick out his eyes*
> > *And eagles eat the same*

At last, she plunges into a nightmarish sleep. *Sharp claws scratch at the window; a red face with fiery eyes peers in; horns butt against the glass: Bartie, trying to break in and carry her down to his pit of fire.* She screams herself awake. Rain pelts the shutters, and wind assaults the stone walls as if to blow them in.

In the morning, her mother orders Jean to pack her grip. Tomorrow they are sending her to Paisley to stay with her aunt and uncle. "Those nosey kirk elders will be beating on the door if they pick up any rumours," her mother says.

She has barely enough time to write to Rab and explain all that's happened; she can't say where her parents are sending her, and he mustn't try to see her until she sends word.

Her brother Adam is a willing messenger. He worships Rab as a model of rebelliousness. They became friends after Rab sheltered him one night at Mossgiel when Adam was evading arrest. He and some other lads had carried Agnes Wilson, a prostitute, astride a log through the village streets. Her mother, Poosie Nansie, sent the magistrate out to hunt them down. Adam showed her the verses Rab had written for him that night, "Adam Armour's Prayer." Jean didn't think much of them; they pardoned Adam and the other yonkers as just lads pulling a prank, and warned jurrs like Agnes about the consequences of whoring. So-called *loose women* had practised their trade since time immemorial because men laid down the boddles for their services, and Jean has always wondered why their customers aren't labelled *loose men*.

The stagecoach rattles over the rutted dirt trail, shaking as it rocks and sways around the curves at a nauseating pace. It stops at every village along the thirty-mile route, dropping off and picking up travellers and mail. Cramped inside the stuffy coach with three men, Jean feels the disrepute of a woman travelling alone. Every glance questions her status, appraises her dress and checks her fingers for a ring. Wearing a grey wool cloak to shield her body from scrutiny, she withdraws behind the wide brim of her silk bonnet and thinks about her aunt and uncle, whom she hasn't seen for a few years. She remembers her Uncle Andrew, a carpenter, as kind and soft-spoken. Aunt Elizabeth, her mother's older sister, was devout and somewhat stern, but she always welcomed Jean affectionately. With no children of their own, they enjoyed having their young nieces and nephews come to stay during the summer months.

Through the slit of a window, she catches fleeting glimpses of the changing landscape: fields purple with harebells, dry stone dykes, copses lush with bracken; greening hillsides dotted white with fat ewes and newborn lambs; cows black as the crows pecking in their dung patties; glens abloom with golden gorse. The smell of peat smoke drifts into the coach with the sounds of creaking harnesses, clopping hooves, the barking of a drover herding his cattle to market.

A sign in the window of the hostelry reads *Paisley Coach Stop and Post*. Jean looks around for her aunt and uncle then surmises they were probably unsure of the time of her arrival. She lugs her grip through the dusky lanes to the cottage on New Sneddon Street that she often visited as a child. When her aunt opens the door, she does not draw Jean against her ample bosom in a warm embrace. She nods a curt greeting, her mouth pinched and unsmiling. It's a look that tells Jean all she needs to know about her aunt's judgment: she is a fallen woman, a burden that must be endured.

A dish of tea is not offered. Her aunt leads her up the attic stairs to a small, windowless room with a narrow cot and a wash stand. *Like a cell*, Jean thinks as she drops onto the hard straw mattress, a place to do penance—to serve her time.

In the morning, Aunt Elizabeth outlines Jean's household duties: cook the meals, do the washing-up, sweep and scrub the slate floors, fetch water from the Cross, empty the slops, wash the linens and the clothes… Their maid-servant has just left them to be married, her aunt says, and Jean must earn her keep. "Least as long as your condition permits," she says, eyeing her niece's belly. Then she shows Jean the scullery and tells her to get started, pointing to the laundry heaped in the wicker basket.

Jean stokes the fire and sets the cauldron on the grate. After filling it with water, she runs out to the pump-well at the market cross to refill the casks. She adds a cup of lye soap to the scalding water and churns the linens with a long stick. The stained table-cloths and napkins need scrubbing against the washboard. Steam rises from the tub and beads her face with sweat. She heaves the scummy water out into the back garden and fetches more buckets from the well for rinsing. Three hours later, she collapses onto a chair and rubs her red, wizened hands—a maid-servant's hands.

She does not sup with her aunt and uncle. She serves them at the mahogany dining table in the spence, then eats the left-overs in the kitchen, alone. Uncle Andrew smiles sheepishly as she ladles cock-a-leekie soup into his bowl and pours his mug of ale. One day, he sees Jean hauling water caddies from the cross and rushes down the street. "Not a job for a lass in your condition," he says, taking the pails from her hands. From then on, the cistern is always full when she comes down in the morning to cook their breakfast.

One Saturday afternoon, Jean answers a knock on the front door, and it takes her a moment to recognize the young man, so stylishly dressed in a charcoal tailcoat and breeches, white cotton stockings, and fine calf-skin shoes. "Robin!"

"Thought you might enjoy a ride in my new gig," he grins. "Have you been to Stanley Castle yet?" During his last visit to Mauchline, Robin says, Mr. Armour told him of her where-abouts. She envisions her father in the background, like a pup-peteer manipulating the strings of her life.

Jean introduces Robin to her aunt, hovering a few feet behind her. Aunt Elizabeth smiles and nods. "A lovely day for a ride to the Gleniffer Braes."

"To be sure," Jean says, delighted at seeing Robin and the prospect of getting out of the house. Then her cheeks flush with the secret shame she will have to disclose. "I only need a moment to change my gown."

The road follows the old cattle droves along the White Cart River, its banks spilling with yellow broom. A warm breeze wafts sweet with spring blossoms, apple and honeysuckle.

They veer onto a lane that twists up a steep hill to a sun-lit meadow sprinkled with purple and red primroses. Robin reins in the horse beside a small, whitewashed cottage. Green-crested lapwings warble and flit from the oaks rising behind it. Its front windows look out upon the river and the gorse bushes gilding the bank.

Jean sighs. "What a peaceful spot."

Robin tells her he'll soon have the money to buy it; the orders are flooding in since he's set up his own weaving shed with eight looms. Jean knows what's coming next. Wringing her hands, she confesses the reason for her stay in Paisley. "I'm sorry," she says, bowing her head. "I've not been honest with you."

He drops the reins, takes a deep breath and slowly releases it. "I half-suspected." He removes his leather gloves, one finger at time then stares down at the river. "I'm sorry for your troubles."

After a long silence, he tilts up her chin and meets her wet brown eyes. "None of this changes how I feel about you, Jean. Just say the word."

"You could accept another man's bairn?"

At that moment she feels, as she never has before, what *love* really means. She knows she'd be foolish to turn her back on such unconditional devotion. Her misery would end. She would gain a loving, prosperous husband as well as her father's blessing. But she would lose Rab. He's part of her now; part of him is growing inside her.

"You truly are the gallant weaver," she says, dabbing her eyes, "and deserve a better lass. One who's still a maiden."

"I will say it again," he says, taking her hand. "Unless you wed another, I am waiting for you." Then he clucks the horse to a trot.

Winding down the narrow track, they notice the first purple blooms of heather on the hillside, and Robin begins to sing softly: *By sea and sky she shall be mine, the bonnie lass amang the heather*.

Every Saturday afternoon Robin comes to take her out for a ride, her only reprieve from the drudgery and her aunt's disapproving looks. He brings her a shawl that he wove in the pink and purple hues of the heather blanketing the braes. Draping the silky wool around her shoulders, he whispers, "*There's ne'er a lass in Scotia's isle, Can vie with ye amang the heather.*" He gives her money to buy the linen and the thread she needs for sewing cradle quilts, flannel petticoats, and the wee mutches she trims with lace. By the end of May, she feels the first fluttering movements in her belly, slowly rising like a satiny mound of dough. In three months—God willing—she could be cradling a baby.

No letters come from home. Then one afternoon, the first week of June, Jean is kneading dough for bannock when a rapping sounds on the front door. After scraping the sticky flour from her fingers, she opens the door and embraces the tall, gangly frame of her younger brother. Kissing Adam on each cheek, she feels the downy black fuzz sprouting above his lip and at the curve of his dimpled chin.

"The old man's more daffed than ever," Adam says, as Jean sets the copper kettle to boil at the back of the grate. "'Tis beyond the ken." He tells her about Rab coming to the house the previous week.

"Did father let him in?"

"In the door, but no further," Adam says, twirling his checked wool cap in his hand. "Rab tried to convince him he could support you and your bairn. Said he'd turn over his interest in the farm to his brother. Or he'd go work in the West Indies for a while. The old man flew into a rage, cursed Rab for defiling his daughter and threatened him within an inch of his life to keep away. He said you've come to your senses and want nothing to do with him."

"Dear God," she gasps. "What will Rab be thinking?"

"A few nights later I met him at Johnnie Doo's, slumped in the back corner with his pint. He looked more wretched than I've ever seen him. Still loves you to distraction, is what he said, and asked me to give you this."

She breaks the red wax seal on the back of the envelope, and her eyes well at the sight of his even, elegant handwriting.

My Dearest Jean,

You poor, ill-advised girl. Why have you deserted me? Have you forgotten our pledge and forsaken me? I hear you're in Paisley consorting with Wilson the weaver. News that has cut my very veins.

May God forgive your ingratitude and perjury to me. I can have no nearer idea of the place of eternal punishment than what I have felt in my own breast on your account. I've run into all kinds of dissipation and riot to drive you out of my head, but all in vain. The only cure I hope for is on a ship that will take me to Jamaica; then Farewell Scotland! And farewell dear unfaithful Jean. Never will I see you more. My heart has died within me.

Le miserable,
R.B.

She covers her face with the letter, her tears blotting out the ink of his words.

"But it was father who sent me here with his carriage," Adam says, setting down his mug. "I'm to bring you back."

Her head jerks up from her hands. "Back home?"

"Ay, Willie Fisher also came to call—God's own messenger service." He retrieves another envelope from the pocket of his breeks.

Her fingers tremble as they split apart the gold seal of the Presbytery of Ayr. She pulls out the thick parchment inscribed in heavy black ink:

Miss Jean Armour is hereby summoned
to appear for questioning before the Mauchline kirk session
on the 12th of June 1786.

*   *   *

The Mauchline Parish Church, with its imposing four-cornered tower, dominates the centre of the village. Built in 1829, the Gothic structure stands in the same spot as the old St. Michael's kirk, and the same flat-toned bell rings from the belfry. I stroll through the ancient burial ground surrounding the church, a maze of flat slabs and tall pillars crawling with moss and lichen. The names on many of the graves—Poosie Nansie, Nanse Tinnock, Gavin Hamilton, Willie Fisher; Andrew Noble, Jean's schoolmaster, and Robert Wilson, "The Gallant Weaver"—are so familiar to me now that they too seem like auld acquaintances.

At last I find the grave I've been searching for, tucked in the far northwest corner: *Reverend William Auld*. It's marked by a large tabular tombstone with intricately carved edges and bulging legs. Reverend Auld, the man who sprinkled Jean's infant head with three drops of his spittle to baptize her, who catechized her in childhood and patted her head with praise: "the flower of my parish."

I spread out my raincoat and sit down on the cold stone table. The sun breaks through the clouds, shafting rays of God light, and the leaves on the gigantic yews glisten and drip, the only sound but for the muffle of cars moving down Loudon Street. The spirits of time past envelop me as I peer though the shimmering green branches at the grey and black headstones. Glimpsing the sandstone wall of the church, I imagine the old kirk that once stood there, the long narrow stone building the Monks of Melrose built in the twelfth century. It's said to have looked more like a barn than a church, with a steep slate roof that rose above an old ash growing by the entrance. Jean Armour attended school there in a small chamber partitioned off at the back. Behind a long wooden table, she sat on a roughly-hewn bench and learned to read and to write. And at the front of that kirk, she sat upon the cutty stool, the seat of shame. The morass of emotions she would have experienced on this ground inundates me as if they've seeped into the soggy, consecrated earth.

I can picture her and Adam arriving back from Paisley late at night, the house dark but for a lamp shining from the parlour, her father waiting up for her. His only greeting would be a nod, followed by a cold-eyed scrutiny of her body. He sits her down at his desk, grabs a sheet of paper, and sharpens his quill. "You will write a letter of confession to the kirk."

She pleads exhaustion after the long journey and asks if it could not wait until the morning.

"Now." He jabs at the paper. "You will write it now, if you want a bed to sleep in." He hangs over her shoulder, exuding whisky fumes as he dictates:

> *I am heartily sorry that I have given and must give your Session trouble on my account.*
>   *I acknowledge I am with child and Robert Burns of Mossgiel is the father.*
>   *I am with great respect your humble servant,*
> *Jean Armour of Mauchline*
> *10 June 1786*

Two days later, Willie Fisher appears at their door. His shifty eyes size up Jean as he reads the kirk's summons in a grating, high-pitched voice: *Jean Armour is hereby ordered to appear on the cutty stool on Sunday, the ninth day of July 1786, to show true repentance for her transgression and receive public rebuke before the congregation.* Satisfaction oozing from his grizzled face, the hound of heaven moves in for the kill: *Refusal to obey this order means banishment from the kirk and deliverance into the hands of the devil.*

Jean knows this decree has caused many a lass to wrap a bundle of clothes and vanish into the night; caused many to take their own lives, their bodies found floating in the Chalk River. And caused many women to try to destroy their unborn babies—drinking herbs, inserting crochet hooks, jumping from hay lofts—and lose their own lives in the process.

She can see the vengeful smirk on old Willie's face as he delivers the kirk's order to Rab. And she can hear Rab delivering a quick rejoinder:

> *When I mount the creepie chair,*
> *Wha will sit beside me there?*
> *Gi'e me Rob, I'll seek nae mair,*
> *The rantin' dog the daddie o't.*

He told her about sitting on the creepie chair with Lizzie Patton in the Tarbolton kirk, and leering at the sour-faced old biddies in the congregation. "I wanted to whisper in their lugs that they'd never be up here," he said. "No man would ever find them worth the temptation."

The following week, Jean hears a knock on the door, her mother's quick footsteps then a loud slamming. Peering out her bedroom window, she recognizes the dark, tied-back hair and the russet plaid draping the sagging shoulders of the retreating figure. *Rab!* She wants to call out, but he's already rounded the corner. Hoisting herself up off the bed, she trundles down the stairs.

Her mother stands in front of the door, hands on her hips. "You've disgraced your family enough." She glares at her daughter like a jailer confronting a prisoner. "You'll not be chasing after that lecher."

"Show some mercy," Jean cries. "He's the father of my bairn—of your granbairn."

"And father of how many others?" her mother sneers. "He's been seen at the castle cavorting with that Campbell lass, even younger than you by the looks of her."

Her words slash through Jean like a knife. "That can't be true," she mutters.

"Now she's gone, all of a sudden. Left Gavin Hamilton high and dry without a maid-servant. Claimed she was needed back in Greenock to nurse her sick brother." She pauses before exacting her final cut. "More than likely carrying his bastard too."

Jean slinks back up to her room like a dog kicked into submission. Lying on her bed, she feels somersaulting turns in her belly as thoughts flip-flop through her mind. Knowing how the village gossip mill can turn and twist and distort, she doesn't believe what her mother said about Rab and Highland Mary. But she doesn't disbelieve it either.

She will know for certain on July 9 when she and Rab sit side-by-side on the cutty stools. She will look into his dark eyes and know the truth.

In the weeks that follow, Jean is forbidden to leave the house. Christina and her other friends do not come to call. They're no longer permitted to associate with the likes of her. In her own home, she's treated like a leper. When her father reads from the Bible on Sunday mornings, he orders her from the breakfast table. During family prayers in the evening, she sits alone in a corner of the parlour. Her father's droning is just noise in the background as she prays to Mother Mary. She feels her answering, reminding Jean of the words of her son, the saviour: *Let he who is without sin, cast the first stone*, words that her parents, and the pious kirk elders and the holier-than-thou gossips in the town have all forgotten.

Soon after the first bell tolls at ten in the morning, Jean crosses the High Street and passes through the iron gates of St. Michael's Kirk. She descends a few steps to an arched doorway. After six centuries, the stone floor has sunk several feet, so it feels like dropping into a cavern, dank with mould and decay. One small window in the north gable lets in a feeble shaft of light.

She slips into the school room at the back of the kirk. Seated at her old place near the front of the room, she recalls her former self, a young lass skipping barefooted to school every weekday for six years of her childhood—except those days when her father was away on a contract, and her mother kept her home to help with her younger brothers and sisters. She remembers the thrill of shaping letters, making them into words on her slate, then writing her name on the inside cover of her Bible. Her signature—none other like it in the world. Best of all she loved the singing. Mr. Noble, the schoolmaster, was also the choir director so they mostly sang hymns. But every now and then he taught them a ballad like "The Flowers o' the Forest" so they'd learn something about Scotland's bloody wars with England. He always called upon Jean to lead the class; she had the gift of perfect pitch, he said. She envied the lads, the clever ones, who got to learn Latin and study the English poets, preparing to attend university and become ministers or schoolmasters.

Their playground was the kirkyard where they clambered over the grey slabs cracked with age, so encrusted with lichen they had no idea whose bones they were trampling upon. In noisy games of hide-and-seek, they hid behind the grand pillared tombstones, the proud family names caked with centuries of moss.

The bell peals again. Benches and stools scrape across the stone floor. The outdoor wooden stairway leading to the balconies squeaks with the footsteps of the estate owners: the Bar-

skimmings shuffling into their loft to the right of the pulpit, the
Loudens directly across from them, and the Ballochmyles and
Auchinlecks, who'll be staring down from their lofts directly
above the cutty stool. Muted voices sound overhead from the
balcony leased by the lesser lairds. As the chanting of a psalm
filters through the walls, Jean can picture Mr. Noble, the pre-
centor—his long, skinny arms swaying as he intones a line in
solo and the congregation repeats it:

> *The Lord is my shepherd; I shall not want.*
> *He maketh me to lie down in green pastures.*
> *He leadeth me beside the still waters.*
> *He restoreth my soul.*

She sings along, trying to find comfort in the lovely words.
Then she paces, expecting Rab to burst in any minute. She imagines him scooping her up in his arms, whisking her away, and
smiles at the thought of him attempting to lift her, no longer the slender lass he embraced three months ago. Her hand
strokes her belly, swelling like a hillock beneath her full breasts.

The bell clangs for the third time. Reverend Auld will soon be
mounting the pulpit. The schoolroom door swings open. Black
bonnet askew on his stringy grey hair, Willie Fisher strides in.
"The kirk awaits you," he wheezes, fixing Jean with his beady eyes.

"But Rab Burns. He's nae here?"

"Ay, seated in his usual place."

"But we are to sit together."

"Did your father nae tell you?" He looks at her sideways.

"What?" She stops at the threshold, but Willie pushes her
forward.

The kirk is packed to overflowing. People line the pews; they
squat on stools and peer down from the lofts. Many are standing

along the walls. It seems as if the whole parish has turned out to witness the spectacle. Jean walks down the centre aisle, holding her head high, keeping her eyes focused on the candles sputtering on the communion table, the silver line of pewter cups, the baptismal bowl she was christened in, and the stool waiting beneath the pulpit where the black-gowned figure of Reverend Auld hovers like a vulture eying his prey—the flower of his parish, deflowered, disgraced.

Whispering hisses through the congregation. Hundreds of eyes sear into her back as Jean mounts the platform and sits upon the high stool. A ray of sun beams through the window between the upper lofts. In the shadowy light, colourful bonnets and black hats frame a blur of faces gawking at her rounded belly. She does not look to the centre pew where her family is seated, but scans the rough wooden benches well behind and to the right. There he sits, arms folded across his russet plaid, head bowed. *Why isn't he up here with me?*

The reverend's voice booms above her as he launches into his sermon: "Man's natural state of depravity is so described in the Holy Scripture. The apostle Mark decrees: *From within, out of the hearts of man, proceed evil thoughts, fornications, murders, thefts, covetousness, lasciviousness, an evil eye, blasphemy, pride, foolishness. All the evil things come from within, and defile the man.* Overcoming those inner desires is your only road to salvation. The damned will be punished in hell in an everlasting lake of fire where you will swim and burn, writhing in eternal pain."

He pauses to mop his face then hammers forth for another hour, his words flying up to the roof beams and bouncing off the stone walls. His fists thump the pulpit; his arms flap above Jean's head. The stench of too many bodies crowded in the musty, airless space has her stomach churning. She pulls a handkerchief from her apron pocket and puts it to her mouth.

"We have two such sinners amongst us," Reverend Auld continues, clearing his throat. "Jean Armour and Robert Burns will rise and stand before this congregation."

Jean trembles to her feet, her cheeks aflame, her eyes lowered.

"You appear here to be rebuked and to make profession of repentance for the sin of fornication."

She breathes in, long and deep, bracing herself for the onslaught.

"We call upon you to reflect seriously in contrition of heart on all the instances of your guilt, on their numbers and unhappy consequences, and say you will do no more." His voice thunders as he hurls his final warning: "Beware of returning to your sin like the dog to his vomit or the sow that was washed to her wallowing in the mire."

The slap of the Bible on the rostrum echoes in the silence. Only then does Jean lift her head to look at Rab. Her gaze pulls his black eyes up to meet hers. She sees a flicker of remorse in them, and sadness, but he cannot face her for long. His quick turning away says more than she wants to know.

That night, Jean lies like an injured animal that can't stop licking at its wounds. The bed seems to have shrunk with her expanding girth. Nelly has moved to the adjoining room to sleep with their younger sisters, grateful to be away from Jean's sullying presence. Down in the spence, the pendulum clock chimes ten times. Flinging a shawl over her bed gown, she tip-toes down the darkened stairs. Light seeps from beneath the parlour door.

Her father's head jerks up. He views his daughter with his usual disdain as she blurts out her question. "Why was Rab permitted to remain at his usual seat in the kirk?"

He tells Jean to sit down, that it's time for her to learn about the underhanded dealings of the reprobate who has ruined her life.

Last week Burns appeared before the session to acknowledge paternity, he tells her, then he applied for a bachelor's certificate confirming him a single man. It was granted on the condition he do penance before the congregation and contribute a guinea for the poor. Swirling the amber liquid in his glass, he says, "Worried about your so-called irregular marriage, I suppose. He's bound for Jamaica soon as he's raised money for his passage. They say he's taking that Campbell lass with him. Planning to marry her." Smirking, he drains the dregs of his drink and says he used his influence so Jean would be free of him altogether. Not even have to sit with him before the kirk.

"Leaving the country?" she cries.

"Dinna you worry," he says, shaking his finger. "The rogue will nae get off that easy." He staggers over to his desk and retrieves a paper from the top drawer. "Had my lawyer draw this up. An official warrant ordering Burns to pay maintenance of a hundred pounds. All that's needed is your signature—there." He stabs repeatedly at the blank space beside Jean's name.

"But he doesn't have that kind of money." Despite all she's just heard, and all she endured that morning, her heart will not harden against him. "He'll be arrested."

"Dinna fash yourself about the skellum. He's nae concern for you."

"I cannot believe that."

"No? Why did he have Gavin Hamilton draw up a deed of trust to his brother? Transferred his interest in the farm so his bastard daughter would be provided for."

"How do you know all this?"

"The whole of Ayrshire knows it. The town crier shouted it three times in Ayr's market cross." Pulling another paper from his desk drawer, he stomps back and forth as he bellows: *"I Robert Burns of Mossgiel intend to go abroad and, having acknowledged myself the father of a child named Elizabeth begot upon Elizabeth Paton; and whereas Gilbert Burns in Mossgiel, my brother, hereby obligates himself to aliment, clothe and educate my said child as if she was his own."*

Jean shakes her head, unable to speak. *Nothing for their bairn?*

"I'll not be shouldering the expense of that villain's bastard," he says, pressing a quill into her hand. "I've eight mouths to feed as it is."

She stares at the black letters inked on the page, at the blank space awaiting her signature. Her mind is fogged with uncertainty: *What if he ends up in jail? Who is betraying whom?* Her eyes are too wet and blurry to see anything clearly. Then a gentle nudge, a wee elbow or foot pressing against her flesh, snaps everything into focus, reminding her whom she must consider first and foremost from now on. She spreads the paper out on the curved table of her belly and signs her name.

By mid-July, Jean can manage only sitting-down tasks, sewing nappies—at least a dozen, her mother advises—and wool flannel pilchers to cover them at night. She cross-stitches cradle quilts and embroiders nightgowns. She waddles about the house, her wrists and ankles swollen, her breath laboured from what feels like a hard ball pressing into her ribs. Her hips and back and shoulders ache. Her breasts and belly are marbled with stretch marks and are bluish-purple with veins. She can't imagine that her skin can stretch any more without splitting. The baby is always moving now, poking her with its limbs as if it needs to get out.

Gauging the size of Jean's belly, her mother says she will surely be brought to bed within a few weeks. Mrs. Armour unpacks a kist of well-worn baby clothes, her eyes tearing as she passes her daughter the bundles of nappies, undershirts, pilchers and flannel petticoats. "I'll not be needing these again, God willing. Eleven weans are more than enough to pass through one woman's body."

Jean witnessed, in various ways, nine of those births. Her earliest memory is her mother screaming from behind the bedroom door, and her father hushing Jean's cries. At age eight, she began assisting her mother in the lying-in room; helped the first Mary, the second Robert, the second Mary, Janet and—finally—the third Robert all make their bloody entries into the world.

Jean has no illusions about what awaits her. Her father never failed to remind her: the pangs of birth are God's eternal punishment on women for Eve's disobedience. And she knows about the unforeseen complications: the long, exhausting labours, the babies presenting feet-first or hiplings that need to be turned, and the infections that can develop after the child is safely here. That her mother survived all eleven of her confinements was a feat in itself. For she also knows of women who bled to death or burned up in fever, never holding the child they bore.

Jean can no longer get down on her knees. But at day's end, sprawled on her bed, she beholds Mary's radiant face and prays: *Holy Mother, help me and my wean survive.*

One evening in early August, Mr. Armour arrives home late for his supper (waylaid at the Whitefoord Arms, Jean assumes from the beery odour of his breath). He scrapes his chair up to the table, grumbling about that black-guard Burns catching wind of the maintenance warrant and skulking from one friend's house to the next to evade it. Then he starts ranting about the book of poems Burns has just published. "Everyone in Ayrshire is singing his praises. Even the Edinburgh gentry are taking notice. The ploughman poet, a genius, they're calling him," he says, scowling between mouthfuls of black pudding. "Now Aiken's pressuring me to drop my writ against the scoundrel. There's talk of getting him a job with the excise, so he won't leave the country. Scotland has to keep its native son, they say. The whole country's gone daft over a bunch of verses. Most not fit to be read in decent company, you can be sure."

But behind his tirade, Jean senses a shift in her father's regard for Rab, a grudging admiration. It's unheard of for someone like him, a farmer, to publish a book. Suddenly, Robert Burns is *someone*. And, she suspects, her father is already counting up the coppers, thinking he can wheedle some of the profits. In just over a month, six hundred copies have sold out at three shillings each. And a second printing is in the works.

A week later on Lammas Day, a humid August evening, Jean is propped against a bank of pillows, stuffing muslin into quilt patches, her window and door wide open to let the honeysuckle breeze blow through. A knock on the door downstairs, her father's heavy footsteps then someone asks after her health. The deep voice sets her blood racing. A few minutes later, her mother pokes her head into Jean's room. "Come down to the parlour," she says. "We've some matters to settle with Burns."

Jean doesn't move. An eddy of tangled emotions swirls through her mind—resentment, bitterness, remorse and an overpowering desire. Sitting up on the edge the bed, she waits for the dizziness to pass then pushes herself onto her feet. She hikes her petticoat above her mountain of a stomach, fastens the ties beneath her bulging under-bodice, and covers it all with a long white apron. Her belly pulling her forward, she totters down the narrow stairway and into the spence.

He's standing in front of the window holding a basket of shiny red apples. His eyes widen, and soften, when she enters.

"The first of the harvest from Mossgiel," he says, handing the basket to her. Their eyes lock. As they look deeply into each other, Jean sees herself reflected in the mirror of his unflinching gaze.

"Sit down, Jean," her father says, calling her back to where he and her mother sit grimacing on the settee. "State your business, Mr. Burns."

"I've come to assure you of my intentions of providing for our bairn," he says, his eyes clinging to Jean's. "I'm not leaving the country." He pulls a book from the breast pocket of his jacket and passes it to her. "My earnings from this will help."

Her fingers move over the grey-blue paper cover embossed with black lettering:

Poems, Chiefly in the Scottish Dialect
by
Robert Burns

She feels the enormity of this slim book with his name on it, his poems in good black print. He has done it; he is an author. Opening the book to the first page, she reads,

For Jean,
Alas! How often does Goodness wound itself,
And sweet Affection prove the spring of woe.
R.B.

Fearing her tears might spill upon the paper, she searches in her apron pocket for a handkerchief and dabs her eyes. She stares at the words, not knowing what to say. After lengthy seconds of silence, she lifts her head and turns to thank him for the book. By then, he is gone.

That night, by the light of the lamp, she reads the book from cover to cover—over forty poems in all. She's heard snippets of many of them, verses he recited when he came to her at night in a fever of composition. But not the first poem, "Twa Dogs," in which Luath, the collie of a ploughman—*a rhyming, ranting, raving billie*—and Caesar, a gentleman's dog, compare the lives of their masters. How fitting, she thinks, for Luath—who brought them together—to have pride of place in his book. Next comes a playful ode to his muse, *guid auld Scotch Drink*. Jean chuckles—he and her father have at least one thing in common. And she laughs again through the mockery of "Holy Willie's Prayer": *But yet, O Lord! confess I must, At times I'm fash'd wi' fleshly lust.*

Some poems he wrote after their parting in April, verses of remorse and despair alluding to *a faithless woman's broken vow: For one has cut my dearest tie, And quivers in my heart.* "To a Mountain Daisy: On Turning One Down with the Plough, in April 1786," leaves her sobbing into her pillow.

> *There, in thy scanty mantle clad,*
> *Thy snawy bosom sunward spread,*
> *Thou lifts thy unassuming head*
> > *In humble guise;*
> *But now the share uptears thy bed,*
> > *And low thy lies!*

> *Such is the fate of artless maid,*
> *Sweet flow'ret of the rural shade!*
> *By love's simplicity betrayed,*
> > *And guileless trust,*
> *Till she, like thee, all soiled, is laid*
> > *Low i' the dust.*

She begins to see it all through *his* eyes then, the forces that overtook their lives: *By human pride or cunning driven, To mis'ry's brink*. Her father's monstrous pride, and her fear of him, trapped them in a maze of misunderstanding. Is it too late for them to find their way out?

Through the long night, her thoughts churn, as if she's tossing on a stormy, black sea with no hope of rescue, no safe harbour in sight. Then she recalls the words of another poet, Solomon the Wise: *Many waters cannot quench love, neither can the floods drown it*. And she clings to this hope, a scant piece of driftwood. Hearing Rab's voice and the pulsing of his heart through his verses, she feels close to him in a way that she hasn't in four long months.

As rosy dawn blooms outside her window and the first laverocks chirrup their morning song, she tucks his book beneath her pillow and floats into sleep, his words humming in her ear and his child stirring in her belly.

*   *   *

Behind a glass display case in the Burns House Museum, a first edition of *Poems, Chiefly in the Scottish Dialect* lies open to its flyleaf, a wrinkled sepia-toned page with faint, faded lettering. The book looks too thin, too insubstantial to have shaken up the literary world as it did. An entirely different kind of poetry: the voice of the common man, a farmer with little formal education. Yet this slim volume transformed lives. It kept Burns from sailing across the sea to become a bookkeeper on a Jamaican plantation, and thereby changed the course of Jean Armour's life as well. He gave birth to a book while she was just weeks away from giving birth to their child.

In late eighteenth-century Scotland, giving birth meant confronting the real possibility of death. I have an inkling of the contradictory feelings Jean would have been facing as the trauma of my own birthing experiences is still so acute in my memory. The first time, it was January in a cabin in rural British Columbia. I laboured for two days with a midwife until the baby showed signs of fetal distress. I lay in the back of a Toyota station wagon, bumping over the dark snow-packed roads, forty-five kilometres to the hospital, moaning through contractions. Then the glaring lights of a delivery room; the cold, hard steel of a suction device thrust into me and clamped onto the baby's head. A few minutes later, a healthy ten-pound boy was wrenched out of me.

It took me ten years to do it again. I had the good sense to be in a hospital this time, but it was another marathon labour that ended with fetal distress, an emergency C-section, and another broad-shouldered son, weighing in at ten pounds, five ounces. During both ordeals, I felt caught in a liminal zone between life and death; I remember thinking, *This could go either way*. If not for twentieth-century technology and antiseptic techniques, my birthing stories would not have happy endings. I understand why in the mythic realm of the Aztecs, mothers who died in child-birth shared a special heaven—*the House of the Sun*—with war-riors killed in battle. Becoming a soldier and becoming a mother both demand the giving over of oneself for the life of another.

In an anteroom of the museum, I pull up a chair to an an-tique fold-top desk, a quill-stand and ink pot sitting on its dark mahogany top. It's quiet; no other visitors have come this mor-ning. Taking out my notebook and pen, I try to imagine what it would have been like to give birth here in Mauchline in 1786. I want to reach out across time and take Jean's hand as she under-goes the most dangerous and transformative ordeal of her life.

It may have been the second night of September when the first tightenings in her belly awakened her. I can see her pushing herself up to the edge of the bed then slowly getting to her feet. Water gushes between her legs. Reluctant to waken her mother yet, she lies back down on her side and shoves a pillow between her knees. *Who is moving through me?* she wonders. *Who will emerge through the door of my body to live in the world?* Stroking her globe of a belly, she softly croons:

> *Baloo, baloo, my wee, wee thing,*
> *For thou art doubly dear to me*
> *O but thy daddie's absence lang*
> *Would break my dowie heart in twa.*

The pangs grip her—sharper this time—and she cries out. She sinks into herself, riding out the waves of pain. When her eyes open, a figure in a white nightdress hovers, phantom-like, be-side her in the dark.

"Mammie," she gasps, grabbing her mother's hand, "my water's broke. The throes are on me."

Her mother pulls a chair up to the bed and asks how often they're coming. Jean answers with a long moan as another spasm clenches her belly.

"Breathe," Mrs. Armour says, patting her daughter's leg, "breathe through them. I'll rouse Adam to fetch Mistress Ramsey." Just the sound of her name is comforting to Jean; Mistress Ramsey, the midwife who safely delivered all her mother's babies.

Jean moves in and out of the contractions while her mother flutters about, heaping quilts upon her, then stacking sheets and nappies on the chest of drawers. She lights several candles and places them around the room, the smell of tallow mingling with the lavender scent of the linens. Mrs. Armour cranks the window closed to ward off any evil spirits that might be lurking, then drapes a dark cloth over the glass to keep out the rising sun. Next to the bed, she sets the oaken cradle that Jean, and all her brothers and sisters, slept in. On the bedside table, she puts a Bible and an open pair of scissors to frighten away fairies that might be seeking a changeling.

Still in her nightdress, Nelly comes in carrying a tray with a steaming cup and a plate of oatcakes. Her mother holds the caudle to her daughter's lips and says it will help to keep up her strength and her spirits. Jean inhales the spicy aroma and sips the hot, sweet ale. Her first time helping in the lying-in chamber, Nelly perches on the chair by the bed as Jean groans through her pangs. She sees her sister's face, pale with worry, and reaches out to squeeze her clammy hand. "Sister," Jean whispers, "sae glad you're here with me." Nelly smiles—an uneasy half-smile—and kisses Jean's cheek, her first show of affection for many months. She unties Jean's hair and brushes it, long smooth strokes to remove any tangles that might slow down her labour.

Mistress Ramsey bustles in. She totes a leather bag packed

with tools that Jean hopes she'll not be needing for her confinement: a set of tongs with curved blades to grip a baby's head, a long iron hook to pierce a skull and haul a dead wean out, piece by piece. Village stories replay in Jean's mind: A classmate returning from school one day to find a puddle of blood on the kitchen floor; red tracks leading into the spence then to her mother's bedroom where, beside a basin of blood, she found her mother, grey and cold as stone. And the tanner's wife in labour with her first child, writhing in convulsions for two days, nearly biting off her tongue. There were the after-birth stories too, mothers burning up and expiring with childbed fever.

The midwife's large bosom heaves as she catches her breath. "Lassie, lassie," she grins, "you'll soon be rid of the weight you're carrying." With a knowing touch, her nimble fingers massage the vast mound of Jean's belly. "An unco wame," she says, her flickering eyes betraying some concern. "Och, you're a good-sized lass yourself," she chuckles. "Like your mither. Wide hips, made for bearing weans."

A steady stream of chatter flows from Mrs. Ramsey as she removes the blankets and tells Jean to draw up her legs. "Spread them wide dearie, so's I can check your privities." Jean gasps as the midwife's cold hand moves into her. "Ah, well stretched already. Ay, there's the wee head, just as it should be."

She brews Jean a cup of her howdie tea—pennyroyal, vervain, birthwort—to speed up the contractions. Her mother and sister take turns walking Jean around the room, and Mrs. Ramsay massages her back and shoulders. Jean loses all sense of time, consumed in riding out the throes; they rise and fall like gigantic waves, mounting slowly at first then swelling to a crest, the pain drowning out everything around her. Hours must have passed, Jean realizes, for sunlight is peeking around the edges of the window covering when the midwife begins rubbing butter onto the crowning head.

"Time to get to the floor lass," she says, rushing around to help Jean out of bed.

Jean squats on the straw mat, and her mother crouches behind, supporting her daughter's arms. She feels an overwhelming urge to push and be rid of the spasms, certain she'll die from the pain.

"That's it, Jean," Mrs. Ramsey coaxes, "the head's out, a black-haired one. Keep pushing." The midwife eases out one shoulder, then the other.

With a mournful scream, Jean bears down with all the strength left in her. A tiny body slithers out into the mid-wife's bloodstained hands.

"A wee lass," Nelly says, cradling the infant while the midwife cuts the cord and ties it with string. Flailing her arms like little wings, the baby lets out her first bleating cry, the most beautiful sound Jean has ever heard.

"Nae as big as I thought," Mrs. Ramsey says, towelling off the baby's blood-splotched face and the white glaze coating her body.

"A bonnie bairn," her mother says, carrying her over to where Jean lies, spent but blissful.

Jean takes her daughter into her arms and wonders at her tiny head, bulged out at the back, covered in downy dark hair; at her bleary blue eyes, wide open, looking right into Jean's as if to say, *Where am I?*

Suckling will help to expel the afterbirth, the midwife says, so Mrs. Armour helps Jean position the baby at her breast. Her pink rosebud lips root out the nipple and soon latch on, drawing out the sweet foremilk. Nelly covers them both with a thick linen cloth warmed by the hearth then runs out to tell the family that Jean has been safely delivered. Jean knows that Adam will carry out his promise and hasten to Mossgiel as fast as the mare can carry him to relay the news to Rab.

But no sooner has the door closed when Jean lets out an ungodly scream that sets her baby yowling. "Tis the afterbirth," Mrs. Ramsey says, feeling Jean's forehead. "I'll try to help it along."

The midwife reaches her hand in to find the placenta; her brow furrows, her jaw drops. "Losh," she says, pulling out a round crimson slab and cupping it her hands. "There's some wee feet right behind it." Jean shrieks and clutches the sheet.

"Twins?" her mother gasps, rocking the mewling baby in her arms.

"Ay, hiplings at that," the midwife says. "Brace yourself, lass. I'm turning it now." A large hand and a small body twist like a vise inside her. Then all goes black.

A raspy voice calls to her through the murk: "The head's down. One strong heave will do it."

Wailing, as if in the throes of death, Jean calls forth her second child. And like a little eel, her son slips into the world.

A few hours later, he's snoozing in the hooded cradle on the far side of her bed out of the draft of the door. Jean has just gobbled a bowl of gruel, ordinary milky oatmeal sweetened with honey, but it tasted like the most delicious meal she's ever eaten. She reaches out to rock her son while her other arm snuggles her daughter at her breast.

She can relax now, knowing her babies are safe. Mrs. Ramsey buried the afterbirths in the garden to protect the house. She brought in a teaspoon of dirt to mix with a few drops of whisky, spooned the paste into the babies' mouths to repel the fairies and purge the dark green meconium from their bowels. The midwife bathed their stubby navels in salt water and daubed the brine on Jean's breasts to preserve her milk. Then Jean took three sips of the salty water, a counter charm against the evil eye. The room is clean and quiet. Contentment encases her like a cocoon. Her heavy lids finally close.

Loud voices, and the door bursts open. Rab's face beams with a broad grin as he kneels by Jean's bed. "Blessings of God Almighty on our daughter."

Jean's eyes brim with pride when she delivers the swaddled infant into Rab's arms. "Ay, your bonnie Jeanie."

"Tis your tyta," Rab whispers. The baby blinks and yawns. He turns and smiles at Jean's father who entered fast upon Rab's heels.

"You need to be asking for a double portion of blessings." Jean reaches down into the cradle and passes him another swaddled bundle. "Enough for wee Robert as well."

Rab's eyes gape. His mouth drops open, and he hoots: "A fine lad and lass in one throw." Cradling a baby in each arm, he kisses each of their cone-shaped heads capped with black hair. "God bless the little dears."

"Ay, ay," Mr. Armour interrupts, "Jean's needing her rest," his tone less commanding than usual.

Rab tucks a baby on either side of Jean. "Such a glowing in my heart I never imagined." He plants a long kiss on her lips. "I hope to return soon to see these angels we've given life to. I've been called to the capital. The literati are eager to meet the ploughman poet," he chuckles. "I'll wear my farm boots caked with Ayrshire dirt. Maybe then they'll subscribe to a second edition."

"There'll be time enough for talking of all that," Mr. Armour scoffs, holding the door open, "and how you'll be supporting your two angels."

Mr. Armour's displeasure hangs over the household like a storm cloud. During the baptism three days after the birth, his lips are taut with disapproval. The custom of naming the first-born for the father's father or the mother's mother does not apply since the babies are branded *illegitimate*. But to her father, the names Jean has chosen are too blatant a reminder of her ongoing attachment to Rab. Then he grouses about the crying disturbing his sleep and the lines of nappies drying by the hearth.

In giving birth to not just one, but two babies out of wedlock, Jean has doubly sinned, heaped double disgrace upon her father's sanctimonious head. To make matters worse they were born on a Sunday. To the kirk, birth on the Sabbath means conception occurred on the Lord's Day—a profanity, even within marriage. But Jean no longer holds her father's and the kirk's views as the gospel truth. Rab has opened her eyes and enabled her to see through the thin veil of their hypocrisy. "They tell us we're born into the world slaves of iniquity, inclined to evil," Rab said. "But I believe the opposite. We come into the world with a heart and disposition to do good." As Jean beholds her babies' innocent faces, she knows Rab is right. And the foundation of her father's and the kirk's creed totally crumbles.

"Don't get too attached," her mother advises in the early weeks. "One of them could be snatched from you at any time." Jean fears it's a warning. Her father fumes about them not having room for two more children and alludes to Burns's family taking one of them. But Jean is sure her father will eventually grow to love both his granbairns as his own. *How can he not?* she wonders, as she lavishes her babies with hugs and kisses, delights in their satiny skin and sweet smell. Love swells in her like a sea, vast and all-consuming. It washes over her as she nurses them, cleans their wee hurdies and lullabies them to sleep. But that love is also frightening in its intensity. Parts of her live in the world now, separate but still connected, the umbilical cord stretching invisibly.

It's that powerful maternal love that keeps her afloat during those first sleep-deprived months; she thinks she might drown in the exhaustion of caring for two babies. Her breasts swell hard as boulders after her milk comes in. Her nipples blister, and suckling is tortuous. She gets Jeanie fed and settled at one end of the cradle then Bobbie awakens. She changes his nappy and nurses him, then his colicky bawling begins. Before long, his sister is howling along with him.

With her mother's and sister's help, Jean learns how to hold, to feed and to burp both babies at once; how to tuck one into the cradle without disturbing the other. She's nursing every three hours, and is blessed with a good store of milk. Her babies thrive. Thrilled to be aunties, her young sisters—eight-year-old Mary and six-year-old Janet—help with changing nappies, rocking the cradle and washing the flannel petticoats. Little mothers-in-training, like Jean was when she tended to them as babies.

During the autumn months, her days and nights are so full with the demands of motherhood that she has little time for missing Rab. But he's there in the recesses of her mind, like a room she visits some nights before dropping into sleep. Her father brings home snippets of gossip from the Whitefoord Arms. "That maid of Gavin Hamilton's, that Campbell lass, died at her home in Greenock," he reports one day. "It was the fever. Some say she bore a wean, premature, and they both died."

Jean glances at her mother whose lips are puckered in a smug expression: *I told you so.*

Another day, her father relays news about the capital's reception of *our bard*, as he's taken to calling Rab. "Hosted in the best drawing rooms," he exclaims, "hobnobbing with professors from the university."

Jean imagines Edinburgh, its wide streets, towered palaces and grand houses; envisions Rab discussing poetry and sipping wine in dining rooms glittering with silver and glass; rich men in fine suits and sophisticated ladies in brocade gowns with flowing trains, all hanging on his words. She wonders how different he'll be when he returns, and looks down at her milk-stained calico petticoat, brushes her fingers through her tangled hair, not remembering the last time she washed it. The skin on her stomach sags in lumpy folds. Her huge breasts are often painfully engorged and leaking. Her body is no longer her own. Nor is her time.

Her only outings are to take her children for walks in the fresh spring air. When Robin Wilson returns from Paisley, they often stroll through the streets, each of them carrying a baby. Robin dotes on her twins. Every visit he brings them little gifts, like the sky-blue lamb's wool jumpers he wove himself. As Jean watches his gentle, loving way with her babies, she knows he'd be a good father. They've not talked of it since that day beside the White Cart River. But he's waiting, patient as Job, still hopeful she'll take him for a husband. She's sorely tempted. Soft-spoken and serious, he lacks Rab's charm and flamboyance. It's not the passion she feels for Rab, but Robin's steadfastness throughout the recent upheavals in her life have made Jean appreciate another kind of love. She needs a bit more time to see her way clearly, until Rab comes home from Edinburgh.

Early in the New Year, a letter arrives.

Dearest Jean,

> *The city's literati have been kind in welcoming me and generous in their patronage of a second edition of my book. They're not sure what to make of me, though—*

"the heaven-taught plowman" in my rough kintra coat
and unpowdered black hair. A little too independent
of mind for my station! I've sat for my portrait in oils
and dined with so many lords I've lost count of them.

I feel a miserable blank in my heart for want of
seeing you and our bairns; I hope to be home with the
arrival of spring. Until then, I remain yours faith-
fully, RB

Her father's eyes spark when she tells him another edition of Rab's poems will soon be published. "Returning to Mossgiel with pockets full o' the yellow Geordies," he says, rubbing his hands together, "enough to provide for all his family."

It's a warm day in early June, the heat of the sun finally drying the ground, sodden for weeks with the spring rains. Jean is sunning the twins in the grassy courtyard adjoining the Whitefoord Arms, trying to keep them occupied with rattles and balls on the patchwork coverlet. But her nine-month-old babies want to move and explore the world. Bobbie pushes himself up on his arms and inches along on his belly. Jeanie has mastered a full crawl on her hands and knees. Every stone and twig and bright primula is a wondrous discovery to be touched and tasted. Jean retrieves a wad of grass from Bobbie's mouth and leaves him screeching while she makes a dash for Jeanie, creeping dangerously close to the road. She scoops her daughter up in her arms and spins around to check on Bobbie. He is not on the quilt.

He's hoisted high in the air, smiling into the face of a man in a wide-brimmed black hat. It takes Jean a few seconds to recognize him in his city attire: navy tailcoat, blue-and-white striped waistcoat, beige buckskin breeches and polished black riding boots. Holding Bobbie out at arm's length, Rab grins at his wee replica; the same sable hair curling around his ears, matching broad foreheads, dark brown eyes. Bobbie squeals, showing off his two front teeth.

Rab takes Jean's hand and leans in to kiss his daughter's cheek. "Image of your bonnie mother," he says tousling Jeanie's black curls, "soft as a raven's wings." He eyes the matron's mutch covering Jean's hair. "You've lost your red ribbon."

"Ay, and a good deal of sleep as well," she laughs. "'Tis nothing compared to what I've gained."

Pulling a package from his coat pocket, he says, "A little something for the bairns." Jean unwraps the shop-paper, and they fit matching pairs of red velvet slippers onto the wriggling feet of the babies. "They're aglow with good health," Rab says. "You too, Jean. Motherhood surely agrees with you." He glances down at her fingers. Probably checking for a ring, Jean thinks. The village chatter about her and Robin Wilson has probably reached him by now.

She's suddenly self-conscious of her plump figure and bare, grass-stained feet. "You're looking fine enough yourself," she says, noticing his starched linen cuffs, smooth hands, fingernails evenly trimmed. A diamond ring sparkles on one finger. "The city seems to have treated you well."

"A gift from Lord Glencairn," he says, eyeing the ring. "His lordship's been a great supporter of the second edition. Introduced me to the publisher and rallied many of his rich friends to subscribe."

"Must be hard returning to Mauchline after mingling in such circles."

"Nae, I'd enough of them. Wigged, powdered and painted. Ladies so tightly laced they can scarcely breathe. The tide that's swept me up will just as soon recede and leave me much as I was. A poor ploughman."

Both babies start fussing at once, and Jeanie tugs on the ties of her mother's bodice. "Feeding time and changing time," Jean says. She passes her daughter into Rab's other arm and gathers up the play things into the coverlet.

"How do you do it?" he asks, struggling to control both squirming, squealing babies. "How do you carry them both at once?"

"Strang arms," she chuckles, "and a bairn on each hip."

"Could I come home with you, Jean? Is it a good time to talk with your father?"

She swallows hard. For months she's been anxious about the outcome of this conversation. "As good a time as ever," she says, meeting his eyes. "He's been waiting for you."

At the sound of the door opening and the babies' whining, Mrs. Armour bustles out from the kitchen, drying her hands on her apron. "Well, Mr. Burns," she says, tucking loose strands of grey hair beneath her frilled mutch, "finally back from the city."

"Guid-day to you, Mrs. Armour," he nods. "Good to be home and see my bonnie bairns."

She shows him into the spence while Jean takes the twins upstairs. After nursing, changing and settling them into the cradle, she pulls out a flowered gown from the back of her press and manages to squeeze herself into it. She removes her mutch, brushes her hair and ties it back with a scarlet ribbon. As she descends the stairs, her father's chortling echoes from the parlour. Rab is in full flight of a story. His little finger pointed up on the handle of his teacup, he lisps in a stuffy Scotts accent. A wide grin on his face, her father leans forward in his chair, drinking in the wit flowing from Rab's mouth.

"Walking through the city's wynds is a risky business," Rab says. "Around ten every evening, the upper windows fly open.

Keep your lugs alert for the cry, *Gardy Loo*. Or you'll have a chamber pot dumped on your head. Ay, *Auld Reekie*, Fergusson called it right. The streets are thranging with randie creatures and reeking with open sewers. Pigs nosing and grunting through the gutters."

Never having travelled to Edinburgh himself, Mr. Armour is so absorbed in Rab's stories he doesn't notice that Jean has taken a seat beside her mother. Perched stone-faced on the settee, Mrs. Armour clears her throat and says she must stir the stew simmering in the kitchen.

"Ay, then, Jean," her father says, his brow furrowing into its numerous folds. "About the care of your bairns. Mr. Burns has kindly agreed to take the wee lad to live with his family."

"Take Bobbie?" Jean's eyes dart back and forth between her father and Rab. "But he's still suckling."

"We'll wait a fortnight then, Mr. Burns?" her father asks, as if these arrangements have nothing to do with her. "Jean can wean the lad. And you'll have time to visit, so the boy can get to know you. Make it easier on him." He winks at Rab. "Let's say... two weeks from today? You and Jean can use my carriage to ride up to Mossgiel."

Head lowered, she can feel Rab's eyes on her. "Dinna fash yourself, Jean," he says. "Bobbie will be well loved and cared for. My mother and sisters are missing a baby to snuggle now that Bess is two years old."

She stares at her empty hands, trembling inside, struggling to keep her tears at bay.

Rab touches her shoulder as her father, blathering cheerfully, escorts him to the door. "Honoured to have you visit, sir. We've followed your success in the capital with great interest. You've done Mauchline proud."

The next day, whenever Bobbie screams his hungry cry, Jean holds the spout of a papboat to his mouth. It opens like a baby bird's waiting to be filled. He smacks his lips as the paste of bread softened in warm cow's milk drools down his chin. The bedtime nursing is the hardest for him to forego, but with a stomach full of pap, Bobbie soon drifts off as she rocks him in her arms, crooning a lullaby.

Her mother has little sympathy for Jean's misery over relinquishing her son. "Praise the good Lord he's alive," she says, "and you can still see him from time to time." Thinking about her mother burying three of her children, Jean knows her mother is right. Every night she thanks the blessed Virgin for her two healthy babies.

She clings to a strand of hope that her separation from Bobbie will be temporary. Her father is bending, even stooping, to win Rab's favour. *Men*, she sighs out loud. One advances and one retreats, like pieces in a game of draughts. While she waits on the sidelines. Every day she expects Rab to visit, and takes extra care with choosing her gown and fixing her hair. But he doesn't come. It's sowing season at Mossgiel, so she supposes he'll be helping his brothers in the fields. But he'd surely be taking time for a pint at Johnnie Doo's across the alley. After blowing out the lamp one night, she looks down to the tavern and sees Rab lit up in the window, swilling his ale and grinning that irresistible grin.

In the morning, they will take Bobbie to his new home in Mossgiel. Already feeling the ache of missing him, she reaches out in the dark and draws him close, straining to hear his soft sleeping breath.

*   *   *

Emerald fields roll for miles into the hilly blue horizon. Buffeted by misty rain and wind, I'm standing at the end of a long gravel driveway that leads up to a white farmhouse on the crest of a hill. If not for the stone marker at the end of the lane, I would never have guessed this site was once the Mossgiel farm of the Burns family. A sprawling two-storey house has grown up and out from the foundations of their but and ben cottage. Still a working farm, it looks prosperous with its surrounding green pastures, a far cry from the clay terrain the Burns brothers tried for years to coax into crops. At least the place was fertile ground for poetry. The fields I glimpse behind the house inspired some of Burns's best known works—"To a Mountain Daisy" and "To a Mouse," an ode to the "cowrin', tim'rous beastie" he saved from the guillotine blade of his plow.

To the east, a mile or so down the Tarbolton Road, looms the turreted tower of the Burns National Memorial, a seventy-foot high monument and museum erected in 1896 for the centenary of Burns's death. A sadly ironic juxtaposition in both time and space, this grand baronial style monument dominates the route that Burns, barely eking out an existence, trudged to and from Mauchline. It's the route that I imagine he and Jean would have travelled the day they brought Bobbie to live at Mossgiel.

I try to envision how the farm would have looked in 1787: a two-room cottage, thatched roof, thick stone walls, narrow windows and low ceilings. In the spence, squat chairs and benches would be clustered around the hearth, an iron pot swinging from a chain over the flames. In the centre of the parlour sits a wooden chair with a large black Bible resting on its tabled arm.

Perhaps it was mid-summer, the sun high in a clear blue sky when Jean stowed a small grip packed with baby clothes into the boot of her father's carriage. Bobbie sits snug between his father's legs, his dimpled hands holding onto the reins as Rab sings:

Horsey, horsey don't you stop
Just let your feet go clippety-clop
Your tail goes swish and the wheels go round
Giddy up, we're homeward bound.

Bobbie giggles and bounces on the seat. Jean feels as if she might throw up any minute. Her stomach is queasy with worry, not only for parting with her baby, but also for meeting Rab's family. She wonders what his mother, a strict Calvinist, thinks of her and how she feels about taking in another of her son's illegitimate children. Their cottage already houses a family of nine.

The carriage climbs the steep hill above Mauchline and clatters along a cattle track, the roadside lush with pink bells of foxglove and honey-scented clover. The peaks of Arran rise grey-blue in the distance. After a couple of miles, Rab points up to a dwelling on the crest of a barren ridge. "That's it," he says to Bobbie. "There's Tyta's house." Jean's heart sinks at the sight of it: an old stone biggen and outbuildings nestled in a copse of hawthorns.

A black-and-white dog bounds out, barking and frisking about the carriage. Bobbie screams and clutches his mother. "Tis Luath," she says, squatting to pat the collie. "A nice doggie for you to play with." Luath licks his hands and Bobbie screeches, clasping Jean around the neck.

The door of the cottage squeaks open. A frail-looking woman appears on the threshold and waves. Her shoulders are bent, her pale face a map of wrinkles. Strands of auburn streak her white hair. "Rabbie's finally brought ye home," she says, smiling at her grandson. "Bless your wee sonsie face." Bobbie tucks his head into his mother's shoulder. "And Jean," she nods.

"Pleased to make your acquaintance," Jean says. Their eyes meet, and Jean sees the same dark eyes and thick eyebrows as Rab's, the same broad squarish forehead.

The entryway smells of stewing apples and cinnamon. In the small kitchen, Rab's sisters are bustling about preparing the tea: Agnes and Annabella, black-haired like their brother; and the youngest, Isabella, with long auburn locks tied back with a green ribbon. A square wooden table, spread with cups and a platter of treacle scones, fills most of the room. Shelves line the whitewashed walls, stacked with earthenware bowls and wooden trenchers. Damask curtains hang along the back of the room, not quite concealing a row of box-beds. An elfin face ringed with ebony curls peeks out between the curtains.

"My bonnie Bess," Rab says, gathering her up in his arms. "Look here. Your wee brother's come to play."

"Baby," she says, patting Bobbie's head. They stare into each other's dark brown eyes. Bobbie grins at the chubby little girl who so resembles his twin sister.

They sip tea in the spence while the children romp like puppies on the timber floor, distracting them from all they are thinking and feeling, but not saying about this new arrangement. Then Isabella takes Bess and Bobbie out to the pond to throw some crusts to the ducks. Jean follows Rab up a ladder and through a trap door to the garret. His room is the middle of three small compartments. A posted-bed is covered with a patchwork quilt. On a small pine table beneath a skylight in the thatch, the sun illuminates a quill, an ink-pot and papers scribbled with verses.

"Gibby doesn't mind the stable loft for a few nights. Bobbie can sleep here with me," Rab says. "When I leave, the lad can share a bed with Bess."

"You're leaving again?"

"Ay, back to the city. Need to finalize details for the second edition. Then I'll be up in the highlands for a few months. Gathering some of the old Scottish airs to write verses for. A publisher in Edinburgh has asked me to contribute to a collection of the old songs, *The Scots Musical Museum.*"

"You'll be gone for a good while then." Jean turns away and covers her face with her hands as the tears she's been stifling all day finally erupt.

"Bobbie will be fine," he says, taking her into his arms. "You can see him whenever you want."

Jean lays her head on his shoulder, breathes in his wood-smoky scent, feels the warmth of his body, the strength of his arms… so familiar and reassuring. Out of the corner of her eye she spies an envelope on his desk—stylish, flowing handwriting, a distinctly feminine script. She pulls away and says, "Best be going now," her cheeks burning.

As the carriage rumbles down the lane, Jean turns around for one last glimpse. Bobbie splashing his arms and legs in the duck-dub, delightfully unaware of her leaving. But she knows before long he'll be calling for Mammie. And she will not be there.

Her arms ache with emptiness. She crosses them over her chest. It's as if she's been split down the middle, one half of her riding forward and the other half remaining behind.

They take a detour by way of Ballochmyle and stop at the Catrine woods where the River Ayr flows between massive red sandstone cliffs. Rab wants to show her his secluded spot for "courting the muses." A path through the woods leads past the bluffs, striped layers of vermillion and grey rock rising up against the cobalt sky. A white waterfall tumbles from a ravine and drowns out all other sound. Marvelling at the ancient faces of the cliffs, Jean feels humbled, as if her life and her concerns are but a raindrop in an eternal ocean. They thrust her squarely into the present moment—this perfect summer's day beside a silver-blue river winding between the green branches and white trunks of birches.

At a grassy clearing on the bank, Rab spreads his black-and-white checkered plaid. They sit in the warm sun inhaling the spice of pine and spruce. Harebells nod their purple heads in the breeze floating up from the river. The water froths and foams over the rocks as if in a mad rush to get to the sea. Above their heads boughs sway, lifting and falling to the rhythm of splashing waves and trilling blackbirds.

"*Summer is a glorious time, flowers of every colour,*" Rab says, lying back and staring up into the blue void. "*The water runs o'er the heugh, and I long for my true lover.*"

There is no thought about what happens next, as inevitable and urgent as the flow of the river. Jean feels her body opening like a rose, drinking him in like water after a long drought, a fluid merging and satisfying of yearning. Her leaking breasts assure her there's no need to worry; she's still nursing Jeanie. Her mother's babies spaced so regularly every two years are proof enough of that maxim.

Afterwards, they lie in a drowsy stillness under the spell of summer. "Is it only the muses you've been courting in this lovely spot?"

Rab chuckles. "Tis here that Coila first came to me."

Jean remembers *Coila*, the ancient name of the Ayrshire district of Kyle where Rab was born, the name he's given to his muse.

"Such a vision she was. A shimmering, green tartan robe. A bough of polished holly leaves and red berries twisted round her brows. But dinna fash yourself, Jean." He turns and pecks her cheek. "You are the only lass I've ever brought here."

"But I'm nae your only lass, am I?"

"Well, it's been over a year since we parted. What did you expect?"

"That we could still be wed—properly—and raise our bairns together."

"We were married once." He sits up and keeps his eyes fixed on the river. "You chose your father instead of me."

"I was afraid. And confused," she says grasping his arm. "I thought father would come to his senses. And he has. You can see for yourself. You've won him over."

"His grovelling sickens me," he scowls. "I'm nae the puppet of James Armour."

"Is that the reason?" She tilts his face towards her and looks into his eyes. "Or do you love another?"

"I'll not lie to you, Jean," he stammers. "There is a lady in Edinburgh I've grown fond of."

"You intend to marry her?"

"She is married, though estranged from her husband. He lives in Jamaica. Our relationship is purely platonic."

"Platonic?"

"Ay, a meeting of minds. Inspired by intellectual beauty."

Jean rolls her eyes. "So she won't be spreading her legs for you on the bank of a river."

He glares at her, aghast. "Such coarseness is unbecoming, Jean."

"Only for a lady," she says, getting to her feet and straightening her clothes, "not for a kintra wench."

She stomps back through the musky woods, a sticky ooze seeping down her thighs. Rab trails far behind her.

Though the sun beats upon the carriage, Jean shivers from the chill of silence in the air between them. She folds her empty arms over her chest and tries to warm herself by envisioning her daughter waiting for her at home. But the only image that will come is the tear-stained face of Jeanie's twin brother.

* * *

The Catrine House is so packed with diners on this rainy Sunday afternoon that I have to wait in line to get a table. The café sits secluded on a road two kilometres west of Mauchline near the village of Catrine, once a thriving mill town on the River Ayr. Una, my gracious B&B host, has just dropped me off after touring me around the rural roads and up to Dumfries House, an opulent eighteenth-century estate furnished with original Chippendale, a soulless contrast to the simple dwellings Jean Armour inhabited.

Finally seated at a small table by the window, I bite into a flaky raisin scone slathered with blackcurrant preserves and sip a cup of freshly dripped coffee. Now I understand the popularity of the café with the locals. Besides Scots pancakes and tattie scones, the menu also offers a *Canadian Farmhouse Breakfast*—a waffle, two rashers of bacon and two scrambled eggs, all drizzled in maple syrup.

The rain has turned to mist by the time I scramble down the muddy path towards the river. A weathered sign, camouflaged on the grey trunk of an aspen, informs me I've found the trail I'm seeking—the River Ayr Way. Running forty-four miles along the river, from its source in Glenbuck Lock to the sea at Ayr, the footpath will take me back to Mauchline through the landscape of Burns's beloved river haunts.

The track winds high above the river, a silver coil flashing occasionally through the leafy branches and white trunks. But its rushing, gushing rumble is ever-present, echoing in the background like a surround-sound system. I slip and slide through the mud, leaping over puddles. My white sneakers are soon caked brown with muck.

When brilliant red sandstone cliffs rise above me, I know this must be Ballochmyle, and the source of the sandstone that built most of Mauchline. Formed three hundred million years ago from windswept sand dunes, these cliff faces are the ones Jean would have seen, fresh patches of green sprouting every year between their striated layers. The two centuries that divide us seem to dissolve, as if we are sharing this moment in time, and the footprints I'm following down a steep trail to the river could be hers. They lead me to a grassy slope, purple-blue with harebells bobbing in the breeze. I sit on a moss-encrusted log and breathe in the verdure, a pungent herbal odour, like camphor. I wonder if this pleasant glade could be that sequestered spot. Fertile ground for courting muses and the beautiful Jean Armour, where a seed was sown on a summer's afternoon that would plunge her into even deeper distress.

The river, muddy brown and frothing, eddies around huge boulders as it charges towards the sea, obliterating all other sound except Jean's voice in my head, insistent as the rushing water, releasing the next turbulent chapter of her life.

After that day on the bank of the River Ayr, her dream of marrying Rab would have faded like a vista she once beheld in the near distance but can no longer see. She is twenty-two years old, and a virtually single mother of two. So I don't doubt that she would have begun to seriously consider Robin Wilson's long-standing proposal.

On a hot, sticky July day, they wander around the grounds of the old castle as Robin tells Jean about taking on a new apprentice at his weaving shed in Paisley. "I've eight looms clacking away now," he says. "Orders are piling up. Can barely keep up with the demand for shawls and blankets."

He grins at Jeanie, snuggled at her mother's hip in the heather-coloured shawl he wove, and asks about Bobbie.

"He's with his father's family," Jean says, swallowing hard to ease the lump in her throat.

When she tells him about her son's new home, Robin stops and says, "I'm sorry. And here I am bletherin' on about my shed." Taking her hand, he leads Jean into the shade and seclusion of the castle's crumbling tower. "You shouldn't be parted from your son," he says, dabbing her eyes with his handkerchief. "The wee lad needs his mither."

A spark ignites in Jean's heart. She puts her arm around his neck, and his tall, slim body moves against hers. Her head resting on his chest, Jean absorbs the steady thumping of his heart. "You are such a good man, Robin." But she must be certain before uttering the words that will change the direction of her life. Inhaling the scent of wild roses brocading the tower, drenched in the steamy heat of the day, they stay close, the hard bulge in his breeches pressing against her, until Jeanie begins whimpering.

Saying goodbye at her front door, Robin is about to kiss her cheek when Jean moves her lips up to meet his. "I look forward to seeing you in a few weeks," she says.

Robin smiles, all the warmth of summer shining in his wide blue eyes.

At first, Jean thinks it must be the same illness from which her daughter has just recovered; she's vomiting in the mornings and too tired to keep up with her toddling one-year-old. At night, she gets up to squat over the chamber pot, checking for signs of menstrual blood. Her monthlies haven't yet resumed, even though her daughter is weaned. On September 6, the night of Jeanie's birthday, Jean puts a needle to soak in her urine. The next morning, it's speckled red. Her blood throbs in her ears.

A few days later, Robin comes by with a present for Jeanie— a soft woollen plaid that he wove in autumn waves of orange, yellow and scarlet. Jean declines walking out, saying she's not feeling well. Disappointment clouds his face as Robin comments on her pallid complexion and her red, watery eyes. "Take care of yourself, Jean," he says, pressing her hand. "Until next month then?"

She watches him disappear down the street, his back so straight in a grey tailcoat, his stride long and confident. Shame washes over her. *How can she tell him? How can she tell her parents?* This time, Rab isn't there to lean on. He's in Edinburgh, sipping tea and culture with his lady, or gallivanting about the highlands searching for lost songs. This time, she's on her own.

In the weeks that follow, frantic thoughts race through her mind like wild horses. They invade her waking hours and trample through her sleep. She could leap from the hayloft, or throw herself down the stairs. She considers the herbs a woman can drink to make away with the child in her womb—pennyroyal, wormwood, rue, sage. *Where would she get them? How much is needed? How long must they be boiled?* There would be nausea and vomiting, maybe convulsions. Some women die. The village abounds with stories of desperate girls sticking knitting needles or meat skewers into themselves; their bodies found cold and sopping in blood.

It's Jeanie who keeps her sane. Curling beside her daughter at night as moonlight silvers her sleeping face, and waking in the morning to her twinkling bubbles of sound: "Mammie up, up." She is the sun during those gloomy days. As she rocks her little girl on her knee singing rhymes, ties red bows in her feathery black curls, feels her velvety cheek brushing her own, Jean is reminded—*Such beauty is budding in me again.* Her daughter instills hope. Rab will soon be back; he'll do the right thing and marry her. Only then can she reveal her condition. To tell her father before this certainty is unimaginable.

Kneeling by her bed, looking upon Mary's ever-serene countenance, she prays: *Holy Mother, grant me the strength to believe: blessed too is the child of my womb.*

October 20, 1787. It might have been a golden autumn day, the yellow leaves of the birches glowing incandescent in the mellow sunshine. Toddling down the leaf-strewn path beside the Mauchline burn, Jeanie stops every few feet to stir a puddle with a stick, pick up some speckled stones and gather the scarlet berries scattered beneath the yew tree. A few yards up from the edge of the stream, Jean spreads her purple shawl under the amber-orange umbrella of a majestic oak. Jeanie unfolds the linen napkin, delighted to find some farls baked with butter and a wedge of cheddar. Eating their lunch, they watch a pair of mallard ducks dabbling through the sedges, a flamboyant green-headed male and a mottled brown female, drab but for her iridescent purple wing-feathers.

"Wa-wa," Jeanie says, getting to her feet and pointing at the water.

"Nae, lambkin." Jean grasps her daughter's arm. "Too cold for paddling. Come, Mammie's got a song for you."

She wraps the woollen plaid around Jeanie's shoulders. They lie back, staring up into the canopy of leaves flaming against the azure sky, as Jean sings:

> *O can ye sew cushions,*
> *Or can ye sew sheets?*
> *Or can ye sing ba–loo–loo*
> *When the bairn greets?*
> *And hee and ba–burdie,*
> *And hee and ba–lamb;*
> *And hee and ba–burdie,*
> *My bonnie wee lamb.*

Jeanie's lids are not long in closing. The burbling of the stream and the breeze sifting through the trees serenade them. And soon Jean too is lulled into sleep.

She's sloshing sheets in the burn, trying to rid them of the black streaks marring their pure whiteness. They're too heavy to lift and wring out. Rab stoops beside her, his wide forehead furrowed in disapproval. Then Luath splashes through the water in a frenzy of barking, barking, barking... that morphs into quacking, quacking, quacking...

The raucousness startles Jean awake. Lying on her side, she extends her arm to feel for her daughter. Jeanie's plaid lies in an empty heap, still warm with the heat of her body and the sun shafting through the branches. Dazed, still half in her dream-world, Jean jolts up. The quacking pulls her eyes down to the stream.

A few feet out, two mallards are circling a small body, face down in a foot of water, white-sleeved arms stretched out like sodden wings.

Jean hurls herself down the bank, slipping on the mossy rocks. She lunges for her daughter and drags her body, sopping, into her arms.

"Jeanie," she screams, squeezing her body next to hers—over and over—as if she can wring her out, revive her daughter's slumping form with her own body's heat and the force of her will. "Jeanie... Jeanie..." A keening that rips through the still air for miles.

She lies still as a broken doll, her head slumped against her mother's arm; her brown eyes vacant, like glass lamps whose flames have been snuffed.

The days that follow blur into nightmarish images. A cavity in the earth waiting to swallow her small body; shovelfuls of dirt thudding on a wooden coffin, no bigger than a cradle. A stony mound of clay, rounded like a pregnant belly.

The October winds strip the ash tree and blanket the grave with greenish-yellow leaves. Jean dreams of leaves falling like snowflakes: *Jeanie running through swirling leaves, tripping and falling. Leaves engulf her, smother her black curls. She's drowning in a blizzard of leaves.*

With the November rains, the leafy shroud changes to brown sludge. The ash reaches its bare limbs into the grey sky. The plain freestone marker settles then hardens in the freezing earth, immovable. The world stripped of colour. Sleet drizzling on the roof, Jean lies in bed, caressing her daughter's woollen plaid, still fragrant with the hawthorn buds in which she rinsed her hair. Sleep is her escape, the only relief from the clamps that tighten around her chest, from the weight of the emptiness. And from the phantoms of guilt.

If she had not begun to feel the first quivering in her belly, Jean may never have left her bed to stagger to the kitchen and gnaw on the remnants of the meal left out for her. Part of her lies in the kirkyard as she struggles to stay alive and nourish the child moving inside her. She goes through the motions of living; stumbles out of bed, splashes cold water on her face, puts on the same black gown and apron. As she stirs the porridge, her little brothers and sisters wait, glum and unspeaking.

Her father doles out his usual platitudes: *The Lord giveth and the Lord taketh away. May the name of the Lord be praised.* Jean ignores him, withdraws from the evening prayers and Sunday morning Bible readings. Her faith in both him and God has completely shattered. Contemplating the Holy Mother, she thinks for the first time about Mary having to witness her son strung up on a wooden cross and tortured. While his father did nothing to spare him. What kind of father is that, she wonders. What kind of God?

Only her mother can see the gaping hole in Jean's heart. She tries to reassure her daughter: "You can't imagine how you'll go on living. But the pain will lessen. They say time heals all wounds." She shakes her head. "Not true. Not when a child's taken from you. The scar remains, invisible. A constant, aching reminder. But the pain eases."

Jean avoids the eyes of her mother and her father. Not only her grief, but her hidden shame keeps her head bowed in their presence. By December, she's five months along; her condition can't be concealed much longer. She can't fathom why Rab hasn't returned, or even written. Surely, he's heard about his daughter's death.

Late on a dreary midwinter's day just before Yuletide, Jean bundles up in her hoddin-grey cloak and crunches across the ice-encrusted kirkyard to the Back Causeway. The hush of the gloaming is settling in, the rising moon ringed with a golden collar. The cold, damp air already smells of the snow that will soon be falling. She stops in front of a two-storey brick house, a sign hanging above its red door: *Doctor and Midwife*.

A lamp glimmers behind the shuttered window. Jean lifts the brass door knocker and raps twice. She shivers on the doorstep, then knocks again more forcefully. Quick footsteps approach, and the door swings open.

"Guid-een," Doctor Mackenzie grins. "Step in, Jean. You look as frozen and white as the snow. Are you alright?"

In the oak-panelled parlour, a fire is well gathered-up in the grate. A book lies open on the tea table next to a red velvet resting-chair and a wrought-iron candle stand. Jean pulls up a high-backed chair close to the marble-framed hearth, and warms her hands over the gleede crackling with birch logs. As the doctor fixes a toddy of brandy at the sideboard, she apologizes for disturbing him, then asks if he's heard any news from Rab.

"Received a letter from him this very morning. He's back in Edinburgh now."

"He knows about Jeanie?"

"Ay, the man's sorely distressed."

"When's he coming home?"

"Hard to say. Fell off his horse up in the Highlands and broke his leg. Could be a while til he can ride again."

"But he *must* return," Jean says, sobbing as she explains her dilemma. "He needs to know. He *has* to come home."

"There now, lass," the doctor says, handing Jean his handkerchief and patting her shoulder. "I'll send him a letter by the morning post."

"Try not to worry," he says, as they walk to the door. "Stay calm for the good of your wean."

Jean wonders how that is possible. Mute and listless, she helps with the minding of the children, cooking and cleaning. But mostly she stays in her garret room and paces. To soothe herself and her baby, she strokes her belly and tries to hum a lullaby. But it reminds her of Jeanie, pinned beneath the frozen earth. And of Bobbie, a constant ache in her heart.

Sowans Night dinner, the eve before Yule, Jean picks at her bowl of sowans pudding, usually a dish she savours; tonight it tastes like slop. Her stomach revolts at the grainy smell of the meal and the gritty texture of the oat husks. Her parents shoot anxious glances at each other when she pushes back her chair and excuses herself from the table.

Later that evening, her mother comes up to Jean's bedroom. "Could you come down for a wee talk with us?"

The spence is fragrant with rowan branches flaming in the hearth, and Jean thinks this might be the right time. The burning of rowan on this eve means that any ill feelings between family and friends will be put aside for Yuletide. Fir bows drape the beams, the only *pagan* decoration her father will allow. Arranging her black shawl close about her, Jean waits as her father snorts a pinch of snuff into each nostril.

"It's been a hard time for you," he says, a rare note of sympathy tingeing his voice, "having two babies to tend to… and now…"

"So, we were thinking," her mother says, "about bringing Bobbie back. Having your lad to care for would help you get back on your feet."

The blood rushes to Jean's face, and pulses in her ears. "I'll soon have another to care for," she says, lifting her eyes. "I've fallen again with bairn."

Her mother lowers her face into her hands.

Her father's eyes pop; his jaw falls. "That blackguard Burns again?"

Jean nods.

"Blastit, fornicating bastard. Son of a bitch! And you… you… shameless hizzie." He springs from his chair and stands an inch from her, shouting Daddie Auld's admonition: "Returning to your sin like the dog to his vomit. Like the sow washed to her wallowing in the mire." He strikes out at her, and Jean's hands fly up to shield her head.

Her mother yanks on his arm, pleading, "Hold off! Tis your daughter."

"She's no daughter of mine anymore. Out with you," he bellows. "You'll not defile this Christian home a minute longer."

Jean skirts around him, her arms guarding her belly, and heads for the door.

Up in her room, she tosses clothes into a grip—petticoat, bodice, sleeves, stockings, shift—until it can hold no more. She grabs her leather-bound Bible, removes the picture of Mary from the wall and stuffs these into the case. When she reaches the front door, her mother darts out from the kitchen and presses some coins into her hand. "God be with you," she sobs.

Fat snowflakes whirl like feathers out of an ebony sky, and Jean lifts her plaid to cover her hair. At the corner she pauses, uncertain where to go. Then it comes to her. She turns right to head up the street when a hand clenches her shoulder.

"Adam," she cries and falls into his arms.

Her brother takes her arm, and they trudge up the snowy street to the Cross. The houses framing the quadrangle glow with lights. The village square, which teems with livestock on summer market days—a bedlam of mooing, oinking, baaing and clucking—is a quiet, deserted tract of pure whiteness. Hanging from a wooden triangular post, the scales shimmer with a glaze of ice under the gas lamp.

They tramp down the Back Causeway and stop at the red door, its overhead sign rattling in the wind. The maid-servant tells them the doctor is out on a call, and she's unsure when he'll return.

They cross the street to Nanse Tinnock's inn. The dim room smells of ale and peat smoke, and of tallow candles that drip in the iron sconces hanging from the low board-ceiling. At a box seat by the fire, a few men—vagrants by the look of their ragged clothes and stubbly faces—hunch over mugs of two-penny ale. A young woman in a red, low-cut bodice slouches alone at a bench in the corner. At a table by the window, they sip their penny-wheeps as Jean tells Adam about Rab's injury and his imminent return from Edinburgh.

"Where will you go in the meantime?"

"Find a room somewhere, maybe here." She glances up the stairs to the second floor.

"Nae," he says, eying the grimy walls and stained tabletops.

"Tis for hussies and vagabonds."

"Ay, poor homeless folk. Like me."

Adam takes a crinkled five-pound note from his pocket and passes it across the table. "I've managed to save a bit."

"You're a good brother, Adam," she says, squeezing his hand. "It's just till Rab gets back. He'll have earnings from his book."

"Don't count on it." Adam glances down at his brown ale, avoiding his sister's eyes.

"Why? What are the tales from the city about Poet Burns?"

"You don't want to know."

"About the married lady he's in love with?"

"That lady has a maid-servant." Adam pauses, then looks up. "That maid-servant is now with child."

Jean shuts her eyes, wishing she could shut her ears as well.

"They say she's taken out a writ against him."

Jean shakes her head. "He's my only hope." She gazes out the window, her care-worn face reflected in the darkened glass. Across the snow-packed street, a cloaked figure stops at the entrance to the doctor's house. The light spilling from the yawning door reveals a man in a black cape and wide-brimmed hat, toting a large satchel.

When they arrive on his doorstep, Dr. Mackenzie is stomping slush off his boots. "Forgive us for calling so late," Jean says, "but I need to know. Have you heard from Rab?"

"Nothing yet, I'm afraid." Wiping water from his spectacles, he sees Jean's eyes welling up and insists they come in to warm themselves by the fire.

As Jean tells him about her circumstances, the doctor rubs his hand against the cleft in his chin. A moment later, he grins and points a finger into the air. "There's a vacant room next door above Archie Meikle's shop. Not much by way of comforts. But I'll be close by when your time comes."

Sweet relief washing over her, Jean smiles at her brother. "I have money for the rent."

Dr. Mackenzie holds up his hand. "I'll settle it with Rab. You'll be needing that for other things."

* * *

Sitting in that small chamber that was once above Archie Meikle's tailor shop, I feel as if I've come full circle, back to this upper room in the Burns House Museum where Jean Armour first implanted herself in my consciousness. Now, after reading about what transpired between these walls over the next year of Jean's life, I can understand why her spirit is still hovering. The plank floor, the wood-beamed ceiling, the wooden chairs by the hearth, the curtained box-bed in the corner and the hooded cradle beside it—all create an impression of what the room may have looked like when Jean lived here two centuries ago.

No one else is around; it's still and quiet but for the hum of the central heating. To block out the bright fluorescent lights, I close my eyes and try to conjure up the room Jean may have walked into that December night in 1787. It would be dark and cold, probably smelling of mouse droppings and soot. By the flickering flame of a candle, she could make out a small table and chair, a box-bed, a washstand, a gridiron hanging in the smoke-stained hearth, and one narrow window glazed in filigreed patterns of frost.

Jean drops down on the chaff-filled mattress. The bed groans under her weight. She stares into the silent darkness, and the reality of her situation hits her. Village tongues will soon be wagging. An unmarried woman lives by herself for one purpose only. She knows how they'll judge her, unwed and pregnant, again.

"Rab will come," she says aloud, as if to make it true. Despite the seeds of doubt that Adam has sown, she has to nurture this belief: Rab has a good heart; he will do right by her.

The morning dawns dull and frigid. Jean's breath spirals into the air. It's Yule. The only sound is of squeaking mice and scrabbling claws overhead in the rafters. She stokes the coals to a blaze then scrapes frost off the middle pane of the window, a patch wide enough to see the kirkyard and Jeanie's grave swathed in snow. The black branches of the ash shiver against the leaden grey sky. A jumble of tombstones stretches between her and her home of twenty-two years. Light flakes drift lazily onto the empty street. She feels utterly alone.

She expects that Reverend Auld's henchmen will soon be stalking her, old Willie sniffing the odour of scandal. They'll not be dragging her onto the cutty stool this time, though. In the eyes of the kirk, she's already sealed her fate. The fires of hell will only burn that much hotter. But Jean knows now that these beliefs are not necessarily the truth. She thinks about Mary Magdalene— even a prostitute was worthy of the saviour's forgiveness.

Then some gentle nudges from within remind her: she is not alone. Another heart is beating in her. *In three months, I will have a baby in my arms, God willing. Rab will soon be here. Spring will come; the world will turn green again.* In the meantime, she must not give in to tears, so as not to give birth to a melancholy child. *You've been through enough already,* she whispers, patting her stomach.

Jean wraps a hot brick in a flannel cloth and tucks it under the quilt. In the warmth of her bed, she caresses her belly and croons:

> *Baloo, baloo, my wee, wee thing,*
> *For thou art doubly dear to me*
> *O but thy daddie's absence lang*
> *Would break my dowie heart in twa.*

A few days after Hogmanay, Dr. Mackenzie drops in to report that he's received a letter. Rab is still confined to bed, but will be home as soon as his leg is strong enough to bear the journey.

A five-pound note is enclosed for the rent of her room. The letter chills Jean more than the bitter winds whistling through the chinks around the window frame. She is just one more problem for him. Another woman to appease, another wean to support.

Jean plods through the sunless days of January and February in her cell-like room. Every morning she coaxes a lump of coal into flame then thaws the ice in the copper kettle. Ravenous, she boils a pot of oats, stirs in spoonfuls of sugar and bathes it in milk. Adam comes most evenings with food he's filched from the larder—barley-scones, a hunk of cheese, a leg of mutton— leftovers, he says, their mother keeps out after supper, never asking where they disappear to during the night. Nelly brings her sister clean clothes and linens and takes her soiled ones for washing. A gloominess has fallen on the household, Nelly says. The wee ones keep asking when Jean is coming home, and their mother and father hardly speak.

In mid-February, Candlemas, Jean lumbers up the stairs after picking a bunch of snowdrops she spied poking through the melting snow in the kirkyard, their delicate, white bells and slender, green stems cheering her with the promise of spring. Though the day has been dim with heavy snow clouds lurking, she's reassured by the old saying, *If Candlemas Day be dark and foul, Half the winter is o'er at Yowl.*

As the grey gloaming brings down the night, Jean lights the candle by her bed. A faint rapping on the door. She draws the bolt and inches it open a crack. The smiling face that greets her is one she hasn't seen in many months. "Robin, what a surprise." Conscious of her belly bulging between them, she feels her cheeks flushing.

"Thought you could use something extra to keep you warm." He holds out a shawl, intricately patterned in curving shapes of azure, turquoise and jade—like the sea, the sky and a grassy meadow swirling together.

"It's lovely." Jean brushes the fine wool against her cheek, smelling the scent of his hands woven into every fibre. A piece of notepaper drops to the floor.

Robin picks it up and hands it to her. "Read it later," he says, blushing. "Are you in need of anything, Jean?"

Shaking her head, she touches his wrist. "You shouldn't be risking your good name by coming here."

She closes the door and leans against it, listening until his footsteps fade on the stairs. Then she unfolds the notepaper: *While vital heat flows in my heart, I'll love the lass among the heather.* Burying her head in the shawl, she wipes away the tears— for all that might have been.

In March, winter finally loosens its grip. Jean yearns to be outdoors inhaling the musk of thawing earth. But her rotund belly keeps her in her room, and mostly in her bed. Her back aches; her ankles and wrists are puffy and stiff. Winded by any exertion, she can't climb the stairs with the water bucket or lug the slop pot down to empty in the midden. What would she do without her brother and sister, her tireless helpers? The baby blankets and linens that Nelly brought from home are stacked and waiting in a kist at the foot of the bed. It's a dismal chamber for her confinement, but she's scrubbed it clean. *You are blessed to have a room at all*, she chides herself, remembering the Holy Mother giving birth in a stable and laying her bairn in the straw of a manger. She beholds Mary's tranquil face above her bed and feels doubly grateful.

Late one afternoon, Jean is sitting up in bed embroidering lavender flowers on a tiny nightshirt. She's imagining the wee body that will soon be filling it and humming an old ballad: *The winter it is past, and the simmer comes at last, And the small birds sing on ev'ry tree.* Three knocks sound on the door. Certain it's the doctor checking on her as he does most days, she calls out for him to come in.

The door scrapes open. Peering around it are those dark eyes Jean has been longing to see. Looking dapper in a dark blue tailcoat and white cravat, Rab steps in, scans the room then settles his eyes on her. "A good cargo you're carrying there," he grins. "Guess you'll be delivering it soon."

"I'm hoping so," she says, attempting to smile at this intimate stranger.

"I've just been to the Cowgate. Tried to reason with your father," Rab says, sitting on the edge of the bed. "But he'll not be moved to take you back."

"I don't want to go back." She clenches his arm. "I want you to take care of us." She takes his hand and places it against the bulges moving in waves over her belly.

"Life," he says, smiling. "Maybe a lass?"

Their eyes meet and well up as they talk of Jeanie, then of Bobbie. "He's the mildest, gentlest creature I ever saw," Rab says, stroking Jean's hair and drying her eyes with his handkerchief.

He climbs up onto the narrow bed. Jean lies on her side to make room for him. She closes her eyes, savouring the warmth of his broad chest pressed against her back. His hand strokes her belly then moves up to fondle her fulsome breasts. "Ah, Jean," he gasps, "what a delicious armful you've become."

He lifts her petticoat and rubs himself hard against her bare buttocks. "You're gantin' for it too," he says, pushing his fingers into her, "so soft and wet."

Though her body craves him, she tries to inch way. "Nae," she says, lifting her head, "the jostling's not good for the wean."

He clasps her more firmly against him. "Won't take long," he says, unbuttoning his breeches.

The old bedframe wobbles and creaks. Jean fears it will surely collapse, as pain and pleasure meld in each pounding thrust. His hand clamps over her mouth to muffle her cries. He buries his face in her hair, stifling a drawn-out moan. Then, only the sound of his breath panting in her ear.

Jean lies paralyzed, dazed by what has just happened, wanting to believe it means a reunion. "Is this your way of saying you've come back to me, Rab?"

"What do you mean?" He lifts his head and fumbles with the buttons on his breeches.

"You once told me, the joining of two bodies in love is akin to a vow of marriage."

"The act of love is one thing," he chuckles. "A little hough-magandie's another thing entirely."

"The act love is reserved for your Edinburgh lady?" Jean says, her heart pounding against her ribs. "And fucking is for servant girls and pregnant women?"

He swings his legs onto the floor and sits with his back to her. "Such language is disgusting coming from a woman," he says. "It only confirms your coarseness."

He picks up his jacket from the floor and straightens his clothes. "You have no claim on me as a husband." He glares at her with narrowed eyes. "You understand that, Jean?"

She does not reply.

He steps back towards the bed and speaks louder: "Do you understand?"

"Ay," she murmurs.

He strides to the door then pauses and turns. "Your mother's assured me she'll see you through your confinement. Good luck," he says, tossing a guinea onto the bed.

When Jean lifts her head from her wet pillow, the room is dark and cold. The rumblings in her stomach prod her to get up and light the lamp, fan the embers, feed the fire, heat some water, boil some brose. She struggles onto her feet. A slimy discharge leaks between her legs. Red splotches stain her white petticoat. She drops back onto the bed, shaking at the sight of the blood. *What have I done? Has my time come? Something's wrong.* She recalls the old wives joking that one of the reliefs of being bairned was not having to tolerate their husbands' demands.

All that wakeful night, she waits for some movement or cramping. It's not until the amber light of dawn is turning pale blue that some jabbing limbs press against her flesh. Then she lets go of her belly and sinks into sleep.

The sun is high in the sky when a knock and a familiar voice startle Jean awake. She drapes her paisley shawl over her nightdress and totters to the door.

"Still abed?" Dr. Mackenzie says, his eyes wide behind his horn-rimmed spectacles. "You're looking awfully pale, Jean. Everything alright?"

Colouring with embarrassment, she tells him about the bleeding. His brow wrinkles, and he warns her not to stir from her bed from now on. "But you'll soon have a more comfortable one," he grins. "Rab dropped by this morning. He's ordered a new bed for you from James Morris."

Jean manages a weak half-smile. Not the expression of gratitude the doctor is expecting; Morris is Mauchline's finest cabinetmaker. A puzzled expression on his face, he tells her to expect delivery this afternoon.

That night she stretches out on a plush feather mattress atop a solid mahogany frame that supports her weight without a creak. Leaning against the carved headboard, she tries to fathom what this luxurious gift might mean. She would like to see it as a sincere expression of Rab's caring, but knows it's more likely an expression of his guilt, if not his remorse, for what he did and what he said; and a way of impressing his friend, the doctor, with his generosity. *Rab be damned*, she thinks, and turns her eyes up to Mother Mary, praying the bed will see her through a safe delivery.

But Jean can't keep her thoughts from leaping ahead: *What will become of us?* Perhaps she could earn her living as a maid-servant, though it's unlikely anyone will employ a woman with a bairn. Or hire herself out as a wet nurse. Would she earn enough? Maybe she'll end up like those gangrels that hang about Poosie Nansie's—begging aid from the kirk, wearing a tin badge to show her beggar's rank and scrounging clothes from the poor-box. Women in her situation usually give up their weans, like Lizzie Paton leaving her Bess at Mossgiel. And her own Bobbie; every thought of him is a stab to her heart. But this she knows for certain: she will not forsake another of her babies. She will find a way. Stroking the downy wool of her paisley shawl, the kind face of Robin Wilson flashes before her.

A week later, Jean awakens before dawn, the mattress wet beneath her and cramping in her belly. It can't be time, she thinks, it's too soon. But the contractions continue; no gradual buildup this time. They hit like lightning, only a few minutes between each strike. She staggers down the stairs and pounds on the doctor's door. When his maid-servant peeks out, Jean is leaning against the wall, doubled-over. "My throes are on me," she groans.

Minutes later Dr. Mackenzie, nightshirt tucked into his breeches, stands at the foot of Jean's bed. His fingers rooting around inside of her, he says, "The head's right there."

Jean feels it crowning, and the overwhelming urge to push. She pants and grunts until she's spent. The head is not budging.

The doctor pulls out a set of black iron tongs.

"Nae," Jean cries.

"No choice," he says.

The hard metal pierces into her flesh and everything turns black.

When Jean opens her eyes, a baby lies on her belly. Her hand reaches out to touch the tiny body, still and cold.

"A pity," says a soft voice, "a wee lass." Jean looks up to see her mother standing by her bed and wonders when she arrived.

"Oh Mammie," she cries, stroking the baby's blue-grey skin. Then a spasm grips her like a pair of claws squeezing her belly. She screams.

Dr. Mackenzie massages her stomach, and a moment later, his eyes bulge. "God be with us," he says. "There's another one."

Gasping, Jean grips her mother's arm. She bears down and, with a surge of strength, pushes out a blood-smeared body into the doctor's outstretched hands.

Stubby arms flailing, the baby lets out a cry, then lies pink with life on Jean's stomach beside her sister while the doctor delivers the afterbirth. Jean takes in their diminutive forms; two heads covered with black hair, four eyes fringed with long, dark eyelashes. Identical twin buds. As the doctor cuts the cord, Jean decides to name her, the one who will never blossom. The old wives said it was bad luck, tempting fate, to think about names before a child was born. But Jean had decided her baby would be called after either the brother or sister who saw her through these last months. Her child, though unbaptized, will not be nameless. *Helen*, she whispers, touching her daughter's head.

Wee Mary—Jean names for her mother, and the Holy Virgin—fusses at the nipple; her lips pucker in and out in a sucking motion, but she draws in little milk. That night, the baby squalls as if in pain, then dozes off before Jean can move her to the other breast. She frets about the yellowish tinge of the baby's skin and the scrawny body, which feels unnaturally warm against her own.

The next day Jean is listless, her head achy, and her stomach distended with cramps. By nightfall, she's vomiting. Her body flames with fever, and her mother bathes her with cool, wet cloths. Then Jean shivers so intensely the bed begins vibrating. Dr. Mackenzie can't hide the fear in his eyes when he looks at the white film coating her tongue.

For days, Jean falls in and out of a delirious sleep where mewing kittens are crawling over her body, scratching and kneading at her breasts.

Her eyes open. The room gradually comes into focus. A shaft of sunlight through the narrow window. The smell of chicken broth. The clicking of needles draws her gaze over to the table where her mother sits, knitting. Jean reaches out and feels for the cradle. Only cold air.

"My wean? Where is she?"

Her mother's head jerks up. "Praise the Lord. You've come back."

"Where's my baby?"

"I'm sorry," Mrs. Armour says, smoothing back her daughter's damp hair, "she's gone to be with her sister."

"Nae."

"Just last night... in her sleep."

Jean lies back and shuts her eyes. "I wish it were me instead," she cries.

"You mustn't say that, dear. God moves in mysterious ways."

"God." Jean spits out the word as if she's expelling poison. "I've no love for a God that takes my bairns."

"Jean, that's blasphemy. The Lord giveth and the Lord taketh away."

"He takes more than he gives."

Mrs. Armour wrings her hands. "How would you have managed alone with two babies? Now you can come back home."

"Never," Jean screams. "I will never go back. Tis no longer my home. What kind of father disowns his daughter when she's in need? Tossing me out like a piece of rubbish. I'd rather be a servant. Or go up the street to Poosie Nansie's and become the hizzie he thinks I am."

"It's hard to understand your father's ways. He's a man of God…"

"My babies died because of father… and God. And Rab. I've no use for any of them."

"You're still feverish, talking nonsense. Here, a bit of nourishment." Mrs. Armour holds a spoonful of steaming broth to her daughter's lips. "You'll recover your senses and come home. You're still young, Jean, and beautiful. And," she says with a little smile, "Robin Wilson is still in need of a wife."

* * *

I kneel on the wet grass beside the moss-encrusted stone that reads *The Armour Burial Ground*, recalling my first visit to this grave two years ago. Immersed in my sister's maternal grief, I was doing research for a book about her son's life and death—a book to help her survive, so tenuous was her hold on life. Reading the inscription on this marker, I couldn't comprehend how a mother could endure the loss of four children. Jean Armour was just a name then, a shadowy figure subsumed under the identity of her famous husband. Now, out of the obscurity of the past, a complex woman is emerging. And I understand how these deaths would have shaped Jean's life.

Our losses transform and define us. When I was seventeen, my father's death shook the entire foundation of my world and propelled me into a premature marriage with an older man. My sister, six years after her son's death, still has one foot in another realm as she continues to search for her lost boy. The myth of Demeter and Persephone encapsulates the devastation of losing a child. When Hades abducts the daughter of the earth-mother goddess and carries Persephone down to his underworld kingdom, Demeter wanders the world searching for her daughter. She abandons all her divine duties. The rain stops, rivers dry up, crops die. The earth becomes a barren wasteland.

Jean lost everything—her children, her home, her family. Surviving physically and monetarily was as much at stake for her as mustering the will to carry on. So the crucial decision she has to make at this juncture in her life, I realize, was wrought by the tiny bones buried beneath this cracked slab of stone.

The day after her recovery, Jean wobbles to the window and turns the crank to let in the breeze wafting fragrant with spring. Larks chirrup and flit about with strings of grass draggling from their beaks. In the kirkyard, the ash is unfolding its first leaves. Red and yellow primroses speckle the grass. Two mounds of freshly dug earth bulge on either side of Jeanie's grave. White coffins for cradles. The endless loop of questions replays over and over in her mind. *Why?* Was it all the fear and worry she'd fed them for nine months? Was it Rab pushing inside her? Those iron tongs gripping that soft head? Maybe malicious fairies or the evil eye. She'd placed the Bible and an open pair of scissors under her pillow. But Dr. Mackenzie didn't heed the same after-birth customs as the midwives, claiming they were fey nonsense, old wives' tales.

Her chest aches as if a weight is pressing on it. She gasps for air and collapses onto the floor. All that's transpired in the last year and a half seems too much to carry: birthing four babies and burying three in the past five months. Her son, her only living child, a stranger to her. Bobbie's face shines before her like a beacon across a dark sea. It pulls her up from her knees as she pledges, *I will find a way.*

That afternoon Nelly arrives with a basket of fresh linens. She washes her sister's stringy hair and rinses it in water infused with hawthorn buds. Changing into a clean shift, Jean notices the pearly scars of stretch marks streaking her shrunken belly and sagging breasts. Her illness melted the pounds from her; a gaunt, sallow face looks back at her from the glass.

"The roses will soon be back in your cheeks," Nelly says, brushing Jean's long black hair. "You'll be bonnie as ever." She sets a pot of hotchpotch to heat on the gridiron. "Eat hearty and sleep well," she says, pecking Jean's cheek. "Until tomorrow then."

Jean drops into the chair and stares out the window at the pink and mauve streaks left by the setting sun. *What now?* she wonders. Her rent is paid until the end of the month. Returning to James Armour's house is out of the question. Two weeks to find work, or a husband. Marriage is the only way to get her son back. Would Robin still be waiting?

A soft knock on the door. Jean knows the voice that calls her name, but does not reply. The door edges open. "Please, can I come in?"

She sits silent, eyes unmoving, as if turned to stone.

Rab kneels by her chair and tilts her head up to look at him. "When I learned about our babies… and you… almost… The load of care has been too heavy for my shoulders. I realize how I've wronged you. That I do love you. Forgive me, Jean."

"Bastard," she yells, pounding her fists against his back. "Is this what it takes?"

He grabs her hands and pleads, "I can make it up to you. If you'll let me."

"Can you raise the dead?"

"Nae. But I can provide for the living. Make a home for you and Bobbie."

"And where would that be?"

"There's a farm in Ellisland, near Dumfries. A hundred and seventy acres on the River Nith." His eyes glow as he describes it. "As sweet a poetic ground as I've ever seen."

"But is it good farming ground?"

He nods. "An old farmer-friend of my father's, John Tennant, surveyed it with me. I've spoken with the landlord about taking out a lease. The old house is falling into ruins. But he'd put up the money to build a new one."

"You want to be a farmer?"

"Tis the only way I know to support a family. I was bred to the plough, yoked to it at nine years old. I've learned a lot from working the land at Mossgiel."

"And your grass widow in Edinburgh?" she says, meeting his

eyes. "Is it all over with her?"

"Ay. Mrs. McLehose will never seek a divorce. Religion has her in its shackles. As good as a chastity belt."

"Her maid-servant satisfied your other needs?"

He puts his hand to his forehead and slowly draws his fingers down over his face. "My wild days would be over if you marry me, Jean. I promise."

She studies his eyes, unblinking. She wants to believe him. She wants to trust him. They would have a fresh start, away from the scrutinizing stare of the village and the kirk, far away from her father. And Bobbie—she'd have her son.

"Could you be a farmer's wife, Jean?"

She shakes her head. "That won't do."

Rab raises his thick eyebrows. "What do you mean?"

"Surely, Poet Burns, you can come up with a more romantic proposal than that."

Grinning, he looks up into the air and closes his eyes. A minute later he tells her that the words are from an old song, one he's been revising for Johnson's book. He gets down on one knee and takes her hand. His voice is rather harsh and off-key, as usual, but he sings the lines with so much feeling:

> *As fair art thou my bonie lass,*
> *So deep in love am I,*
> *And I will luve thee still, my dear,*
> *Till a' the seas gang dry.*

> *Till a' the seas gang dry, my dear,*
> *And the rocks melt wi' the sun!*
> *And I will luve thee still, my dear,*
> *While the sands o' life shall run.*

Jean cups his face in her hands. The grooves in his wide forehead are too deeply etched for his twenty-nine years. She strokes his bristly sideburns. "If you write verses like that, but let me sing them," she says, touching his lips with her fingertips, "then a farmer's wife I'll be."

*   *   *

A few weeks later, in early May of 1788, Jean Armour and Robert Burns strolled down the Back Causeway to the home of Rab's good friend Gavin Hamilton. They said their vows before a justice of the peace. So the story goes, Ian Lyell tells me as we stand in the flowered courtyard of the large L-shaped house once occupied by Gavin Hamilton. Although the home is privately owned, Mr. Lyell—honorary president of the Mauchline Burns Club—has permission to bring the occasional visitor into the grounds. He points to one of the lower windows. "It was in there," he says, "in the dining room, that they were married." That original part of the two-storey house is now linked to the old castle tower, its fifteenth-century stone wall an incongruous backdrop for two white, plastic lounge chairs.

A member of the Burns Club for fifty years and the local Burns expert, Mr. Lyell tells an endless stream of stories as he tours me around the village. Within the eighteenth-century walls of Poosie Nansie's Hostelry, he shows me the small wood-panelled room where the Burns Club meets. Then we stand at the top of Loudon Street, the old village cross, as Mr. Lyell points out all the buildings Robert Burns would still recognize, the past still alive in the present. I have to listen carefully; my guide speaks at a rapid pace with a pronounced Ayrshire accent full of rolling r's: the Cowgate is the *Coogate*, a house is a *hoose* and Ayr is *ear*. As much as I prod, I learn nothing new about Jean Armour or her family. No Armour descendants live in the village; no Armour graves are identified in the kirkyard but for Jean and Robert's children.

When I tell Mr. Lyell about the subject of my research, he regards me quizzically. "Why would you want to write about her?" he asks.

That evening, I return to the red sandstone building in the Back Causeway and look up to the second-storey window of Jean's room. Then I walk the approximately three hundred yards she would have walked with Rab to Gavin Hamilton's home—too short a distance it seems for the radical shift it affected in the course of her life. The white stucco back wall of the house is grimy with soot, and the lower window is curtained with gauze. I try to peer through it, but only my own reflection greets me.

In my mind's eye, though, I can see Jean dressed in a black silk mantle with scarlet knot and a red plaid of the finest wool, a wedding gift from Rab. After they exchanged vows, her husband slipped a slender gold band onto her finger—almost weightless, but so heavy with meaning. Rab insisted on inviting Jean's parents to attend as witnesses. But the Armours sent word that they would be away that day. Jean knows it's her father's way of stating that the only marriage he condones is the holy matrimony of the church. So be it, she shrugs, no longer caring what her father thinks. She's a respectable married woman, wife of the famous poet and soon to be mistress of her own home.

Villagers who shunned her in the past months as if she carried the plague now nod when they pass her in the street: "A guid-day to you, Mrs. Burns." The first time, she swivelled around to check behind her before realizing the merchant was addressing her. Jean Armour has dissolved into the mist of the past. Jean Burns has taken her place. In relinquishing her father's name, she feels released from his power over her, freed from the fetters of the kirk.

And free to enjoy the pleasures of married love. In the weeks after they wed, she appreciates the perfection of the term *honeymoon*. As a young lass, she imagined a brilliant crescent moon with a man and woman nestled in its crook, their legs dangling in the star-studded sky. Now she savours the *honey*, the sweetness of love without fear. Though their home is but that small dingy room in the Back Causeway, it has a bolt on the door and a feather bed where their bodies lie entwined all night long.

United too in the misery of their losses, they stare out the window at the three small graves. Then find solace in their melding bodies, the only salve for the ache in Jean's heart. An act of creation, she hopes, in defiance of death.

On Whitsunday, the middle of May, Rab takes over the lease of the farm and begins work on its restoration. As it turns out, not only must he replace the rundown farmhouse, but new outbuildings also need to be constructed, the open fields enclosed with stone dykes; drains have to be dug, and a sheltering berm of trees planted between the house and the River Nith. He stays a mile down the river from the farm, near the tower of Isle in an old hut—or hovel, as he calls it. *Pervious to every blast that blows and every shower that falls*, he writes to Jean. *I'm only preserved from being chilled to death by being suffocated by smoke.* A Dumfries contractor is building the five-room house with Rab's help. *Not a palace*, he writes, *but a plain simple home for a family.* Adam joins him on the weekends to assist with digging the spring into a well and carting lime and stone for the foundations.

When the weather's fine and he can spare the time, Rab rises at three in the morning, mounts his roan mare, Jenny Geddes, and gallops the fifty miles back to Mauchline. If Jean knows he's coming, she strolls out in the evening along the dusty Cumnock road to meet him. They find a secluded glade and Rab spreads his plaid in a grove of myrtle. They lie amongst the white blooms fragrant with minty pine and honey. As the gloaming sifts down over the braes, Rab lifts Jean onto the back of Jenny's saddle and they trot home.

One evening when she meets him a mile or so outside the village, he's bursting with verses he's been composing along the way. "As I jogged on in the setting sun, I was taken by a poetic fit," he says. "Just listen to the galloping rhythm." As the stars brighten the sky, they ride into Mauchline while Rab croons his *honeymoon song*:

> *Of a' the airts the wind can blaw*
> *I dearly love the west,*
> *For there the bonie lassie lives,*
> *The lassie I lo'e best,*
> *There wild woods grow, and rivers row,*
> *And monie a hill between,*
> *But day and night my fancy's flight*
> *Is ever wi' my Jean.*

Jean knows such adoration cannot not last forever. But for those halcyon honeymoon months, she delights once again in her role as Rab's chief muse. *I only live to love thee.*

During the week he's home, they ride out to Mossgiel. Bobbie—nearly two years old—eyes his mother shyly at first, peeking out from behind the folds of his Aunt Agnes's petticoat, his wavy black hair curling around his ears like his father's. Before long he's climbing up on Jean's knee and calling her *Mammie*, for she often stays on at Mossgiel when Rab returns to Ellisland. Knowing nothing about work on a farm, she wants to learn how to be a good farmer's wife.

Milking a cow is harder than it looks, she realizes, perched on a one-legged stool at the hind end of a mottled white and reddish-brown Ayrshire. Between her legs, Jean braces a luggie beneath the bulging, pink udder and watches Agnes crouched at the cow beside her.

"Squeeze and pull, squeeze and pull," Agnes says, rhythmically squirting a steady, white flow into her pail. Jean's thumbs and forefingers clamp the tops of two elongated teats. She pulls and squeezes, pulls and squeezes. The cow turns her massive head with its curved horns, her large brown eyes staring blankly at Jean.

"No, squeeze and pull," Agnes laughs. "Don't yank. Be firm, but gentle."

The cow bawls, annoyed with Jean's inexperienced hands. By the time Agnes, Isabella and Annabella have finished milking the other six cows, Jean has drained her first one dry. She stands, wipes her hands on her apron, admiring her brimming pail. She bends to hoist it up and display her accomplishment. The cow steps back. A white stream floods the clay floor of the milking-sheil. Luath and the byre cats bound out of nowhere, lapping and slurping this rare treat.

The three sisters are patient with her fumbles. They're kind and light-hearted, much like their oldest brother in many ways. During meals they each sit with a horn spoon in one hand and a book in the other. As they churn butter and roll it on the board to remove the last of the whey, they recite poems and trill songs like "The Ballad of Sir James the Ross," and sometimes the Psalms of David. Unlike Rab, they've been blessed with their mother's melodic voice. Mrs. Burns nurtured a love of singing and rhyming in all her children, Agnes says. She was always crooning the old ballads as they washed clothes, cooked meals, spun yarn and waulked the wool.

"It relieves the drudgery. Just like the thrush's sweet song eases your cares for a moment," Agnes says. "But after Daddy died, Mammie changed. Seemed to bury her voice in the grave with him. Now she's all glunch and gloom."

The only one besides Bess and Bobbie who makes Mrs.

Burns smile is Gilbert, the good son in her eyes, sensible and reliable—more like her side of the family, the Browns. The two brothers are like night and day. Gilbert is tall and thin, his face pinched and serious, his movements slow and methodical. He seldom talks, and Jean has never heard him laugh.

Rab is the wayward son, a disappointment, Agnes confides to Jean one afternoon as they're packing curds into the cheese moulds. "Mammie can't forgive him for shaming the family with his illegitimate bairns," Agnes says. "She was adamant Rabbie should marry Lizzie Paton. Thank the Lord I convinced him otherwise."

"Why was that?"

"Lizzie's plain and uncultivated. I knew Rabbie would soon be disgusted with her. Though the poor creature loved him with a beautiful devotion."

"Maybe that's why your mother's nae so fond of me."

"Nothing to do with you," Agnes says, shaking her head. "It's Rabbie and his verses. Mammie reads only the Bible. But she overheard the gossips jawing about one of his poems. You know the one, Holy Willie's Prayer?

> *O thou, who in the Heavens does dwell,*
> *Wha, as it pleases best Thysel,*
> *Sends ane to Heaven an ten to Hell,*
> *A' for Thy glory.*
> *And no for onie guid or ill*
> *They've done before Thee!*

True though it may be," Agnes chuckles, "tis blasphemy to a die-hard Calvinist like Mammie."

"You've read all your brother's verses?"

"Ay, often before anyone else." A sly smile turns up the corners of Agnes's mouth. "When Rabbie was out plowing, I'd sometimes sneak up to his room to see what he was scratching onto his slate late into the night. One day he and Gibby came in for dinner, and Rabbie headed straight up to the garret without a bite. After they returned to the field, I slipped up. His composing book lay open on his desk. *Wee, sleekit, cowrin, tim'rous beastie, O what a panic's in thy breastie.*"

"*Thou need na start awa sae hasty*," Jean chimes in, "*Wi bickering brattle.*"

"Have you ever seen such a heart open on the page?" Agnes asks, her brown eyes welling up.

"Ay. He sees the same things as us—ordinary things, a field mouse or a daisy—but he sees them differently."

Agnes's face clouds over as she rinses her hands in a bucket of water. "'Twas the siller he earned from his verses that saved us. If Rabbie hadn't loaned Gibby two hundred pounds to keep the farm going, heaven knows where we'd be." Then a grin lights up her eyes, so much like her brother's lightning changes of expression. "And with those earnings, Rabbie ordered enough mode silk from Glasgow to make us all new cloaks and bonnets for kirk."

"Surely your mother was pleased about that," Jean says, pressing a weight atop the mould to force the liquid from the curds.

Agnes grimaces. "*Pride goeth before a fall*, Mammie said. What she always says when we praise Rabbie's achievements."

During her apprenticeship, Jean learns to make sweet, buttery Dunlop cheese from the unskimmed milk of the Ayrshires, to feed turnips to the cows with a long-forked tattie spade and muck out the stable with a graipe. She grows strong and stable enough to carry two full milk buckets on a shoulder yoke without spilling a drop. Every night, she falls exhausted into her bed in the garret and snuggles up next to her son, his quiet breath soothing her to sleep.

In mid-September, a letter arrives.

> *My Dearest Love,*
>
> *I received your kind letter with a pleasure which no letter but one from you could have given me. I dream of you the whole night long, but alas! I fear it will be three weeks yet ere I can hope for the happiness of seeing you, my harvest is going on; I have some to cut down still but I put in two stacks today, so I am as tired as a dog. The apples are all sold & gone.*
>
> *I have written my long thought letter to Mr. Graham, commissioner of Excise, and have sent a sheet full of poetry to Johnson besides. Now I talk of poetry, I had a fine strathspey among my hands, to make verses to, for Johnson's collection, which I intend as my honeymoon song.*
>
> *I am ever, my dearest Madam,*
> *Your faithful husband & humble servant,*
> *Robt Burns*

Rab often talked of applying for the Excise, whose officers roam the countryside searching out illegal whisky stills and goods smuggled over from France. Now that he's married and nearly settled in his own home, the Service will regard him as a worthy applicant. "A backup plan, should fortune not favour me in farming," he said. "I have no great faith in her fickle ladyship."

In November, just after Martinmas, Jean opens a letter that makes her heart trill. Though their house is only half-finished, Rab has found a place they can both live in for the winter. *In the very neighourhood of our farm, a couple of furnished rooms in a large house. I'm extremely happy at the idea of your coming, as it will save us from these cruel separations.*

On a morning in early December, a fresh skiff of snow whitens the roads and hoarfrost gilds the hedgerows. Huddled by the door of the tailor's shop, Jean's mother, little sisters and brother wave goodbye to Jean and Rab as the cart bumps over the icy cobbles of the Back Causeway. Jean wipes her eyes, thinking about the three frozen mounds in the kirkyard that she's abandoning. But she does not look back. Her eyes stay fixed on the hazy horizon. Her yearning during the past eight months of married life has finally been answered. She is, joyfully, with child.

PART II

The Mistress of Ellisland

1789–1791

But pleasures are like poppies spread,
You seize the flow'r, its bloom is shed;
Or, like the snow-fall in the river,
A moment white, then melts forever.

AN EARLY MORNING SHOWER HAS LEFT THE SIDEWALKS glistening, and the sun is winking through the clouds as I pull my suitcase up Loudon Street. I'm a familiar presence now and pedestrians nod in a friendlier way. Before turning down Earl Grey Street to the bus stop, I pause at the corner to take one last look at Jean, standing timeless on her pedestal at the Cross. She looks different from that first day I beheld her statue. After following closely in her footsteps and reliving three years of her life, I now see a spirited woman behind that enigmatic half-smile, a woman who rose out of the ashes of her great losses to begin anew. I'm eager to follow her and become more acquainted with this eighteenth-century woman who has come alive for me in the present. In these past five days, I've experienced the flow of time in an entirely new way, more as the thirteenth-century Zen master Dōgen Zenji explains it: "Every being that exists in the entire world is linked together as moments in time, and at the same time they exist as individual moments of time."

I wave goodbye to the Belle of Mauchline and board the coach that will take me fifty miles southeast to the home of Jean Burns, the mistress of Ellisland farm.

Ellisland Farm is said to have changed little over the centuries. It remained a working farm until 1921 when a trust was formed to preserve the property for the nation. After refurbishing the house and outbuildings, the trustees handed the farm over to a local group of volunteers, the Friends of Ellisland, who maintain the site as a museum.

A long driveway leads up between tall, overhanging trees. Strolling up the gravel lane beneath the leafy archway, it feels as if I'm stepping back into a different century. The swish of traffic from the highway recedes, the only sound a chorus of bird calls. Robins and magpies dart between the aspens, starlings swoop over my head. Kelly-green fields open up on either side of the lane, bordered with mossy stone walls and thick, thorny hedgerows that look as if they've always been here. The dykes have been rebuilt over the years, but some of these amorphous grey stones would surely have been gathered by the hands of Robert Burns.

At the crest of the hill, a small house and outbuildings appear. Whitewashed and trimmed with green, they form a quadrangle around a cobblestone courtyard. An orchard of gnarled apple trees is just coming into bloom, as it would have been on May Day 1789 when Jean and Rab moved into their new home.. In this eternal moment in spring, I envision them performing the traditional Scottish settling-in ceremony of *freit* as curlews whistle from the hawthorns, their pink blossoms swirling down like confetti.

Their maid-servant crosses the threshold first. On her head, Liza balances a bowl of salt atop the new family Bible Rab ordered from London. The word of God and the staff of life will thus bring them, the first tenants of the house, good fortune. Rab gathers Jean up in his arms and carries her through the green door. "Goodness lass," he pants, lugging her into the kitchen, "can you be carrying a pair again?" He tells Jean to close her eyes; he has a surprise for her.

"A Carron Range," Jean cries. In the centre of the hearth gleams a black cast-iron stove, the most modern and efficient cookstove to be had, a coal-fired range with an oven for baking and top grates for cooking. "What a luxury," she says; no more making meals over an open fire.

"Only the best for the best," Rab says, kissing her.

He takes Jean's hand and leads her into their bedroom. Next to the window stands a heavy mahogany four-poster bed with an arched canopy, side curtains and valances. "A wedding gift from Mrs. Dunlop," Rab says.

Jean knows the elderly lady by name only. Mrs. Frances Dunlop, a member of the Ayrshire gentry, was given a copy of Rab's poem "The Cotter's Saturday Night" when she was suffering a deep depression after her husband's death. So moved by the poem, she wrote to Rab asking for six copies of his book, and invited him to visit her at Dunlop House just north of Mauchline. Since then they've maintained a steady correspondence. His poems, she's told him, have transformed her life.

"I'll feel like a queen sleeping in such a grand bed," Jean says, sinking down onto the floral coverlet.

"The dear lady knows the importance of the nuptial couch," Rab grins. "She blessed her husband with eleven bairns."

"Does the dear lady approve of the wife you've chosen?" Jean has already felt the sting of disapproval from many of the gentry in Dumfriesshire. Elizabeth and Robert Riddell, their closest neighbours downriver at the estate of Friar's Carse, invited them to their table sparkling with silver and gilt-edged china. Beneath the candlelit chandelier, Jean sensed their appraisal of her plain frock, her broad Ayrshire accent. *An uncultured lass with country ways*, their eyes said. *The bard has clearly married beneath him*. Rab has coached her—which piece of silver to pick up first, how to eat her soup without slurping. He's bought her silk stockings, gold earrings, colourful shawls and kid gloves smuggled from France. Wanting his wife to be the best-dressed woman in the kirk, he ordered fifteen yards of the finest black silk for her gowns, costing over four pounds—more than six months wages for a farm worker. Jean cringes at such extravagance. And new furniture, ordered from John Morris in Mauchline, shines in the parlour: an oval dining table with six matching chairs and a mahogany-cased clock.

"I told the good lady I've captured the lass with the handsomest figure, the sweetest disposition and the warmest heart in all of Scotland," Rab says, stretching out on the bed. "Not to mention the most extraordinary twin-bearing capacity. I reckon on twelve times a brace of children against we celebrate our twelfth wedding day. These would give us twenty-four christenings."

"Easier said than done," Jean laughs, nestling against his broad chest. A breeze blows up from the river ruffling the lace curtains. Lulled by water lapping on the bank, they breathe in the musky scent of hawthorn blossoms.

"I hae a wife o' my ain, I'll partake wi' naebody," Rab whispers.

With child, with husband, in her own home, Jean smiles and closes her eyes.

It starts off well enough. As if the slate of the past has been erased and they can write their lives anew. Those first May mornings when they rise at the break of day seem as fresh as the dawn of creation. The chirruping of larks fills the air and dew glistens on the fields like bits of glass. Jean watches Rab stride along the newly ploughed rows in tan breeks, an old working sark and a blue bonnet. He reaches into the white sowing sheet slung over his shoulder and scatters seed for corn and oats. Long-eared hares, brown as the soil, hop ahead of him; iridescent-black rooks trail behind, pecking in the furrows.

Jean trundles between the kitchen and the dairy, eager to do more than her expanding belly will allow. She plants a vegetable garden by the back door and helps tend the herd of ten Ayrshires—the best milk-producers, Rab believes. She churns butter and makes cheese; pitches hay into the stalls of the four strapping Galloway horses that pull the plough and harrow. A flock of black-faced sheep graze in the meadow, thick with wool that Jean will spin into yarn.

The month of June turns cold and wet. Jean has never seen such rain, sheets of grey rolling down the glen. The Nith swells and swirls with muddy foam. Squalls tear through the woods, ravage the apple trees and fell a birch. The fields turn into a quagmire.

"The dirt's soft with lime and drains poorly," Rab says, squeezing a sodden clod in his hand. Already Jean sees the first doubts surfacing, like weeds poking a few tendrils out of the earth.

Rab grins and throws the clump of mud across the field. "It may not have the soil," he says, "but it's got the soul. I never hear the solitary whistle of the curlew at noon, or the wild cadence of a troop of grey plover in the morning, without feeling the pleasure of poetry."

Every evening, whatever the weather, he saunters down to the river, "to take a gloamin' shot at the muses," he says, putting on his blue cap. The water's gurgling ripples stir his imagination, and he returns bubbling with lines and verses. "As if carried down by the current itself," he says, "gifts from Coila, my early sweet inspirer."

One night, it's after dark and he hasn't returned. When rain starts splattering against the windows, Jean throws on her cloak, lights the lantern and tramps out to the haugh where he often paces when he's thinking on a poem. From the edge of the broom, she spies him in his black-and-white checked plaid, drenched, waving his arms and shouting into the wind while the waves roil and splash upon the bank.

"Come in before your catch you death," Jean hollers.

Back in the house, Rab retreats to his desk beneath the gable window in the parlour. For the rest of the evening, Jean hears the scratching of his quill and sometimes a sigh or a gasp. Before retiring to bed, she peeks in to say goodnight. He's hunched over his paper, writing at a furious pace. On either side of his desk, leather-bound volumes line the shelved presses, the gold tooling on their spines glinting in the lamp light: *Poetical Works of Alan Ramsay*, *Essais de Montaigne*, Shakespeare, Chaucer, Spencer, Milton, Dryden, Pope, Goldsmith, Voltaire, Rousseau... *The heaven-taught ploughman* indeed, Jean thinks, as she leaves him undisturbed.

The next morning, Rab can't wait to read his verses to her. Jean stirs the porridge and bakes bannock as he recounts a long poem about a drunken farmer riding through the darkness to his wife waiting at home. Galloping past the old Alloway kirk, Tam spies through its lit-up windows witches and warlocks dancing with the dead. Captivated by a young lass dancing in a *cutty sark*—a skimpy dress—Tam yells, *Weel done, cutty-sark!*

And in an instant all was dark. The witches and warlocks turn on Tam and chase him down the road to the River Doon. He thinks he's escaped when he reaches the bridge—witches can't cross moving water—but just before his mare steps upon the bridge, the lass lunges and grabs Maggie's tail: *The carlin caught her by the rump, And left poor Maggie with a stump.*

Breathless at the end of his recitation, his dark eyes shining, he glances up from his notebook. "Well, Jean, what do you think?" His usual question after reading one of his poems, which she always answers honestly.

"A rollicking, good story. Though the rhythm needs polishing here and there. It's got a good lesson behind it." She gives him a knowing look. "One that many a man should heed." His face breaks into a wide grin.

He scribbles away with his stumpie while Jean boils the water for tea and slathers the warm bannock with butter and blackberry preserve. Half an hour later, he lifts his head. "Is this to your liking, Mrs. Burns?"

> *Now, wha this tale o' truth shall read,*
> *Ilk man, and mother's son, take heed:*
> *Whene'er to drink you are inclin'd,*
> *Or, cutty sarks run in your mind,*
> *Think! ye may buy the joy's o'er dear:*
> *Remember Tam o'Shanter's mare.*

"Ay, you've put it well," Jean says, wielding the knife in front of his face.

He chuckles. "It might be the best poem I've ever written. But you never know. Making a poem is like begetting a son. You can't tell whether you have a wise man or a fool until you produce him to the world and try him."

Many evenings they work together on the songs Rab is amending for a third volume of *The Scot's Musical Museum*. The words of many old tunes are missing, so he composes lyrics for them, re-arranges the verses of some, and condenses or expands others. Jean knows all the country ballads by heart and sings the melodies for him. One afternoon, he comes home from market day in Dumfries all atwitter about a verse he heard an old man crooning over a pint at the Globe Inn. Rab is sure the words he took down have never appeared in print. When he hums the tune, Jean recognizes it and sings the familiar chorus about the olden times:

> *For auld lang syne, my dear,*
> *For auld lang syne,*
> *We'll tak a cup o' kindness yet*
> *For auld lang syne!*

"A heaven-inspired poet penned that glorious fragment," Rab says. "There's something in the old Scots tunes. A fire of native genius that marks them from English songs and our modern song-wrights." He writes two more verses for the song and includes it in the parcel of compositions he posts to James Johnson every fortnight. And the publisher is clamouring for more.

Summer bursts wild with flowers, the meadows fragrant with briar rose, foxglove and purple harebells. The corn grows tall, like row upon row of sentries. Grain shoots up into a green wave rippling in the breeze blowing up from the river. One morning in early July, they're watching the sun rise above the Dalswinton hills purple in the distance. "Red sky in the morning, shepherd's warning," Jean says. "You'll not be scything the field for a few days yet."

"Good time to make that trip to Edinburgh," Rab says. "I've publishing business to see to." Then, with a sheepish look on his face, he adds, "And I have to settle things with Jenny Clow."

The sound of her name is like the rattling of bones: Jenny Clow, the twenty-year-old maid-servant of the married Edinburgh lady, Nancy McLehose. Letters arrive regularly from Mrs. McLehose. Jean recognizes the feathery script on the thick vellum envelopes. Rab assures her it's only a friendship. When the lady wrote last November to report that Jenny had given birth to his son and named him Robert Burns Jr., Jean prickled with the heat of jealousy: How dare she appropriate his name, *her* son's name. Then she chided herself: all this happened before they wed; forgive the mistakes of the past and enjoy the blessings of the present. *Commune with your own heart and be still.*

"Jenny's nae doing so well," Rab says. "She's struggling to provide for her lad."

Jean can well imagine the misery of the young woman's circumstances. *There but for the grace of God go I.* "Do you want to bring him here?"

"You'd do that, Jean?" He stares at her, dumbfounded. "Bobbie and Bess will soon be here with us. And in a couple of months, you'll have a new wean to care for, God willing."

"Another bairn to love is nae hardship," she says, "until the lass gets on her feet. If that's what she wants."

"How do I deserve such a wife?" He pulls her in for a hug, barely possible now with her mountain of a belly between them.

Rab hires two men to take over the farm work while he's away, and his mother and sister Agnes come to relieve Jean of the household and dairy chores. With them, they bring Bobbie—three years old now—and his four-year-old half-sister Bess. The skipping footsteps and sweet voices of children fill the house and Jean's heart. Having her son, at last—after two long years—eases her constant yearning for her three lost daughters.

Lying alone at night, she wonders if Rab will once again be captivated by the city's culture and seduced by its fine ladies, or fawning barmaids. Will he regret his humble life as a farmer? She feels his love in the marrow of her bones, but their bodies have not joined for months. The outcome of her last pregnancy has made them wary. He'll be visiting Jenny as well as his old flame, Nancy McLehose—or *Clarinda* as she signs her letters to him, her *Sylvander*. Jean read one of them; it lay open on his desk like an invitation. Mrs. McLehose was not pleased with him marrying; charges of "villainy" and "perfidious treachery" peppered the letter as she accused him of being tied to Jean while courting her. So, Jean suspects, he'll have to set things straight with this woman as well.

A fortnight later, in the middle of the night, a horse snorts and whinnies outside her bedroom window. Rab scuffles in and collapses onto the bed. Groaning, he pulls off his riding boots and rubs his feet. "I'm fair hashed," he says, burrowing close to Jean. "Sae good to be home." He tells her about meeting his eight-month-old son, Robbie, black-haired and brown-eyed; and about Jenny's determination to find the means to raise him herself. Then he rants about the city and the condescension heaped upon him—a peasant with mud still sticking to his boots. "They expect me to talk in the dialect of my poems," he chuckles. "They're shocked when I speak better English than most of them. Ay, Auld Reekie. Tis all worship of rank and privilege. A business of sickening disgust." His arm around Jean's big belly, his hand fondling her ballooning breasts, he sighs, "I'd nae trade places with King Geordie himself, for I reign in Jeanie's bosom."

On August 18, near midday, a squawking cry comes from behind the bedroom door. Minutes later, Rab is at Jean's bedside. "The handsomest child I've ever seen," he beams, cradling his son.

"And the easiest one to birth," Jean says, "so eager he was to be born."

Rab peers into his son's opaque blue eyes. "Welcome, Francis Wallace." Then he turns to Jean. "Does the name not suit him? Look at the manly swell of his little chest. And his wee head, so nobly shaped. Shows the promise of an independent mind."

"Ay, suits him well." Jean smiles, pleased with the name he's chosen to honour his friend Mrs. Frances Dunlop and the Scottish patriot William Wallace, one of Mrs. Dunlop's ancestors. But Jean knows the name will not meet the approval of Rab's mother, who has stated unequivocally that children should be given family names; one more disappointment in her oldest son.

Jean witnesses another side of her husband emerging. He revels in being present, for the first time, to observe all the day-to-day changes in his infant son. When Frankie howls during his colicky bouts, Rab paces the floor with him at all hours of the day or night. "You have a pipe," he says, looking into his son's rosy face, "as loud as the horn your immortal namesake blew as a signal to take out the pin of Stirling Bridge."

When the day arrives for Rab's mother to return to Mossgiel, young Bess cries and clings to her grandmother, the only mother she's ever known. "Och, Rabbie, we can wait till she's older then," Mrs. Burns says, her veiny hand patting her granddaughter's black curls. Then she clasps Bess's hand and leads her out the door.

In September, golden fields of ripened grain undulate against a sapphire sky. By the end of October, the fields are stripped bare, the last sheaf cut. Jean admires the piles of the hay and grain stacked in the byre, the mounds of oats and barley stored in the stockyard. But Rab shakes his head. "Not near enough to see us through the winter," he says. So on Hallowmas Eve, he insists they observe the old traditions. "Tonight witches and devils and fairies will be haunting the braes and glens," he says, "looking for places to cast their evil spells." Jean and Agnes stare at the heap of fat turnips he wants them to carve into lanterns. "Make scary faces to frighten away any malicious spirits," he says with a wink. "This farm needs all the help it can get." As Jean watches him binding stocks of dried kail to make torches, the tremulous half-smile on his face tells her what's hiding beneath his words—those weeds of doubt, taking hold and spreading.

As the gloaming descends, they place the glowing lanterns with their leering faces into the windows. Then they gather in the middle of the field where the farmhands have set a peat fire blazing. Lighting their torches, they spread out and march around the stone-dyke border of the farm. As Jean follows the flame of Rab's torch far ahead of her, she begins to feel uneasy and stumbles in the ruts of the stubbly field. Footsteps tromp behind her, and she swings around. Agnes's torch glows in the dark distance; a sliver of a moon blinks in the sky. Jean's never believed the superstitions, and knows that nothing tangible is tracking her, nothing visible—only her own fear, her dread of something she does not want to see.

"Ever think your life would end up so bloody?" Rab asks, rubbing his hands against his red-stained smock.

It's late November. Jean has just finished salting the marbled pink flesh of a freshly butchered hog, and Rab is hanging the meat on hooks to smoke over the range.

"One more thing about a being a farmer's wife you failed to mention," Jean laughs. Yesterday she was up to her elbows in pig fat, cooking it into lard then adding lye she'd made from wood ash. She boiled the mixture in the copper kettle until it hardened, enough soap to do them for a year of washing and cleaning. Now she scoops oatmeal into a large bowl half-filled with blood. "We'll have a tasty black pudding," she says, chopping a slab of suet. She dumps the pieces into the bowl with some minced onion and a teaspoon of salt then grabs her wooden spoon. "And all the bacon, ribs and roasts should see us through the winter."

"Not likely. We'll be scrounging." Rab rinses his hands in the bucket and says, "So I've decided to accept that offer. Fifty pounds a year would take the pressure off."

For the past week, they've been mulling over a letter from the Excise Service offering Rab a commission as a riding officer. He'd be searching out old wives' liquor barrels and hunting down smugglers. Coming from a long line of whisky traders himself, Rab has misgivings about taking such a job. As a lad he'd spent a summer on the coast, learning mensuration and surveying, and befriended many men in the smuggling trade.

"Are you sure?"

"I nae fancy being a stool pigeon, and I don't pretend there's honour in the profession. But I have a family to feed. All around, it's not a bad settlement for a poet." He explains that the commission also includes lifelong provisions for widows and orphans.

"No need to think about that," Jean says, glancing up from the length of intestine she's stuffing. The salary would be a luxury, but she can't imagine how he'd manage it all: ride over ten parishes on his rounds, write his poems and run a farm. She loves this place. The house with its bright airy rooms; the quiet mornings when the mists rise like phantoms off the river; the stunning sunsets, mauve and saffron washing over the fields. "What about the farm?"

"We can hire another worker and switch to dairy farming." Grinning, he adds, "Grass is one crop this land can grow."

"Ay," Jean says, a quiver of hope tingling down her spine. "The Ayrshires' milk makes wonderful cheddar."

She stuffs the bloody mixture into the long casing of intestine while Rab lifts the heavy hanks of pork and skewers them onto meat hooks. Broad-shouldered and muscular, he's stronger than most men Jean knows. She's seen him sling twenty-stone bags of meal onto his back while still laughing and talking. He can load a cart with sacks of corn and plow a field twice as fast as the farm hands. But she can also see the drudgery leaving its mark on his body, his shoulders stooping as if he's carrying a massive burden.

"I'll go answer that letter," he says, "and join thae curst horse-leeches o' the Excise."

Jean watches him trudge from the kitchen. From the back he could be mistaken for an old man. Yet he's only thirty years old.

*   *   *

Pre 1780 reads the sign in the old byre. Corroded farm implements, worn leather harnesses, wooden milking stools, pails and butter churns are stacked like relics of a dream that turned to rust. Smoke plumes from the chimney of the farmhouse across the courtyard. Chilled from standing around in the damp air, I'm drawn to the warmth it promises, looking forward to sitting quietly by the hearth and communing with Jean in her kitchen. I almost expect to smell the savoury aroma of a black pudding baking or see strips of salted pork dangling above a Carron range.

But when I step inside the green door, I'm greeted by a hubbub of conversation and many people seated around a large wooden table sipping tea and coffee. A short, grey-haired man in a brown tweed jacket rises to introduce himself—Les Byers, curator of the museum—and introduce the Friends of Ellisland. The men are here for a workday, as they are every Wednesday all year round, repairing the buildings and maintaining the grounds. Coffee break over, their chairs scrape back on the wood floor, and they button up plaid jackets, zip up fleeces and pull on work gloves.

The original stone fireplace dominates the small kitchen, throwing off a lovely heat and the fragrance of woodsmoke. The cast-iron stove, Mr. Byers tells me, contains parts of that first Carron Range. The oven is the very one in which Jean Armour baked her scones, bread and oatcakes. I take hold of the curved black handle, melding my handprints with hers. The room has a rich, comforting aroma that reminds me of my grandmother's farm kitchen in Nova Scotia—a room where food has been smoked and boiled and baked for years, so that all the smells have seeped into the wooden rafters and wide floorboards.

Since part of the house is occupied by the curator, the only other room open to the public is the parlour. Entering the room, I'm momentarily disconcerted. A black-haired figure in a dark blue suit is seated at a fold-top desk in front of the window—a mannequin. Robert Burns sits, quill in his white-gloved hand, eternally writing, his sightless eyes staring out at the green bank of the river that inspired some of his best poems: "Tam O'Shanter," "A Rosebud by My Early Walk," "To a Blackbird." Glass cases line the walls displaying the poet's most ordinary possessions—a rust-speckled dressing mirror, a clothes brush, a small wineglass—endowed with the status of sacred artifacts. Mr. Byers tells me the spence is essentially unchanged since Burns's time, but the atmosphere is sterile and museum-like; nothing of the spirit of the place or its inhabitants lingers.

I head down to the River Nith, taking a route the Friends of Ellisland have recently laid, the Jean Armour Path. The well-trod trail along the river meanders between lofty beech trees and gorse bushes stippled with golden buds. On this day of low, brooding clouds, the wide river flows with a silver sheen. On the far bank, black-faced sheep and lambs dot jade pastures that stretch for miles. I follow the path north to Friars' Carse, the former estate of Robert and Elizabeth Riddell, Jean and Rab's closest neighbours, now the opulent Friars' Carse Country House Hotel.

With a bit of searching, I find the Hermitage secluded in the trees above the river. A remnant of the monkish origins of the estate, the old stone hut served Burns as a writing retreat. A wrought-iron fence prevents me from peering in the one small window facing the river. I rest on a stone bench, and the sun finds a space between the clouds to warm my face. Birds trill their myriad calls, a light breeze riffles the leaves as the river gushes over the rapids, rushing like the passing years… Jean's yesterday flowing into my today… today flowing into tomorrow. I inhale the damp, earthy smells, the centuries of composted leaves in the spongy ground beneath my feet. *Life is but a day at most, Sprung from night in darkness lost*, Burns wrote from this very spot, this timeless refuge. Sweet poetic ground indeed. I understand how 130 poems and songs could have sprung from Burns's pen during his brief time in Ellisland, and why Jean loved living here. *Ay, as close to Eden as you can imagine.* Her voice sounds wistful inside my head, for the story of paradise is also a story of temptation, and a story of loss.

The autumn of 1789, the hawthorns hang heavy with shiny red berries, a feast for the flocks of blackbirds twittering in their branches. Many jars of ruby hawthorn jelly line the shelves of Jean's pantry, but she fears such abundance could mean a long, hard winter. She frets about Rab having to ride two hundred miles every week across his Excise division. In the sleety dribble of November, she watches him slog into the house, drenched and shivering. And for the next week, she nurses him in bed with a cold and fever.

She seldom sees him in the evenings; he works into the wee hours compiling his accounts and writing a daily journal of his visits, distances, calculations, measurements. With farm work on top of it all—plowing up the stubble, threshing and flailing and winnowing the wheat—he complains there's no time for writing verse. "I'm a poor, rascally gauger," he moans, "condemned to inspecting dirty ponds and yeasty barrels."

Winter offers a respite. Many days Rab can't ride out through snow drifts tall as a man. The roads turn to rivers of ice. In the evenings, they curl around the ingle blazing with a peat fire; the kettle steams and hisses as the north wind howls about the house. In the corner, Agnes spins sheep's wool into thread, singing along with the steady birr of the wheel and treadle. One foot on the pedal, Jean rocks the cradle while darning socks in the lantern light. Bobbie nestles in his father's lap as Rab recites rhymes and spins yarns of ghosts and fairies, tales that fired his imagination as a young lad.

"Tyta, can you sing the story about rantin Robin?" Bobbie asks.

"If your mammie will carry the tune. I've the gift of a silver tongue," Rab says, winking at Jean, "but your mither's blessed with the golden voice."

They all sing the verses Rab set to an old melody with only one strain, the story of his birth on such a stormy winter's night. Riding off to fetch a midwife, his father came upon an old woman wandering by the River Ayr. She'd lost her way in the storm, so he gave her shelter at their cottage. When their baby was born that night, the crone looked into the cradle and made a prophecy.

> *There was a lad was born in Kyle,*
> *But whatna day o' whatna style,*
> *I doubt it's hardly worth the while*
>   *To be sae nice wi' Robin.*
>
> *Our monarch's hindmost year but ane*
> *Was five and twenty days begun*
> *'T was then a blast o' Janwar win'*
>   *Blew hansel in on Robin.*
>
> *The gossip keekit in his loof,*
> *Quo' she, Wha lives will see the proof,*
> *This waly boy will be nae coof:*
>   *I think we'll call him Robin.*
>
> *"He'll hae misfortune great an' sma'*
>   *But ay a heart aboon them a'.*
> *He'll be a credit to us a':*
>   *We'll a' be proud of Robin!"*

Between each verse, Bobbie joins in the chorus, clapping his chubby hands:

> *Robin was a rovin boy,*
> *Rantin, rovin, rantin, rovin,*
> *Robin was a rovin boy,*
> *Rantin, rovin Robin!*

On such evenings, when they're all together and Rab is cheerful, Jean wishes time would stop, preserve their snug fire-lit circle—forever warm, forever content.

For the winter also brings out Rab's "blue devil hours," as he calls them. Jean watches his moods change as suddenly as the weather; from sunny singing and joking one day, to brooding clouds of depression the next when he withdraws behind his dark brows in silence. The excise work is sucking everything from him. His only poems come from musings as he gallops across the county.

For three weeks in February, Rab lies in bed with a nervous headache, scarcely able to lift his head from the pillow, the same rheumatic fever he often suffered as a child. "This farm has undone my enjoyment of myself," he rails. "Tis a ruinous affair. Let it go to hell." Jean wants to believe such ranting is fuelled by the generous doses of mercury, port wine and laudanum that Dr. Mundell has prescribed. But all that winter, threats of forsaking the farm hang in the air, heavy and ominous as the grey snow clouds.

The same month, her baby takes ill. At first, Jean thinks it's just a milk rash. Frankie howls whenever he tries to suckle. His gums are speckled with white splotches like milk-curds, and pink sores sprout on his face. The sores spread to his chest, his arms, his legs, and change into oozing pustules. Then he's burning with fever. Dr. Mundell confirms her worst fear—smallpox, the infection that's afflicting the country.

Through the long nights, Jean rocks her sick baby in her arms, her ear pressed against his tiny chest, straining to hear his wheezing. Agnes wants to take over so Jean can get some sleep, but Jean will not leave his side for a minute. She remembers too well her mother losing two babies to this disease, and the ghosts of her lost daughters haunt the dark places in her mind: *Jeanie, Helen, Mary.* She must be vigilant.

After two weeks, the blisters crust over with scabs. A good sign, Dr. Mundell says. Jean prays to Mother Mary, even to God, asking for his forgiveness. She wonders if this is why Frankie is spared.

Sitting on a stone bench outside the byre, Jean tilts her face up to the sun. Swallows glide in and out in a flurry of nest-making. In one of the stalls, a newborn calf is wobbling to its feet. Fuzzy yellow chicks peep around a flock of hens clucking and pecking in the dirt. The bleating of sheep pulls her eyes to the far pasture where snow-white lambs frisk beside the lumbering ewes, and red sodger bees hover over purple and yellow primroses. Down on the riverbank, ferns uncurl their fiddleheads, and ducklings waddle a cheeping trail behind their mother. Jean fills her lungs with the promise of this loveliest season on the farm.

With the coming of spring, she's relieved to see Rab's energy and health returning. The most demanding season of the excise business is over, so he often stays late at the Globe Inn in Dumfries or attends private parties with his hard-drinking gentlemen friends. Lying awake, Jean hears him staggering into the dark house, singing: *We are na fou, we're nae that fou, But just a drappie in our e'e.*

In the morning, he's droning a different tune. "My head's

addled as an egg," he whines. "Hard drink's the very devil of me."

"As ye sow, so shall ye reap," Jean replies. She hates her scolding voice, the self-righteous tone that brings her father to mind, a voice she's not heard for a long while. Neither he nor her mother has visited the farm, not even to meet their new grandson. Rab has encouraged her to invite them, and she's done so in many letters. Jean has not been back to Mauchline since she left almost two years ago. And that, she suspects, is the problem. It's time for them to make their peace, she decides: *Jesus taught us to pardon our trespassers. Forgive and ye will be forgiven.* Nothing can change the past. But she can try to change the present.

In early June, Jean steps down from the Camperdown coach in front of Poosie Nansie's. The hostelry looks seedier than she remembers, its whitewashed front stained brown as tea in many places. Clutching her grip in one arm and Frankie in the other, she strolls to the corner. Instead of turning left to the Cowgate, she heads down High Street. The same shops and taverns line the curving main road—all looking so familiar yet somehow different. She passes through the iron gates to the kirk where the gargoyles guarding its entrance still glower. Abbot Hunter's ivy-covered tower in the old castle has crumbled a little further into ruin. A strange sensation overcomes her. Not much has changed, yet nothing is the same: the streets seem narrower; the burn but a trickling brook compared to the rolling Nith; the bleaching green, a meagre field in contrast to Ellisland's wide pastures. She's viewing it all through the eyes of a twenty-five-year-old wife and mother of five.

Her lost daughters are still alive in her, each one a distinct presence in her thoughts. *Who would each have become?* Jean wonders as she kneels by the little mounds in the kirkyard. They've sunk deeper into the earth, and a dense thatch covers them. Peering up through the leaves of the ash, Jean can see into the second-floor window of the red sandstone building in the Back Causeway, one small room teeming with memories. She lays Frankie down on her shawl and stretches out beside him, her arm reaching across the three green humps. Breathing in the grassy scent, she wonders if they live again in these green blades. *Baloo, baloo, my wee, wee things, For thou art doubly dear to me.*

The savoury aroma of roast duckling and gooseberry sauce fills Jean's nostrils when she steps through the door. Her father welcomes her home like a prodigal daughter, embracing her with an affection he's not displayed since she fell in with Rab five years past. Her little brother and sisters, whom she's not seen for two years, stand in a smiling row before her—all so changed and grown up. Nelly, a young woman now with a shapely figure; seven-year-old Robbie grinning with new front teeth that seem too big for his mouth; Janet and Mary, nine and eleven, bonnie lassies with thick black hair tied back with red ribbons. They all dote on their ten-month-old nephew, and Frankie charms everyone, showing off two pearly bottom teeth when he smiles.

"So good to hear a baby's laughter again," her mother says. She regales Jean with all the village gossip: the couples who've been called before the kirk session; the poor girls who've borne children out of wedlock; and the lucky ones who've made good matches. Jean's old friend Helen Miller married Dr. Mackenzie last year. And Christina Morton, Jean's former companion at singing classes, is betrothed to handsome Robbie Paterson, a Mauchline draper.

"And poor Reverend Auld," Mrs. Armour says, "died last fall. Eighty-two years old. He served the parish well for fifty years."

Just the mention of his name makes the blood rush to Jean's cheeks. After a moment she asks, "And Robin Wilson? Do you hear anything of him?"

"Ay, still in Paisley. Doing well, they say. A master weaver now."

"Married?"

Mrs. Armour shakes her head. "Guess the right lass hasn't come along yet," she says, meeting her daughter's eyes.

Jean nods. She often thinks about him, that devoted lad of her youth, and the road she didn't follow. And not without some regrets. Life with Rab, she's come to realize, will always be turbulent. Though she feels his devotion to her and the children, she also feels his restlessness, like a horse confined to the stable that yearns to run free. That untameable *rantin' rovin' Robin* spirit. Those nights he stays at the Globe Inn in Dumfries, sometimes it's inclement weather keeping him there, and he says the town allows him easier access to his excise territory. One day Agnes overheard the farmhands joking about Rab keeping company with the barmaids. Jean shrugged it off as rumour. "You know your brother. He dearly loves the lassies," she laughed. "Our Rabbie should've had two wives."

Jean knows that a beautiful woman is a direct channel to his muse: that merciless mistress of his soul, unrelenting in her demands for young female flesh. He once told Jean that the first poem he ever penned was inspired by a sweet sonsie lass he'd met while harvesting grain. "It was a little before my sixteenth year," he said, "that I first committed the sin of rhyme. After that my heart was completely tinder, eternally lighted up by some goddess or other."

Jean hasn't been looking, or feeling, much like a goddess of late. She hasn't regained her figure since Frankie's birth. The skin on her stomach sags like a deflated balloon; her breasts, as big as boulders, seem always to be leaking. Rab constantly makes cutting remarks about her stoutness: "You lay as lustily about your breakfast as a reaper from the corn-ridge." She tries, but fails, to remember the last time their bodies met in anything more than a comforting embrace. This fortnight apart, she hopes, may be good fuel for rekindling the spark.

As Jean is packing her case for home, her father comes into her room with a square wooden box, a golden plate engraved on its lid: *For Jean and Robert Burns.* "A somewhat belated wedding present," he says, clearing his throat. Jean pulls out a large marble punch bowl rimmed with silver. He crafted it himself, he tells her, out of the rich chestnut and black-veined marble from Inveraray. Jean smiles, knowing she's been given a tremendous gift, one she didn't realize she wanted, until now: her father's blessing.

Morning sunlight dances around the walls and the wooden floor as Jean flutters about the parlour dusting, sweeping and setting things in order. It's as if the sun is shining inside her too, so happy she is to be home and the glow still lingering from last night with her husband. Her first night back, she moved Frankie into Bobbie's bed. And she and Rab enjoyed a languid, tender coupling, like in their honeymoon days. She touches her belly, wondering if that warm afterglow might mean another new life.

The usual pile of books, papers, music sheets and envelopes clutters Rab's desk. Mrs. Dunlop's most recent letter lies on top. While Jean was in Mauchline, she finally met her husband's dear friend. Mrs. Dunlop sent her carriage to convey Jean for a visit at her estate in Stewarton. "You've made quite an impression on the lady," Rab told her last night. Curious to read what she's written, Jean picks up the letter and strains to make out the cramped, rather illegible script: *Mrs. Burns I found in all the rosy bloom of health and beauty. I was delighted with the cheerful openness in her countenance, the intelligence of her eyes and her easy, modest, unaffected manners.* Jean is taken aback at such praise from someone of her station. Although Mrs. Dunlop welcomed her effusively, and Jean instantly warmed to the elderly lady's maternal nature, she knows you can't always trust the gentry. They often say sweet words to your face, and bitter ones behind your back.

She smiles at this small victory, until her father's admonishing voice echoes in her head: *Pride goeth before a fall.* Jean puts the letter down amongst the disarray. She never attempts to tidy Rab's desk, knowing there is order for him in the disorder. *Essays on Songwriting* lies open next to his commonplace book. Pleased to see that he's found some time to work on his verses, she flips over his notebook and reads what he's composing.

> *Yestreen I had a pint o' wine*
> *A place where body saw na;*
> *Yestreen lay on the breast o' mine*
> *The gowden locks of Anna.*
>
> *The hungry Jew in wilderness*
> *Rejoicing o'er his manna*
> *Was naething to my hiney bliss*
> *Upon the lips of Anna!*
>
> *The Kirk an' State may join, and tell*
> *To do sic things I maunna:*
> *The Kirk an' State may gae to Hell,*
> *And I'll gae to my Anna.*

The words blur. Her heart stops. She closes the notebook and places it back on the desk. Standing by the window, she scans the words Rab engraved on the lower pane—*An honest man's the noblest work of God*. His favourite line from Alexander Pope. Just so many words, she thinks, as she stares out at the river glinting through the trees. Across the muddy path that her and Rab's footsteps have trod into the bank, something quick and brownish-green slithers into the tangled underbrush.

An owl *who-whoos* from the hawthorn tree, and the scent of honeysuckle, twined around its trunk, floats into the bedroom. Beside the open window, Jean sits with her red plaid draped over her nightdress, the shawl Rab gave her when they wed. She hears his footsteps, then the door to the children's room creaking open. No matter how late, he always tiptoes in to look at his boys before snuggling into bed beside her.

He steps into the darkened room and gasps: "A vision etched in the moonlight." He bends to kiss her cheek, sweet wine heavy on his breath. "What a glorious ride," he says, dropping to the floor beside her chair. "The night's oozing a thousand scents of summer. Pegasus galloped like she'd sprouted the wings of her immortal namesake."

"You stopped at the Globe Inn?"

"Ay, a quick pint after a long day in the saddle."

"A pint of wine—with Anna?"

"Anna?" he stammers. "You mean the barmaid?"

Jean pictures her then, Anna Park, the niece of Mrs. Hyslop, proprietor of the Globe. "Fits the description," she says. "Long, gowden locks. She serves more than wine to her patrons?"

His eyes flit about the room then narrow to a slit as they meet hers. "You've been reading my writing."

"As I always do."

"The poem's but a drunken flight of fancy."

"Tell me the truth."

His head sags. He lets out a long sigh and glances up at her. "'Twas only one night when you were away. I was fou as Bartie. Guid drink goes in, guid sense goes out."

"Nae so fou you couldna recall the hiney bliss of it all."

"Those verses were meant for no eyes but mine."

"You betray your wife. You fuck a young lass. Then write a poem about it?"

He flinches. His mouth opens, nothing comes out. A loud silence fills the air between them. "My sins are staring me in the face. Each one tells a more bitter tale than his fellows." He reaches up with his handkerchief and wipes her cheeks. "I'm sorry, Jean. 'Tis no reflection on my love for you, believe me."

She brushes his hand away. "Was it your golden-haired muse firing your ardour yester evening?"

He shakes his head. "A cursed business, this rhyming. Like a hunger that demands to be fed, else it withers and dies." He grasps her hands. "You and the children are my rock. All that keeps me steady. God knows what I'd be without you."

Jean glares at him. His words, true though they may be, provide no balm for the hurt in her heart.

His dark eyes plead with her. "Can you forgive me?"

"I don't know."

"Never again, Jean. I promise."

Another promise. Uttered with such remorse, such conviction. She wants to believe him. She wants to trust him. What choice does she have? For better or for worse, she's in this for life. Those words she repeats every night in her prayers—*Forgive us our trespasses as we forgive those who trespass against us*—are easy to say. But heeding them, she knows, is a more complicated matter.

Nine months later, on the ninth day of April 1791, Jean brushes the nipple of her breast against the soft cheek of her newborn son, trying to coax him to his first suckling. Her husband grins, perched on the edge of the bed, crowing about his brawny new lad, William Nicol's worthy namesake. Chuckling, Rab says he can already see in his son's dark blue eyes the same fondness for witty mischief.

Jean frowns and voices her misgivings about the name—or rather the namesake, William Nicol, Rab's companion on his tour of the highlands and the sot described in his poem "Willie Brew'd a Peck o' Maut," an ode to drunken dissipation. Rab laughs off her objection. William Nicol is a model of learning, he says; the man studied theology and medicine at the University of Edinburgh and is a classical master in the Edinburgh High School.

"I want all my children to be named as tributes to my friends," Rab says, taking his sleeping son into his arms. "And may heaven be so obliging as to let me have them in the proportion of three boys to one girl. I'm not equal to the task of rearing girls. I'm too poor. A girl should always have a fortune."

"I've done just fine without one," Jean says, aglow with that after-birth euphoria—both she and her baby alive and well. "But I hope to give you a set of boys to honour your name." In her heart, though, she pines for a daughter to pacify those female spirits that haunt her still.

It's a sunny May morning aglitter with dew when a soft knock comes at the door. Jean has just nestled Willie into his cradle; her hair is still uncombed, her harn gown stained with milk. She's about to call out for Agnes. But her sister-in-law left yesterday to return home to Mossgiel. Rab has taken the children down to the Isle by Friar's Carse to fish for trout, and the maid-servant is out in the dairy. Reluctantly, Jean throws a shawl over her gown, tucks her hair under a mutch, and opens the door.

On the stoop stands a young woman. Short and buxom, she wears a blue plaiden gown that accentuates the cornflower blue of her eyes. Her long hair shimmers in the sunlight like spun gold. She holds a baby in her arms. "Mrs. Burns?"

"Ay." Jean puts her hand to her eyes to block the glaring sun.

"I'm Anna Park."

She does not look like the brazen hussy Jean has imagined. She looks like a frightened young mother. Jean blinks several times, as if her mind can't process what her eyes are seeing. She hasn't been to Dumfries for months, such is her embarrassment with her husband's transgression, and she keeps herself isolated from the rural gossips.

"I see," Jean says. "Step in."

As she follows Jean into the parlour, the baby awakens and begins whimpering. "She needs changing and feeding, if you don't mind, Mrs. Burns. We've had a long ride in the cart from Leith."

"You'll be in need of a dish of tea then," Jean says. In the kitchen, she puts the kettle to boil and sets out her best porcelain teapot—white, painted with pink flowers; its curved handle and spout display an elegance she hopes will compensate for her own dowdiness. *Why should you care?* she thinks, spooning the curly dried leaves from the wooden caddy. *Why are you making tea for the young hizzie that seduced your husband? Her baby's still in swaddling clothes, about the same size as Willie.* Head spinning, she arranges a plate of gingerbread cakes and her rose-and-thorn patterned china on the tray.

Sipping their tea, Anna tells Jean that her daughter was born a month ago—on March 31—and she named her Elizabeth after her mother. A yowling erupts from the bedroom, and

Jean scurries in to the cradle. When she returns with a swaddled infant in her arms, Anna's eyes bulge in disbelief. "I had no idea," she says.

"My son is nine days younger than your daughter," Jean says. They sit across from each other, two mothers nursing their babies. With the contented sounds of their suckling, Jean feels the frozen lump of bitterness in her throat melting away. "You need not worry," she says. "My husband will help provide for your bairn."

"Mr. Burns is an honourable man. Not like some." Her cheeks aflame, Anna looks down at her baby. "I want to raise her. But my aunt won't let me keep my job if I do. My family's near disowned me. I've been staying with my sister. But her husband says he's got too many mouths to feed already."

Jean nods, her stomach churning, the young woman's situation all too familiar. She understands then why Anna is here, and Jean knows what she must say. "Do you want to leave your lass with us til you're able to care for her? I've plenty of milk on me. Plenty enough for two."

Anna bites her lip, her eyes turn glassy. "I want what's best for Betty." The baby nuzzles into her shoulder as Anna pats and rubs her back. "She'd have a better life here than what I can give her. And she wouldn't be an orphan." A thin smile turns up the corners of her mouth. "I overheard your farmhands jawing at the inn. They say you're a good mither, and kind."

Jean gazes at the back of the baby's head, downy with light brown curls. "She's but an innocent lammie, worthy of love as any child." Then, darting a knowing look at Anna, she adds, "My Rab has his faults. But as a father, none has a more tender heart."

They carry their sleeping infants into the bedroom and lay one at either end of the cradle—like twins. Jean leaves Anna there, rocking the cradle with one hand, dabbing her eyes with the other, softly singing.

> *Hush–a–ba birdie croon, croon*
> *Hush–a–ba birdie croon*
> *The sheep are gone tae the siller wood,*
> *And the coos are gone tae the broom, broom.*

When they step out the front door into the warm spring air, Anna's brother-in-law is waiting in the cart. He tips his peaked tweed cap and nods a curt greeting at Jean. Anna climbs up onto the seat and wraps her arms about her as if shivering from the cold. A flick of the reins, and the cart rumbles down the lane. Anna does not look back.

A few hours later, Jean is settled into her low wooden nursing chair in front of the parlour window, a baby at each breast. Rab and the children come trundling up the path from the river. Frankie rides high on his father's shoulders, bouncing and giggling. Beside them, Bobbie lugs a basket with the morning's catch. *One two, three, four, five,* he sings. *Once I caught a fish alive.*

Rab spots her through the window, and his jaw drops.

"Mammie's had another baby," Bobbie shouts.

They bustle about her, admiring the new bundle crooked in her arm. "The white stork dropped her down the chimney," Jean says. "Knew we needed a bonnie lass in the family." Once the boys toddle off to play, she tells Rab the whole story.

"Anna didn't tell me," he says, cuddling Betty in his arms. "She disappeared from the inn a few months ago, and I wondered. Mrs. Hyslop said her niece went back to Leith to care for her sick mother."

He kisses his daughter's forehead. "Welcome, my sweet wee lady," he says, looking into her blue eyes. "God grant you may inherit your poor daddy's spirit and not his failings." Then he looks at Jean and shakes his head. "You are a far better wife than I deserve. Are you sure you can manage with two babies?"

"I've another chance to find out," Jean says. "Maybe the third time will be lucky." She smiles down at Willie then up at his sister, really believing for the first time that God does indeed work in mysterious ways.

Late one afternoon, a few weeks later, Jean is in the dairy shed, carefully skimming the thick yellow cream off the milk in the setting trays. The cows keep them well supplied, though the dairy is not bringing in much money. With two babies to nurse, along with house and farm chores, she doesn't have the time to make it profitable. But their money worries have been alleviated, she hopes, with Rab's raise of twenty-five pounds a year. She smiles at her five-year-old helper plunging the dasher up and down, up and down in the churn.

"Come butter come, come butter come," Bobbie chants. "Frankie stands at the gate, waiting for a butter cake."

Just then the maid-servant rushes in with Frankie in her arms. "Some visitors here, ma'am, an older lady and gentleman."

Jean sets down the skimming spoon and lifts her apron to wipe the sweat from her forehead. "Keep at it, laddie," she says, patting Bobbie's head. "You'll soon have your first batch."

Rounding the corner to the front of the house, she recognizes the carriage and the chestnut mare tethered by the door, as well as the backs of the grey-haired couple gazing down at the river. "You've come at last," Jean says, hugging her parents and wondering if Eliza has swept the floor yet, or seen to that mound of washing on the table.

"Sorry we've come unannounced. Didn't want you to go to any bother. We overnighted in Sanquhar at Bailie's Inn," Mrs. Armour says. "We've been anxious to meet our new grandchild."

Jean shows them into the parlour, picking up the children's playocks scattered on the floor. "Swith awa', Mailie," she says, shooing a fat ewe asleep beside the cradle. "Rab's gimmer-pet," she laughs.

Mr. Armour raises his bushy grey eyebrows and peers over his pince-nez at his wife. "Like baby Jesus in the manger," Mrs. Armour titters. They tiptoe over to the cradle and lift the muslin covering. Their heads slide back and forth, from one end of the cradle to the other.

"We didn't know you had twins again," Mr. Armour exclaims.

Jean smiles. "The wee girl belongs to a lass who lives up river. I'm caring for her wean til she gets on her feet."

"As if you've not enough of a brood to mind already," her father says, eying the clothes draped over the chairs and the heap of nappies on the table. Mrs. Armour says nothing, but fixes her daughter with one of her comprehending looks.

Mr. Armour takes in the view from the bay window—the green bank lush with bracken and the river gleaming through the trees. "You've done well for yourselves," he says, "all things considered." He rubs his hands along the thick mahogany casing of the clock. "Rab's doing well in the Excise?"

"Ay, just got a promotion to the Port Division. A bigger territory and longer days," Jean says, folding the nappies into a neat stack. A few minutes later, hooves clomp and a horse neighs outside the front door.

Rab's face lights up with a grin when he enters the parlour. "We've long been awaiting this occasion," he says, shaking Mr. Armour's hand and bowing before his mother-in-law. "Tis the perfect time to christen your handsome gift." From the top shelf of the cabinet, he pulls down the square wooden box. "An exquisite work of art," he says, opening the lid.

"Lapis-ollaris, the finest stone to be found," Mr. Armour says, his chest puffing out. "Acquired it while working on the Duke of Argyle's home."

"Ah, the water of life," Rab says, inhaling the peaty, smoky aroma of the Highland whisky he pours it into the marble bowl. He stirs in some water and sugar then ladles the amber liquid into four horn glasses and passes them around. Raising his glass, he says,

> *Ye whom social pleasure charms*
> *Whose hearts the tide of kindness warms,*
> *Who hold your being on the terms,*
> > *"Each aid the others,"*
> *Come to my bowl, come to my arms,*
> > *My friends, my brothers.*

"Sláinte," they chime in unison as their glasses clink together. Such a satisfying sound, Jean thinks, like the relinking of a broken chain.

The summer of 1791 is scorching. In the parched fields, corn withers on the stalks; the oats shrivel brown in the fields. One evening in mid-August, Rab gallops in at twilight looking wearier than Jean has ever seen him. In the saddle for twelve sweltering hours, he dismounts and collapses onto the ground.

"All my hurry of business, grinding the faces of the publican and the sinner on the merciless wheels of the Excise," he moans as Jean fixes him a nipperkin of toddy. "Then making ballads and correcting the press-work for publication. And this accursed farm. I've worked as hard as an Edinburgh bawd on a Sunday morning, and it doesn't yield enough to pay for the lease. We're better off moving to Dumfries."

Jean sets the glass on the table and gapes at him in horror. "Nae, we'll not be giving up our home."

"There's no security in farming," he says, draining the glass in one gulp. "You're at the mercy of fate. Poor soil, or foul weather, or bad seed..." He bangs the glass down on the table. "The book of Genesis is missing a verse: *And the Lord riddled all creation— and the riddlings he threw in Ellisland.*"

"But your salary's increased. And you'll have earnings from Johnson for all the songs you've contributed."

He frowns at her, aghast. "I've refused to accept a penny. To talk of money would be downright sodomy of soul. I vowed from the outset, *That I for poor old Scotland's sake, Some useful plan or book could make, or sing a song at least.*"

"But the endless hours you've spent collecting and rewriting those songs. And me as well, singing them over and over to get them right. You're not appreciated for all you do for Scotland."

"Dinna worry lass," he chuckles. "I'll be much more appreciated a hundred years from now."

"A lot of good it'll do us then," she sighs. "We'll never find a home like this in Dumfries. We could keep just a few cows and hens. I can grow enough vegetables to feed us year around. And the river's teeming with fish."

"The city's smack in the middle of my new territory. My hours on horseback would be cut in half. I'd have more time at home."

"More time to spend at the Globe Inn." She folds her arms and glowers at him across the table.

"Blastit, Jean!" He pounds his fist on the table and leans toward her. "I'll not be a slave like my father. All toil and seriousness. Not an hour to sip a pint and blether with friends."

"But think about the children. The city's no place for raising bairns."

"We need to think about *educating* the children. Dumfries has a fine grammar school. I've a thousand reveries and anxieties about our little charges and their future. They'll not be harnessed to the plow like I was. I can't give my sons a fortune. But I can grant them the means for a sound education, like my father did for me."

Jean knows the story well. When Rab and Gilbert reached school age, and the little school in Alloway had no master, their father hired a private tutor to teach them English speech, Latin and mathematics.

She concedes that he's is right about the schooling. There's nothing close to Ellisland, and Bobbie will soon be six years old. She lowers her head in resignation.

In Ellisland, she reclaimed her firstborn son. She birthed two more sons and gained a daughter. In Ellisland, nobody died.

The next day Rab rides out to inform Mr. Fintry they'll be stopping their lease in November. By the end of September, they've sold most of the farm stock and dairy utensils—the cheese presses, butter churns, milk tubs and pails. The remaining animals will be going to the slaughterhouse except for a few pet sheep and Jean's beloved Ayrshire cow, which she insists on taking with them. "At least the children will still have fresh milk to drink."

On a bitterly cold Martinmas morning, the house stands hollow. Only powdery ashes linger in the grates. Wooden shutters cover the windows. Jean slips into the darkened byre to pat the sheep one last time; the Riddels at Friars' Carse will take them over to graze in their vast meadows. She inhales the sweet hay and pungent manure, an elixir. She fastens the leather

thong around the door handle and climbs up onto the cart beside Adam, who's taken a day off from his masonry work at an
estate downriver.

Rab finishes carving into the grey bark of a hawthorn, its bare
limbs shaking in the wind: *R Burns 1791*. A mixture of sadness
and relief on his face, he takes a slow look around—at the thorn
hedges, at the beech and birch trees he planted, at the dykes he
built stone upon stone. Then he swings up into the saddle and
prods Pegasus to a slow trot. The cart rattles behind, piled high
with furniture and crates packed with clothes and kitchen utensils. Willie and Betty are bundled close beside Jean in a fleece-
lined basket. In the back, Bobbie and Frankie huddle together
under a woollen blanket. Tethered at the rear, the brown-and-
white cow bawls as they wind down the ice-furrowed lane. Every
few minutes Jean turns around. The white farmhouse on the hill
and the fields, silver with hoarfrost, grow smaller and smaller,
then disappear.

*　　*　　*

By the time I get back to the farmhouse at 4:30, the Friends of Ellisland have left. There's a deserted feeling about the place; the kitchen is quiet, the fire is out. The curator appears from his part of the house, anxious to be closing up for the day. I ask if he knows when I might catch the next bus into Dumfries. He says I shouldn't be standing out on that narrow road flagging down a bus and kindly offers to give me a drive.

We hurtle down the highway at a speed that seems far too fast. Mr. Byers isn't driving much over the speed limit, I realize when I glance at the speedometer. But I've been living this day at the eighteenth-century pace of horse-drawn carts and meandering rivers.

Mr. Byers tells me he's been living at Ellisland for twenty-five years now. "It's such a beautiful, peaceful place," I say.

"It's a bloody lot of work," he says, "and never enough money for the upkeep." He explains the struggles of fundraising and hosting events to maintain the property: Burns Suppers, St. Andrew's Night celebrations, concerts, ploughing matches. After ten minutes, we're crossing a bridge into the city. "The new bridge," Mr. Byers informs me and points further down the river to the old bridge, an elegant red sandstone structure built in the fifteenth century, now a pedestrian walkway. People stroll across the curved span and snowy swans float beneath its semi-circular arches.

We drive along the Whitesands, the main street fronting the River Nith. A broad greenway and paved walkway, lined with shade trees, stretch along the riverbank as far as the eye can see. The word *regal* comes to mind and already I'm sensing the aptness of the city's moniker, *The Queen of the South*.

"All the information you'll need is in there," Mr. Byers says, pulling up to the tourist centre. "Be sure to visit the Globe Inn."

PART III

The Wife of the Famous Poet

Dumfries, 1791–1796

The best-laid schemes o' mice an men
Gang aft agley,
An' lea'e us nought but grief an' pain,
For promis'd joy.

I'M WALKING UP ONE OF THE OLDEST THOROUGHFARES IN Scotland, Friars Vennel, a medieval route between the River Nith crossing to Galloway and the town of Dumfries above. Shops, cafés and crumbling brick buildings with historic plaques line the shaded, narrow road. Colourful murals decorate the frontages, one depicting Robert the Bruce slaying the Red Comyn at the Grey Friars Monastery that stood here in the thirteenth century. At the top of the vennel, I turn onto a broad, cobbled pedestrian street humming with people. It's like stepping from the constricted gloom of history into the spacious brightness of today.

Dominating the central square, a white marble statue of Robert Burns towers above the busy flow of life on the street, a figure from the past eternally presiding over the present. Beds of red and white flowers surround the pedestal where he sits upon a tree stump, a collie dog curled at his feet. I find a seat on one of the benches encircling the statue and stare up at his face, wondering what he would make of all the acclaim: fifty-five statues dedicated to him worldwide, more than any other secular figure after Queen Victoria and Columbus. Just then, a pigeon lands on the poet's white, marbled hair. It cocks its iridescent green-and-purple head, while greyish droppings ooze over Burns's broad forehead. I can almost hear him chuckling, *A man's a man for 'a that.*

I should be heading north to a street called Lover's Walk, the location of my B&B. My stomach is grumbling and my legs are weary, but I can't resist walking further down High Street. The city map shows that the Globe Inn is close by. I pass the Midsteeple, a three-storey stone building with a square clock tower that once served as the town hall and guardhouse, *1707* incised above its door. At this main plaza, Jean Burns would have strolled through the busy weekly markets, appraising the pyramids of carrots, cabbage and leeks; and the fishmongers' booths, odorous with salmon, flounder, mackerel and skate from the Solway Firth.

My historic destination is so well concealed that I miss the entrance and have to retrace my steps to find the alley tucked off the main street. I tread upon the original grey flagstones down the shaded close to a wooden sign suspended between two brick buildings. The door to the Globe Inn opens into a small, musty-smelling foyer. Beyond the unattended reception desk, a narrow, low-ceilinged dining room has various sized portraits of Robert Burns covering every inch of the walls. A couple of men sit at a snug bar in the corner, sipping their pints.

I eat my smoked haddock cakes while drinking in the unassuming atmosphere of one of Scotland's oldest hostelries, established in 1610. It feels authentic, the tourist appeal of Burns's watering hole not overly exploited. There are few other diners, and from the bits of conversation I overhear, their accents suggest they are probably locals.

Paying my bill, I ask the manager about the rooms in the inn associated with Robert Burns. She's happy to give me a tour and shows me into a private chamber on the other side of the foyer. Encased in the dark wood-panelling of two centuries ago, this snuggery was the original *howf* that Burns frequented. "His usual seat was right there by the hearth," she says, "and that's the very chair he sat upon." At her prompting, I sit for a moment in the curved wooden armchair with a checked, padded seat. *A chat and a glass beside the fire before heading home to Jean.* But the clutter of Burns memorabilia and the modern tables and chairs distract me from sinking into that other realm of time.

My guide then leads me upstairs and unlocks the door to the bedroom where the poet stayed when he overnighted at the inn. As I enter the dimly lit room, it feels like Burns could have slept here just last night. In the corner stands a plain box-bed covered in a patchwork quilt; directly across, two small windows are etched with the poet's handwriting. One has a verse in praise of the lovely Polly Stewart, and the other engraved with a well-known song—before its final revision:

> *Gin a body meet a body*
> *Coming through the grain*
> *Gin a body kiss a body*
> *The thing's a body's ain.*

How fitting, I think, in this bedroom where Burns most likely shared a pint of wine—and more—with Anna Park. The manager talks about the reputed affair between the poet and the barmaid, and about the ghost that's said to haunt the inn, an unnamed servant girl who died in the late- eighteenth century. As if viewing it all through Jean's eyes, I feel a sting of betrayal. Then guilt washes over me as I realize my complicity in playing that same role—*the other woman*.

Stepping out the door of the inn, I glance to the left and do a double-take. Tethered to a picnic table is a black-and-white collie. "Luath," I exclaim. The dog tilts its head, nose quivering in the white hour-glass surrounding its black snout. Walking out the alley, I turn around for another look, as if to ensure that it wasn't an apparition. The dog sits still on its haunches, patiently waiting for someone to return.

The next morning, I'm awakened by bells clanging and sunshine streaming through the wide bay window of my room in Dumfries Villa, a lovely Victorian townhouse with high ceilings and ornate mouldings. Across the street, the red brick spire of St. John's Scottish Episcopal Church reaches into a clear blue sky. After a big bowl of creamy porridge (cooking the oats with milk is the secret, my host discloses), I set out to find Jean's first home on Bank Street, a steep road that runs from High Street down to Whitesands on the river.

At the bottom of the street, I spot a long three-storey building with the blue-and-white flag of Scotland flying from its roof. A small plaque between the second-floor windows reads, *Robert Burns, the National Poet, lived in this house with his family in 1791.* Below the plaque, signs hang for the businesses on the first floor. I can have coffee at the Burns Café, get my hair styled at the Burns Hairdressing Salon, then browse the Burns Gift Shop for shot glasses, tea towels and cups imprinted with mugshots of the poet.

From a bench on the greenway, I have a clear view of the building with its fresh white paint and brown trim. It bears little resemblance to the tenement house Burns moved his family into, and the street itself is a much sanitized version of the close that was then called the Wee Vennel—or *the Stinking Vennel* by the locals.

It's grey November and, I imagine, pouring down rain the day the cart pulls up in front of the tenement house. Raw sewage and rubbish stream down a gutter in the middle of the street. The stench mingles with the odour of the ebbing tide and the reek of tanneries on the riverbank. Though it's only a hundred feet from the river, Jean can't see the water from the front window of their middle-floor flat. But she can hear the droning down on the bank from the timber yards, breweries and tanneries, and from across the street, the laughter and screams that leak through the walls of the Coach House Tavern and the brothel on its second floor.

The small kitchen overlooks a back alley of belching chimneys. Shaking mats from the window, Jean breathes in the brownish-yellow smoke that lingers like a fog, stinging her eyes. She can even taste it, acrid, on the tip of her tongue. The rear courtyard is hardly big enough for Rab to stable his horse. Not a green patch to be found, and Jean has to part with her cow. The two front rooms are the size of bed-closets, so Rab's desk and bookshelves must be jammed into a recess between them.

"Better a wee bush than nae bield," Rab chuckles as they move in. But before long, he's pacing like a prisoner in a cell, unable to write. His temper flares at the children's constant whining.

"What do you expect?" Jean scolds. "Yanking them from the braes where they frolicked like spring lambs and caging them in this hell-hole." Still nursing two six-month-old babies, she has little time for taking the children outside. Bobbie pleads to go down to the Nith with his two-year old brother to watch the river cascading over the weir, a small dam that reroutes the water to drive the woollen mill on the opposite bank. But Jean fears letting them go out alone. The wide, rushing river looks dangerous and unpredictable, completely unlike the friendly Nith that flowed by the Ellisland farm. And the boys are unaccustomed to the traffic, the rumbling carriages and galloping horses that speed down the narrow wynds like loose cannons.

As Jean peels potatoes and slices turnip in the cramped scullery, she darts accusing looks at her husband. *I told you so* screams in the frosty silence between them. Her shrewish comments, the bawling of the babies and the children's brattle inevitably send Rab down the creaky stairs to see his friend John Syme, the collector of stamps for the district, whose office is beneath their flat. Jean knows they'll head up the street to the Globe for a pint or three, and that Rab may well be out for the rest of evening. He often dines at Syme's villa across the river in Ryedale. Well known by the city's cultured gentlemen, Rab is often invited to their fancy tables. "You're welcome too," he says, putting on his best tailcoat. But Jean knows she doesn't fit into that society and makes no pretense of trying. Its judgmental gaze has already classified her: *Not the right kind of wife for a poet*.

With four children to care for and no maid-servant, Jean lets the order of her house and her appearance slip. Anxious about her dressing well, Rab buys her a costly gingham gown with a lace collar—the latest fashion—to wear to St. Michael's Kirk. At his insistence, they start attending regularly. "Every little creature that calls me father will be taught the doctrines of religion," he says. "Religious faith makes us better and happier people." Jean begins to believe him; his approach to religion is so different than her father's was—force-feeding the scriptures and wielding them like weapons to induce guilt in his children.

After supper, Rab usually sits with Bobbie at the kitchen table, tutoring him in catechism. The Bible open between them, Rab patiently answers his son's questions and explains things Bobbie doesn't understand. Every night, he tells the children stories from Shakespeare's plays: *Once upon a time in the city of Verona, there were two noble families called the Montagues and the Capulets. They were ancient enemies.* He always stops at a suspenseful part, so Bobbie and Frankie are waiting the next night for their father to come home before bedtime. *Will Romeo arrive on time to save Juliet?* "Probably not," Jean overhears Bobbie telling his brother. "Tyta said it's a *tradegy.*"

At these moments, Jean's heart surges with love for her husband. He instills respect rather than fear. When the children lie or misbehave, he's quick to forgive. "Though they go a-kennin' wrang," he says to Jean with a knowing look, "to step aside is human." She wishes he'd been her father.

One day in early March, Jean is flipping through her well-used copy of *The Art of Cookery Made Easy*, searching for a way to transform a scrawny fowl into something delicious. Scotch Barley Broth sounds simple enough, and all the ingredients are in the larder except a few marigolds for seasoning. She sets the water to boil, chops carrots, celery and onions, then dumps the vegetables into the pot along with a pound of barley. Rab trudges into the kitchen, an envelope dangling from his hand. He slumps into a chair and says a letter has come from Mrs. Nancy McLehose. That cold, dank winter of 1792, mail arrived weekly addressed in her familiar feathery script. Jean hasn't given in to the temptation to read them, bundled away in a drawer of Rab's desk, but he'd told her Mrs. McLehose was making plans to sail to Jamaica with her four children and reunite with her long-estranged husband. This news has dulled the knife of anxiety that ordinarily cut through

Jean whenever she spied one of those envelopes on his desk.

"*Obliged from all symptoms of rapid decay to quit her service, Jenny Clow is gone to be in a room unattended,*" Rab reads in a quavering voice. "It's the consumption. The poor girl's distress makes my heart weep blood."

When Jean asks who is caring for Jenny's boy, Rab shakes his head. "I have to go and see what can be done to help them. She's dying."

Jean goes to the window and looks out at the smoking chimneys and slate roofs slick with rain; she envisions a young mother shut away from the world and the small child she must leave behind, an orphan. Turning to Rab, she says, "You could bring the wee lad home with you."

He buries his face in his hands. After a long silence, he lifts his head. "I'll have to offer."

"Ay."

"I'm sorry, Jean," he sighs, scanning their two-by-four kitchen. "Hard to picture one more bairn under this roof."

"Tis not me you need to be sorry for, but Jenny. And the poor lammie who's losing his mither."

Rab nods. "I didn't want to say anything til it's certain. But the district supervisor is taking a leave. I may be replacing him. An extra thirty pounds a year would get us out of this hovel."

Jean smiles, and hope flutters in her like a fledgling bird fearful of trying its wings: escape from the Stinking Vennel, more room for their growing family. She too has been harbouring a secret, waiting for its certainty before telling her husband.

After Rab leaves for the capital, morning sickness hits Jean full force. She's also weaning Willie and Betty, and they're cranky with the switch to cows' milk. Bobbie has to watch over the little ones while Jean scurries out to buy a knap bone or mutton ribs to make a pot of soup. Six years old now, he's strong enough to lug the chamber pot down to the Nith and fetch water from the well on the riverbank. "What would I do without my big boy?" she asks, hugging him. Children, she's come to realize, repay your affection tenfold. So if her husband brings home another little Robert Burns Jr., she knows there will be plenty of love for this child as well.

But Rab comes back with empty arms. A childless couple of Jenny's acquaintance has taken her boy to raise. "He'll be well cared for," Rab says. Jean hears relief in his voice, but remorse as well: a son he'll never know. At least he sees Bess now and again, though he's more like an uncle to her than a father.

In the days after his return from Edinburgh, Rab mopes about the house when he isn't on his excise rounds. In the evenings, he hunches at his desk, scratching away in his commonplace book, sighing and moaning as if in the throes of labour. Jean suspects he visited someone else in the city, and there's someone on his mind besides his lost son.

Once evening just before twilight, Rab grabs his hat and gnarly walking stick and says he's heading up the river to Martingdon Ford, his musing ground. Rural and secluded, only rushing water and rustling leaves, it's like the river walk in Ellisland, where ideas surface, images appear and his verses take shape.

A few hours later, he dashes in the door muttering some lines. He pulls up a chair by the hearth where Jean sits with a basket of mending. "Coila came smooth gliding without step and whispered me the following," he says. Balancing on the back legs of the chair, he rocks back and forth humming some lines. "Do you ken the air, Jean?"

"Sounds like *Rory Dall's Port*."

He runs to his desk and retrieves his notebook. "I've tried to set these verses to the tune. Could you try them out?" Then he bows his head and closes his eyes as if in prayer while she sings:

Ae fond kiss and then we sever!
Ae farewell, and then forever!
Deep in heart-wrung tears I'll pledge thee,
Warring sighs and groans I'll wage thee.
Who shall say that fortune grieves him,
While the star of hope she leaves him?
Me, nae cheerfu' twinkle lights me,
Dark despair around benights me.

Reaching the second verse, Jean almost stumbles over the words, *Naething can resist my Nancy, For to see her was to love her.* But she continues on into the third verse, relieved to be singing a song about parting forever.

"Do the words suit the measure?" he asks. Jean points out a couple of places where the rhyme or the rhythm is jarring, and he retires to his desk to polish the rough spots.

A few weeks later, Jean is taking Rab's blue tailcoat off the hook to mend a tear when her fingers touch something hard in the corner of the pocket. She pulls out an ivory breast pin, a silhouette of a woman, a bosomy figure with wavy, upswept hair. Her fingers brush the carved surface of the two-inch miniature: a memento of a lost loved one. "Fare-the-weel, Mrs. McLehose," Jean whispers, tucking the pin back into the bottom of the pocket.

This infatuation, she knows, will be replaced with other muses groomed in the finishing schools of Edinburgh or Dumfries. She can't keep up with their ever-changing names in his poems and songs: bonnie Lesley, charming Deborah, lively Maria and Chloris, "the lassie wi' the lint-white locks." She has accepted that Rab needs two women: a wife to keep his home and raise his bairns, as well as a charming goddess to inspire his songs. As long as that other woman remains the *platonic love* he claims, she has no complaint; and since his last indiscretion, she's had no reason to suspect otherwise. He's happiest when he's writing, and he is the weather glass of their household.

Even in the Wee Vennel, the least inspiring of dwellings, Rab churns out scores of songs, some for another volume of Johnson's *Musical Museum* and many for a new publication, a collection of the best Scottish airs. After twelve hours of excise duties, he races up the stairs with a song on his lips: *Ye banks and braes o' bonie Doon, How can ye bloom sae fresh and fair.* In the evenings, he cuddles the children on his knee, teaching them rhymes and ditties. Jean too is always trilling as she goes about her chores, trying out his latest compositions.

"It's the Sanghoose o' Scotland," Rab says, his black eyes flickering with memories. "Like when I was a lad, and the light of Mammie's voice lifted us above the gloom of our miserable poverty."

On the twenty-first day of November 1792, the midwife lays a crying infant onto Jean's belly. Smiling and weeping at the same time, Jean reaches out to touch the cheesy-coated body—after five years of missing and pining, her own sweet daughter. She can't take her eyes off the baby's long eyelashes, her rosy bow of a mouth, her wavy black hair that curls around the nape of her neck concealing a brown berry of a birthmark. But Jean resists praising her daughter's beauty; the bonniest weans are at risk of being stolen away by the fairies. Jean hovers over the cradle, reluctant to leave her baby for a minute. She heeds all the old customs: decorates the cradle with a sprig of dill, pins a tiny bag of salt to the blanket, and laces a string of coral beads around her daughter's neck.

"But you already have two Elizabeths, a Bess and a Betty," Jean objects when Rab wants to name their daughter as a tribute to the wife of his good friend, Robert Riddell, who composed airs for some of Rab's poems. The Riddell estate, Friars' Carse, bordered the Ellisland farm, and Rab often wrote in the old hermitage on their property.

"I've enjoyed more pleasant evenings at the Riddell fireside than at all the houses of fashionable people in the country put together," Rab says. "I'm indebted to them for many of the happiest hours of my life." As usual, Jean allows his enthusiasm to prevail, and Rab inscribes the name of their seventh child into the family Bible: Elizabeth Riddell.

During the bone-chilling dampness of the winter months, a blanket of smog from the mill shrouds the city, blocking the sun's feeble attempts to penetrate the clouds. Throughout January, Rab is plagued with aching joints and a cold. Jean fears he might have consumption or rheumatism, common ailments in the city due to the surrounding bogs. A family of seven confined to three small rooms, she frets that her husband's coughing and sneezing might infect the children, especially Elizabeth, not nearly as hearty as her baby boys were. Her tiny body feels almost weightless in Jean's arms, like a fairy baby who might vanish at any moment. She drapes a muslin sheet over her cradle and prays: *Mother of God, guard my precious daughter*.

In February, a third edition of Rab's poems is published in two volumes. Jean expects it will bring in some money, so they can settle debts with the butcher and the tailor. But Rab tells her his sole payment for fifty pages of new poems is twenty copies to give to his friends. He'd sold the copyright to his Edinburgh publisher with the second edition. "A hundred guineas seemed fair, even generous at the time," he says, "now I'm not so sure." Living in Dumfries is costing considerably more than he anticipated, but he loves coming home with little luxuries—a sheep's head to season a pot of broth, a stylish new hat for Jean, a bag of boiled sweets for the children. When Jean chides him about the expense, he kisses her cheek and chuckles, "Carpe diem."

One evening in mid-April, Jean has just settled the children into bed. Quick footsteps pound on the stairs as if someone is running up two steps at a time. The door flies open. Rab pulls her into his arms and swings her into the air. "Start packing, Jean," he grins. "Supervisor Burns at your service." He doffs his hat and sweeps into a low bow. "Ninety pounds a year!"

Jean cannot speak for laughing. They dance about the room, stumbling on the furniture, and end up on the floor rolling around like a couple of giddy children. Then on those rough wooden boards, their bodies merge with all the ardour of their younger selves.

*   *   *

I'm scribbling so rapidly that the words in my journal are barely comprehensible, as if the faster I write the sooner Jean will get out of the Wee Vennel. My table in the Hullabaloo, a restaurant on the second floor of a converted eighteenth-century woollen mill, gives me a commanding view of the Nith gushing over the weir in a curling waterfall, and of the turreted city of Dumfries spread out on the hillside above. Through the casement window, with two-foot-wide stone sills, I spy the second-storey window of Jean's former home at the foot of Bank Street. She would have looked out her window across the river to this red brick building, and up at this window. Imagining our eyes meeting across a portal of time, I raise my glass of Rosé Cabernet: *To your escape from the Stinking Vennel.*

I cross the Nith on the arched stone footbridge, the fifteenth-century Devorgilla Bridge that Jean would have crossed to get to Maxwelltown. On a sand spit in the middle of the river, seagulls preen and spread their grey-white wings to dry; a blue heron spires on one leg as eddies swirl around it. Flowering trees line the greenway of Dock Park, their bright pink and white blossoms tracing the curve of the river.

Heading up Bank Street, I follow the route Jean and her family would have taken on Whitsunday 1793, the day they followed the loaded wagon up the Wee Vennel. They were moving up—in every sense of the term—above the noisy, smelly streets by the river into a more genteel area. I picture a shining day in mid-May: Jean carrying baby Elizabeth, her blue eyes wide under her lace bonnet; Bobbie and Frankie gripping the hands of Willie and Betty; Rab turning around from his seat on the cart, grinning and waving at his gypsy brood. The first left brought them onto Irish Street, at that time an avenue of brick townhouses and fancy gardens banking the river. Then they turned right onto Shakespeare Street with its freestone houses, carved doorways and terraces; they could hear blackbirds twittering and smell the cherry trees, rosy with blossoms.

From Shakespeare Street, I hurry across the busy intersection to get to Burns Street, formerly Mill Hole Brae. The cobbled lane twists up a hill, and on its crest sits a red sandstone house; the sun illuminates its beautifully weathered stone front and the scarlet tulips and golden primroses blooming on either side of the doorstep.

Across from the house, I sit in a small park-like area with flower beds and benches, breathing in the unlikely quietude of this mid-city setting. No cars or pedestrians, not even the sound of traffic from the surrounding streets; it's like an insulated pocket. The house itself remains largely unaltered since Jean occupied it. After her son William bought it in 1851, he signed it over in trust to the city to maintain in his father's memory. But it was really Jean's home; she lived here for thirty-eight years after her husband's death. White-framed windows, three across the bottom and three across the top, seem like so many eyes reflecting her resolute spirit. Even from the outside, I sense her lingering in this dwelling, the place of her greatest trials.

But on that first day, I can well imagine Jean's delight. Though only a short climb from the Wee Vennel, arriving at 24 Mill Hole Brae would have been like landing in a different country. If they'd moved into the house directly after Ellisland, she may not have thought much of it. No place could match their farmhouse with its light-filled rooms and its vistas, so soothing to the eye and the soul. But compared to the Wee Vennel, her new two-storey home would have seemed like a palace. She would have loved the commodious kitchen with its stone-flagged floor; the cast-iron fireplace and sandstone chimney piece in the parlour, its walls washed in sky blue; the stone stairs, scoured white, leading up to two bedrooms and a small chamber for Rab's study; and the garret that made a cozy bedroom for the children.

No more footsteps tromping over their heads. No more smoke or clamour filtering through the windows. Jean throws open the back door to let the cooling northwest breeze blow through without having to worrying about the children tumbling down a steep staircase. They have space to romp in the backyard. Jean plants a vegetable patch and fills the window boxes with primroses. She can breathe again.

But not for long. The hot, dry fever of summer inflicts drought and famine upon the country. Leaves curl up and apples wizen on the trees. In the autumn, a shortage of meal and corn has prices soaring. The poorest folk are starving. No money can buy a speck of grain, and many nights a pot of muslin-kail is all Jean can set upon their table. The political climate heats up as well. Infused with the spirit of the peasants' uprising in France, people are demonstrating in the market square. Mobs seize grain carts and break into the town's main granary. Because of England's war with France, two regiments are stationed in the city. Soldiers in red tunics patrol the streets; tension and the smell of horse dung fill the air. Jean keeps the children inside until things settle down.

One day that fall, Rab bustles into the kitchen with a pamphlet in his hand. Elizabeth is gurgling and splashing in the washtub as Jean trickles warm water over her skin. "You have to read this," he says. "*Liberté, Egalité, Fraternité*. Dammit Jean, this is the kind of world to work for—democracy instead of kings and courts."

As Jean lifts Elizabeth dripping from the tub and lays her onto the towel, he relays the story in the *Weekly Journal* about the guillotining of Marie Antoinette. "Nothing wrong in delivering an unprincipled prostitute to the hands of the hangman.

Ay, my wee, sonsie lassie," he says, tickling his daughter's feet, "a man's a man for a' that." Then he scurries from the kitchen. "Be right back," he says, pounding up the stairs.

Jean dries Elizabeth's satiny skin, ties on her nappy and undershirt, all the while crooning—*And hie and baw birdie, and hie and baw lamb, and hie and baw birdie my bonnie wee lamb.* An hour later, she's asleep in Jean's arms when Rab returns with his commonplace book, the black ink scarcely dry on the page.

"They say love and wine are the exclusive themes of songwriting," he says, "so this isn't really a song, I suppose."

Jean lays Elizabeth in her cradle, and rocks it with the foot pedal as she tries out the tune Rab has set to the verse:

> *What though on hamely fare we dine,*
> *Wear hoddin grey, an' a' that?*
> *Gie fools their silks, and knaves their wine—*
> *A man's a man for a' that,*
> *For a' that and a' that!*
> *Their tinsel show for a' that,*
> *The honest man, tho' e'er so poor,*
> *Is king o' men for a' that.*

Jean thrills at the radical ideas she's singing about. To suggest a man's worth is in his character, not in his money or class, is next to heresy in Dumfries. Anti-French sentiments are running high. Last week's sermon at St. Michael's warned about the terrors of revolutionary France and the dangers to be fought in their own community. A few months ago a young Glasgow lawyer, leader of a democratic reform organization, was convicted of treason and imprisoned. Jean cautions her husband about being too outspoken in his views.

"Ach," Rab chuckles, "a man of independent mind looks and

laughs at a' that." He concedes to submitting the poem anonymously to the newspaper then runs off to compose another verse.

Jean shakes her head. She loves the way her husband gets fired up about his beliefs, but his quick tongue—especially when heated with wine—burns many bridges. His vocal support for the French Revolution has already created rifts with some of his wealthy friends. Mrs. Frances Dunlop, whose daughter is married to a French royalist, has stopped writing to him.

"How was the play?" Jean asks, setting three horn glasses on the mahogany table beside the bottle of Richardson's port that John Syme has brought. Son of a laird, John started visiting after they moved into a more respectable dwelling. Jean has felt him looking down his pointed nose at her—peasantry. He and Rab have just returned from the Theatre Royal with Maria Riddell. She has a private box at the opulent new playhouse, just around the corner on Shakespeare Street, and Rab often accompanies her.

"*Incroyable*," Maria gushes. "Especially the prologue our brilliant bard composed for Miss Fontennelle. *While Europe's eye is fixed on mighty things, the fate of Empires and the fall of kings.*" Chestnut hair upswept with golden combs, nineteen-year-old Maria flounced into the house in a fitted scarlet silk and high-heeled shoes with silver buckles, her hazel eyes darting around the unkempt parlour. Her painted red lips flash Rab a wide smile. "The mention of *Ça Ira* in the last line got everyone's attention."

"A sure way to cause a stir. As well as not standing to sing *God Save the King*," John says, grimacing. "We're servants of the Crown, laddie. Watch it, or you'll be joining Muir behind bars at Sydney Cove."

"Not rising for the anthem?" Jean glares at her husband.

"Enough lobster-coated puppies there to sing the monarch's praises," Rab says, grinning at Maria.

"Those dashing officers in scarlet uniforms?" Maria titters. "I do believe you're jealous, *mon ami*."

Jean pastes on a smile as she passes a glass to each of her guests. Five months pregnant and depleted after getting the children into bed, she hasn't changed out of the rumpled gown that stretches tightly over her bulging belly.

"I've always wanted to write a play," Rab says. Jean's not surprised at this pronouncement. Whenever he doesn't have to rise early, he stays in bed reading from his musty volume of Shakespeare's plays. At every meal, the book lies open beside him at the table.

"*Vraiment?* A play? About what?" Maria leans forward in her chair, her tightly laced bodice pushing her breasts up like two ripe apples. "Perhaps we could write one together." She fancies herself a poetess and has written a book about her travels in the West Indies where she met her husband, Captain Walter Riddell.

"One the Scots would appreciate," Rab says, swirling the ruby liquid. "A play about liberty and independence." He winks at Maria.

Rab strides about the parlour, hands behind his back, head down. Then he halts, thrusts his fist into the air and roars, "Robert Bruce addressing his troops at Bannockburn:

> *Scots, wha hae wi' Wallace bled,*
> *Scots, wham Bruce has often led,*
> *Welcome to your gory bed,*
> *Or to victorie!*
> *Lay the proud usurpers low!*
> *Tyrants fall in every foe!*
> *Liberty's in every blow!*
> *Let us do or die!*"

"Bravo!" Maria cries, applauding. "Encore!"

"Ay, a tribute to one of the great saviours of our country." John bangs his glass on the table then peers over at Jean knitting in the corner. She seldom joins in their repartees. No longer cowed by class, she stares back at him as if to take his measure, and her direct gaze makes him uncomfortable.

"*Magnifique.* Kilted warriors marching about the stage," Maria says, as Rab tops up her glass. "I love men in kilts." She giggles, blushes and hides behind her fan. The two men chuckle and refill their glasses. "And sporrans," she says. "Whatever do they keep in those pouches…" And they all three break into uproarious laughter.

Jean manages a weak smile, stifles a yawn and glances over at the bottle of port—only half empty. How much longer will she have to listen to this woman toss her French words around the room? Jean was up all last night with Elizabeth. A year old, her daughter is frequently ill with one thing or another, no sooner recovering from a fever then she's down with a cough. The city borders on the Solway marshes, so the air is always damp. Elizabeth's delicate body seems prey to every germ. Rab too; in such pain with rheumatism during the winter, he couldn't pick up his quill for weeks.

An hour later, the bottle drained, Maria teeters to the door, John stumbling behind her. She embraces Rab and whispers in his ear while looking over his shoulder at Jean. "*Bonsoir, chéri,*" she smirks. "*À la prochaine.*"

Jean eyes her with indifference. She has deeper concerns than this latest incarnation of the beautiful young muse.

Four months later, in August of 1794, Jean sits in her low wooden nursing chair, petting the downy black hair of her swaddled newborn. Rab lingers by her side, gazing above her head at the plaque of the Earl of Glencairn. He tells Jean that the Earl's patronage rescued him from wretchedness and exile, saved the home that sheltered his aged mother, two brothers and three sisters. He wants to make all his children's names altars of gratitude, he says, smiling down at his fourth son, James Glencairn.

Jean watches the smile slowly fade from her husband's face. Worry lines furrow his brow. "As you hang delighted over the sweet little leech at your bosom," Rab says, "do you ever think where the poor little fellow may wander or what his fate may be?" She knows he's brooding about his ability to provide for six children. His replacement term as district supervisor has ended, his salary reduced. Last week he shelved his pride and solicited a loan to reduce the arrears in their rent. And now he's hanging onto his job by the thinnest of threads. The Excise Board has been scrutinizing his political conduct and questioning his allegiances. In a meeting with his superiors, he was warned: your business is to act, not to think; to be silent and obedient.

In early January of 1795, Jean's mouth drops open when her husband strides through the door. He wears a short blue coat studded with brass buttons, a white woollen waistcoat and breeches, and a round hat topped with bearskin, like the helmets of the Horse Guard—the uniform of the Royal Dumfries Fusiliers. Scotland is without a militia, and the government is encouraging districts to raise volunteer units to defend against a possible French invasion.

"Just swore my Oath of Allegiance. Private Burns at your service," Rab says, with a brisk salute and click of his heels. "It's a way for me to affirm my loyalties and find forgiveness for my political sins. My first duty is to my family."

Jean sidles up to her husband, who seems to stand taller, shoulders straight back, head held high. "You cut a braw figure," she says. "Hard to resist a man in a uniform."

He chuckles, then tells the children about the first two books he read by himself: *The Life of Hannibal* and *The History of William Wallace*. "I used to strut up and down after the drum and bagpipe and wish myself tall enough to be a sodger." Marching out for an evening of drill and target practice, he chants:

> *O, why the deuce should I repine,*
> *And be an ill foreboder?*
> *I'm thirty-six and five feet nine,*
> *I'll go and be a sodger.*

Awed by their father's transformation, the children beg to go down to Dock Park and watch the troop parade amongst the lime trees. "When I get big," Willie says, wide-eyed, "I be a sodger too."

Jean fears this latest venture will be yet another drain on Rab's weakening constitution. He's just recovered from his last bout of rheumatic fever. How will he manage the drill practice in the evenings on top of riding all day and working on his verses? He already frets about not meeting deadlines for Thomson's collection.

That winter is the worst anyone can remember—four-day blizzards and snow piled up to second-storey windows. Roads blocked with ten-foot drifts keep Rab stranded many nights in rural inns. Riding through sleet and hail in sodden clothing lands him in bed with a cold and fever for a few weeks. But throughout the spring and summer months, he seldom misses the drill and target practices. Those nights, he's so knackered that Jean helps him out of his uniform and bathes his calloused feet.

Then in late August everything changes.

"Mammie, Mammie." The wailing from the bedroom across the hall rouses Jean in the middle of a humid August night. *Elizabeth*. Nearly three years old, she hasn't yet moved up to the garret with the other children since she's so often in need of attention during the night. Jean hastens in to find her daughter drenched in sweat and flaming with fever.

"There now, lambkin, Mammie's here," Jean says, removing Elizabeth's damp nightdress. She sponges her daughter's body with cool water, feeling her ribs jutting through a meagre layer of flesh. Jean boils sage and peppermint and sweetens it with honey, a brew to open the pores and release the sickness. Spooning the tea into Elizabeth's mouth, Jean persuades her to part her lips by telling a story about a mamma bird feeding her baby. Then she crawls into the box-bed beside her daughter and sings her to sleep: *Leiger m'chose, my bonie wee lass, An leiger m'chose, my dearie.*

In the morning, Elizabeth has a rasping cough; her cheeks are flushed and burning. Wiping saliva from her daughter's mouth, Jean notices smears of blood on the handkerchief. Alarm bells go off in her head. Rab hurries out to fetch his friend Dr. William Maxwell, who lives around the corner on Irish Street.

As he steps into the darkened bedroom, the doctor smiles at the angelic face, ringed with black curls, lying against the pillow. "Hello, Elizabeth," he says, in his soft-spoken way. "Your daddy's told me what a big, brave girl you are." Her glassy eyes inspect his wired spectacles and dark, wavy hair cropped close to his head. Rab cradles his daughter in his arms while the doctor puts his ear to her chest, then presses his fingers against her wrist.

Jean accompanies Dr. Maxwell to the door and asks the dreaded question. He sighs and shakes his head. "Ay, many signs of the consumption."

"What can we do?"

"Get her out of Dumfries, the sooner the better. This cursed climate's the worst thing for her. She needs the pure, dry air of the countryside."

Ellisland. She sees it through a golden haze of memory—fields of wildflowers, crisp morning air, the smell of hay, lapping water, fresh milk, juicy apples… *That is where we belong.*

After two weeks in Mauchline, Elizabeth revives like a wilting flower that's finally felt the sun. She slurps her grandmother's chicken broth and gulps down the milk that her Uncle Gilbert brings from Mossgiel. "Fresh air and exercise, the best tonic," says Dr. Mackenzie when he comes to check on her.

Jean lets her daughter get up from bed to play hide-and-seek with her own siblings, Robbie and Mary. In the warm evenings, Elizabeth sits on the stoop with her grandfather, giggling as he bounces her on his knee, chanting: *Trot trot to market, trot trot to glen. Watch out little girl, you don't fall in.* Elizabeth whoops as she sinks between his legs, and her grandfather chuckles, hugging her close. Jean perceives a new tenderness emerging in her father, a chink in his armour that lets the light of grandfatherly love shine through.

On a clear day in early September, the first reds and oranges are tingeing the leaves of the maples along the Mauchline burn. Elizabeth skips down the pathway singing, *Skip, skip, skip to my lou, Skip to my lou my darling.* As Jean watches her daughter's black ringlets bobbing in the sun, it all comes flashing back—that autumn day eight years ago and little Jeanie toddling down this path. The place on the bank is just ahead.

Beneath the giant oak, a patch of mauve Michaelmas daisies has sprung up, their yellow centres humming with bees. Jean and Elizabeth stop to pick a bouquet, and Jean kneels in the feathery grass, inhaling the honeyed scent, mesmerized by the burn rippling down to the River Ayr. Elizabeth ambles along the bank, stooping and tugging at the tough stalks. *Like Persephone gathering flowers. Herself a fairer flower.* Jean remembers Rab reading from the Greek story: *The earth opened. The god of the dead grabbed her, carried her down to his kingdom.* "Come, lambkin," Jean calls. "We'll take the daisies to your sisters."

Their graves no longer protrude in little mounds. The grass fronting the grey headstone lies flat, as if their bodies have sunk into the belly of the earth. "For Jeanie, for Helen and for Mary," Jean says, as Elizabeth places the flowers in three little bunches.

"Where my sisters go?" Elizabeth asks, burrowing into her mother's arms.

"Up to heaven."

Elizabeth looks up into the sapphire sky mottled with pillowy clouds. "Why?"

Jean hesitates, not wanting to say *Tis God's will* as she was taught by the kirk and her father. "I don't know. But I know Mother Mary is taking care of them."

"Who that?"

Jean tells her the story about Mary and her baby as Elizabeth's eyelids close. She watches the faint rise and fall of her daughter's chest, and notices the rosiness of her cheeks—surely a healthy sign. They can soon go back home to Dumfries. Jean longs for her other children, and remembers Jamie grabbing her gown, whimpering, as she was leaving, "Mammie, Mammie." Rab's letters assure her they're all fine; their maid-servant is taking good care of them.

The next morning Elizabeth's eyes are glassy and her forehead is hot. Perhaps too much exercise the day before, Jean worries. Her daughter sleeps all the afternoon, then shakes her head at the brose Jean tries to feed her for supper. Throughout the night, Elizabeth coughs and snivels, "A mousie's chewing in my throat." Her body feels as if it might catch fire. Jean cleans the phlegm from her daughter's lips and holds the cloth under the lamp light. The red streaks set off a hammering in her chest.

Over the next week, Elizabeth grows thinner and weaker, as if she's slowly taking leave of her body. When Jean looks into her daughter's face, pale as alabaster, and hears her straining to breathe, she knows what she can no longer deny. On September 15, she writes to Rab and tells him to come—now.

That night, Jean awakens with Elizabeth limp and still in her arms. She holds her until dawn slithers in and boot-heels clop on the cobbles. Then she bathes her daughter's shrunken body and dresses her in a white gown embroidered with rosebuds. As Jean lays her out in the small wooden box, her daughter's body feels hollow, like a shell; her face fixed in an unfamiliar expression. Her Elizabeth has gone elsewhere.

When they lower the coffin into the ground beside the three small graves and shovel dirt upon it, Rab is not there to hold Jean up, to keep her from crumpling onto the ground. He's so ill with rheumatic fever that he can't get out of bed. So the day after she buries her daughter, Jean boards the Camperdown Coach and rattles over the potholed roads to Dumfries. She needs to look after her husband. She needs to hold her children in her empty, aching arms.

*   *   *

The kitchen, with whitewashed walls and a flagstone floor, looks and feels as if Jean herself could walk through the door at any moment and offer me a cup of tea. She would set the copper kettle to boil on the cast-iron range built into the hearth, then take the pottery cups and tea caddy from the oak sideboard. She'd fetch a plate of freshly baked raisin scones from the larder, bright with sun streaming in the small back window. We would sit here at the long plank table beneath the two windows facing the street. I would meet her brown eyes, puffy and darkly circled. I'd say… No words can be found. I take her hand, and hold it in my mind. She is my sister; she is every woman who has lost a child. And, after travelling the years with her, she's an auld acquaintance whose losses trigger my deepest fear. The phone ringing in the middle of the night; the police car pulling into my driveway: *Are you the mother of…?* A curtain drops. I cannot look beyond it.

The staircase, thirteen stone steps, winds up to a landing with a bedroom on either side and a narrow door that leads up to the attic. In the small room to the left, I picture a little black-haired girl sleeping in the box-bed, a coal fire glowing in the hearth. Then the image morphs into a dark-haired man lying in that bed, ashen and gaunt… I shut my eyes. We'll not go there yet.

Stepping into the other bedroom, spacious and bright with windows on two sides, I'm struck with that same sensation— Jean could still be living here. On one side of the hearth sits the low wooden chair where she nursed her babies; on the other side, the rocking chair waits for her to lullaby them to sleep. A hooded cradle rests within arm's length of the curtained bed where two worn feather pillows lie side by side.

At the other end of the room, an open door leads into an alcove. I'm not sure if it's the way the light from the window illuminates the antique desk where a frayed copy of *Essays on Songwriting* lies open, or the way the white feather stands in the quill holder, or if it's the old wooden chair whose brass plate reads *Burns's Chair from Ellisland*, but this small study has the aura of a sanctuary. Here, he literally left his mark—on the window pane, diamond-etched in his bold script, *Robert Burns*. He had so little time left to do so, to make his indelible mark.

Perched on the edge of the bed, I try to imagine all that transpired in these bedrooms in the ten months after Elizabeth's death—the dreams that were dreamed and the nightmares that were lived.

Four little girls, lithesome as fairies, skip through the yellow furze and up the heathery brae, black locks blowing in the wind. No matter how fast she runs, she can't catch up to them. Breathless, she calls— wait. They turn and wave, beckon for her to follow, then vanish over the crest of the hill.

"Please, don't go," Jean pleads. Rab's arms enfold her, pulling her back into the grey dawn. "I almost had them," she cries. Every morning they wake to a dull, flattened world, as if a hurricane has struck and left them lying in a heap of rubble. They have no will to sort through the pieces. Jean knows this domain too well, knows you have to plod on for the sake of the children. Do not look back, or you'll harden into stone.

Rab cannot write. His other lost daughters hadn't rooted in his heart; he hadn't rocked them in his arms, soothed their cries, dandled them on his knee, crooning, *Oh she's the lassie o' my heart, My lassie ever dearer*. So, until now, he hadn't known about living with the void, the aching hollow in your heart. A gill of whisky clenched in his hand, he slouches at his desk staring at the unopened letters and his notebook, twiddling his quill. When Jean suggests that writing might help to relieve the weight of the emptiness, he says, "The words have died. My finest creation lies in the Mauchline kirkyard."

Jean wonders if he'll ever pen another verse. The blue devils have him in their clutches throughout the autumn, usually his best time for writing. He struggles out of bed and climbs into the saddle to make his excise rounds. During his illness he earned only a half-salary, so the rent is past due and bills are piling up.

Then in November, Rab opens a letter from Gilbert and learns that Luath is gone, killed one day while out wandering. "A gash and faithful tyke," he says, teary-eyed. "Led me to a lass e'er sae loving."

"Your wish was surely granted," Jean says, stroking his arm. "As loyal as your dog."

On Hogmanay, the Midsteeple bells peal at midnight as pots and pans clang from windows throughout the city streets. But there is no celebrating at 24 Mill Hole Brae. The first day of 1796, they wake to a wintry blast, and Jean makes Rab a toddy to toast the New Year. He sips it with a blank eyes. "Man was made to mourn," he sighs, talking about a song his mother used to croon to his blind grand-uncle. The old man would sob and moan as she sang:

> *O Death! the poor man's dearest friend,*
> *The kindest and the best!*
> *Welcome the hour my agèd limbs*
> *Are laid with thee at rest!*

"Give over," Jean says, and reminds him of the old saying: *Those that cry and fret on New Year's Day will be crying and fretting all the year to come.*

January 25, Jean adds to their debt at the butcher's, buying all the fixings for a special supper: Rab's thirty-seventh birthday. He's fond of plain things, and hates tarts, pies and puddings. But there's one dish he relishes above all. She spends the afternoon in the kitchen, boils the sheep's pluck—liver, kidney, heart, lungs and suet—then minces the meat and mixes it with diced onions, pinhead oatmeal and broth. She stuffs the mixture into a scoured sheep's stomach, stitches it with twine at either end, and sets it in boiling water to cook for three hours.

That snowy evening, Rab steps in the door and sniffs the aroma oozing from the kitchen. "Ach," he grins. "Gie me a haggis!"

The children giggle with the excitement of staying up late and supping at the big table in the spence. Bobbie, a stocky nine-year-old, sits to the right of his father at the head of the table. To Rab's left is six-year-old Frankie, much slighter in build than his big brother, a gap-toothed grin on his freckled face. Then the four-year-olds: black-haired Willie, with the same stub nose and short neck as his father; and across the table Betty, their golden-haired daughter. They haven't seen her mother again, though Rab has heard that Anna is working as a domestic servant in Leith. At the foot of the table Jean holds eighteen-month-old Jamie, bobbling on her knee.

The haggis steams on the trencher, its beige skin sweating with amber beads. Beside it sit heaping bowls of creamy mashed tatties and golden neeps slathered in butter. Rab lowers his head into his hand and says,

> *Some hae meat and canna eat,*
> *And some would eat that want it;*
> *But we hae meat, and we can eat,*
> *Sae let the Lord be thankit.*

As he picks up the knife to slit the bursting mound, Bobbie asks, "Please, Tyta, could I address the haggis?"

"Ay, laddie." Rab's eyes gleam with surprise. "Go fetch the book."

"I've no need of it." Bobbie scrapes back his chair and gets to his feet. Gazing at the haggis, he launches into the ode his father wrote a decade ago:

> *Fair fa' your honest, sonsie face,*
> *Great chieften o' the pudding-race!*
> *Aboon them a' ye tak your place,*
> *Painch, tripe, or thairm:*
> *Weel are ye wordy of a grace*
> *As lang's my arm.*

Jean marvels that he's so much his father's son, not only in looks—the large head covered in dark, wavy hair; straight, even teeth; dimpled chin—but also in his remarkable memory. The works of the English poets, mathematics, English grammar, Latin and Greek, they all come easily to Bobbie. "The smartest pupil in the class," his schoolmaster has reported. "A boy of uncommon talents."

As Bobbie recites all eight verses without forgetting a word or stammering over the broad Scots dialect, pride shines on his father's face. The children sit completely still, awed by their big brother's recital. Then Rab slices into the stuffed stomach; the entrails gush out, infusing the air with a livery aroma. "Ah, warm reekin' rich," Frankie says.

At the end of the meal, the children chant their father's birthday song, *Rantin, Rovin Robin*, but Rab remains silent. "How can I sing," he says, "when one sweet voice is always missing?"

The children put to bed, Jean fans the coals with the bellows then curls up on the settee beside Rab who is sipping his whisky and staring into the orange tongues of flame. Sleet pelts the windows, and the peats sputter and hiss. "What a transient business life is," he says. "Just lately I was a boy. The other day I was a young man. And already I begin to feel the stiffening joints of old age. On what a brittle thread of life does man hang."

"He's always compleenin frae morning to eenin. What can a young lassie do wi' an old man?" Jean laughs. "Nae, you've still a few oats to sow yet." But running her fingers through his sable hair glinting with silver, she can't deny how he's aged in the past year. His once-muscular body seems to have shrunk, and his clothes sag on his thin frame. He no longer strolls in the gloaming to his haunts along the Nith. Walking exhausts him and causes his heart to race.

"Sowed too many wild ones," he says, "in my misspent youth."

"Well, my old man," she says, patting his hand, "you've a few left, enough to plant another seed in your wife."

"Is it so, Jean?" His eyes brighten. "Blessed with another bairn?"

"God willing. Carrying one at thirty-one is nae the same as at twenty-one."

"My love," he chuckles, then scoops her up in his arms and dances her around the room, singing:

My love, she's but a lassie yet,
My love, she's but a lassie yet!
We'll let her stand a year or twa,
She'll no be half sae saucy yet!

"Age has nae improved your ability to carry a tune," she giggles as they flop onto the settee.

"Tis why I have you," he says, panting and red in the face.
"When?"

"About six months from now."

"Around July 25 then—high summer, a glorious time to come
into the world." He strokes her belly and whispers, "Maybe a
wee lass?"

She shakes her head. "Not a wish to be making. Our four
sons lie warm in their beds. Our four daughters lie cold in the
kirkyard."

"You're fit to be the mother of a regiment," he says, taking
her hand. "You've passed on your good health and happy disposition to our boys, the finest creatures in the world. But their
daddy," he grins, "now he's another story."

Early the next morning, Rab writes an apology to George
Thomson for falling behind in his promised contributions to
Select Scottish Airs. He flings himself into the project once again
and talks excitedly about publishing a collection of the songs
he's written for both Thomson and Johnson's *Scot's Musical
Museum*—close to three hundred all told. "At least all the songs
I want to be called author of," he says. "To do justice to my muse
lest I be blamed for trash I never wrote. Or defrauded of what
is my own." But after an hour at his desk, he has to lay down his
quill. His temples throb and his eyes burn.

With the coming of spring the city turns green and lush with
blossoms, but Jean doesn't feel its rejuvenation as she normally
does. Her lower back aches, and her legs bulge with blue rivers
of varicose veins. She can't be long on her feet, so their maid-
servant takes over all the cooking and cleaning. Jessy Lewars,
from across the street, comes to care for the children and for
Rab, unable to work for the past month.

Jean watches her husband perk up every morning when

eighteen-year-old Jessy walks through the door in her print jacket and homespun skirt. Tall and graceful with a tiny waist and a mane of auburn hair, Jessy is like a flower in full bloom. She waits on Rab, serving him a bowl of brose or a glass of toddy. She takes his arm when he strains to rise from his chair, and massages his neck and shoulders to relieve the shooting pains.

As she sings to the children, Jessy's melodious voice brightens the house like dancing sunbeams. One day, she's crooning an old Scots song about a robin and a wren. "Tis a lovely air," Rab says, "but the words are trash."

That evening Jean hears him scraping away on his fiddle, trying to fit some words to the tune. The next day, he hands Jessy a paper with two verses he's written and asks her to try them out to the air of "The Wren's Nest."

"Be honoured, Mr. Burns." She stands and clears her throat, her eyes brilliant as emeralds, her cheeks flushing pink as she sings:

> *O, wert thou in the cauld blast*
>   *On yonder lea, on yonder lea,*
> *My plaidie to the angry airt,*
>   *I'd shelter thee, I'd shelter thee.*
> *Or did misfortune's bitter storms*
>   *Around thee blaw, around thee blaw,*
> *Thy bield should be my bosom,*
>   *To share it a', to share it a'.*

Rab hangs on every note, enchanted by this goddess of song. Jean has read, and sung, many of the verses his countless muses have inspired, but it's the first time she has beheld one, in all her youthful beauty, singing his lines—while she plods about the house, bulbous with child and peevish about her discomfort.

Jean is glad this lovely lass can fire his blood and his quill, provide him some relief from his achy body. In their eleven years together, many sirens have beckoned him. But Jean knows she has always been the anchor on the stormy sea of his life.

Dr. Maxwell's large hands roam over Jean's belly, touching and pressing the taut mound. "Bed rest," he says. "Complete bed rest til you're delivered." While undressing the previous night, Jean noticed blood stains on her petticoat. Her heart started thumping; she has still a month to go until her confinement.

Rab shuffles into the bedroom in his carpet shoes, a fur hunting cap drawn about his ears though it's a scorching midsummer's afternoon. As he sinks into the armchair beside the open window, the doctor gasps at the sight of his friend whom he hasn't seen for a few weeks. "My God man, you're wasting away."

"I fear my spirit's fleeing," Rab sighs. "Pain, rheumatism, cold, fever. At night I close my eyes in misery. And open them in the morning without hope."

Pulling a chair up beside him, Dr. Maxwell examines Rab's gaunt face, his dark sunken eyes. "It's likely flying gout. Sea bathing and country air could help. Brow-Well would be the place to go." A clachan ten miles south on the Solway Firth, Brow-Well has a few rundown cottages and an inn on a windy spit of land. The iron-rich water from its spring is said to have healing properties.

Rab arches his bushy eyebrows. "'Tis a damn frigid sea even in the summer. I have to get back to work. That rascal Williams will land me in jail." He rants about owing the haberdasher eight pounds for his Dumfries Volunteers' uniform and about falling behind in the rent. "I'll end up like my father," he says. "If the old man hadn't died of consumption, he'd likely have been sent to debtor's prison."

The doctor grimaces and removes his wire-rimmed spectacles. He looks hard at Rab. "It's your best, maybe your only, chance of recovery. You should wade into the sea every day, up to your chest. Take in the salt air. Drink from the spring. Best to stay the entire season."

"But Jean could be put to bed any day now."

"Dinna fash yourself about me." Jean reaches for Rab's hand and forces a smile. "I've done this a few times before." Her words mask her uneasiness. She remembers the women who attended her mother's final lying-in, talking about the increased risks with each pregnancy—for the mother as well as the child. And Rab, teetering on this cliff. *His only chance of recovery?*

At dusk, the St. John's Day bonfires blaze on the mountainsides around the city. Lying sleepless, turning one cheek to the pillow then the other, Jean smells the smoke drifting in their bedroom window. On Midsummer's Night, the veil between this world and the next is said to be sheer as gauze; fairies and witches can steal you away. She doesn't put much stock in the superstitions, but had their maid-servant pick sun-soaked bunches of St. John's wort and rue to hang above the front door.

The next day Rab bends over his desk, his bony fingers struggling to grip his goose-quill. Jean has finally convinced him to write to Thomson, from whom he's never taken a shilling for his contributions to *Select Scottish Airs*. He asks for five pounds and promises his editor five pounds worth of songs as soon as he regains his health. Then he writes to the Commissioners of Excise requesting they grant him full salary while on medical leave in light of his dire domestic situation. His final letter is to Jean's father, asking if Mrs. Armour can come as soon as possible to aid Jean in his absence.

On the morning of July 3, Jean packs a small grip for her husband with a change of clothes and his writing materials. Rab mounts the gig he's borrowed from John Syme, a woollen muffler wrapped about his neck and a thick quilt covering his legs. Jessy and the children cluster on the stoop, waving. Jean peers from the upstairs window, blinking back tears as he flicks the reins and disappears down the cobbled street. He will follow the river south to where it flows into the sea, its journey's end.

Every day, reclining in her bed, Jean imagines Rab limping along the barren shore, his feet slimy with mud, stumbling into the icy waves, his skinny body quivering and shrinking with the cold. She fears his blood will cease to flow, his heart seize up from the shock of it all. She's come to realize that faith in the ways of doctors is like faith in the ways of God. You trust in their mysterious powers. Trust and hope.

Not since being pregnant and alone in her small room in the Back Causeway has Jean lived with such trepidation. The letters that arrive do nothing to quell it. The Excise refuses Rab's appeal for full salary. Thomson writes that a five-pound money order will soon be in the mail, and suggests that Rab collect the poems from his manuscripts and publish a volume by subscription if he's in need of money. Her father's reply is abrupt: Mrs. Armour is in Paisley, helping at the bedside of her sick sister. Jean knows he's miffed. She's not been in touch with her parents since Elizabeth's death. A few weeks ago, her father wrote to say that he feared she'd forgotten them altogether.

Jean tries to steer her mind elsewhere, to feed loving thoughts to the baby pushing against her skin. It's dropped in the past week, the bearing-down of a wee head announcing that her time is nigh.

In the middle of July, she opens the long-awaited letter.

My Dearest Love,

I delayed writing until I could tell you what effect sea-bathing was likely to produce. It would be injustice to deny that it has eased my pains, and I think has strengthened me; but my appetite is still extremely bad. No flesh nor fish can I swallow: porridge and milk are the only things I can taste. I am very happy to hear, by Miss Jessy Lewars, that you are all well. My very best and kindest compliments to her, and to all the children. I will see you on Sunday.

Your affectionate husband, R.B.

Jean knows not what to think or how to read between these lines. Is he returning because he's feeling better, or because he's given up? But it's his handwriting—no longer a straight, even script with flourishing capitals, but an unsteady scribble—that tells her more than she wants to believe.

Two days later, a muggy Sunday afternoon, Jean waits, stretched out on the settee, staring above the mantle at Nasmyth's portrait of her husband. Such a good likeness of him ten years ago, so young and darkly handsome, when his eyes still shone as if lit from behind. Jessy has taken the four little ones to play at Dockside Park. Bobbie is attending the service at St. Michael's—to pray for Tyta, he said. Jean closes her eyes and takes in the fragrance of wild briar roses floating in the breeze.

The clopping of hooves and the clatter of carriage wheels come to a halt outside the front door. Jean eases herself up and peeks out the window—*Rab*, looping the reins around the iron railing. She pads across the carpet on her swollen bare feet and flings the door open. He hobbles up the steps, clutching the rail, his breath heavy as if he's been running. His legs buckle on the threshold, and he falls into her arms. "Ah, Jean," he pants, "I'm not long for this world."

She grasps his arm and helps him into the parlour. Collapsing onto the settee, he squints into the glare of the sun on his face, pale as powder. Jean reaches up to close the curtains. "Nae, let him shine," he says, lowering his eyelids. "He'll not shine on me for long. My life's day draws near the gloamin'."

Jean tries to mask the horror welling in her. "Naw, you canna give up," she says, smoothing the tangled hair from his forehead. "I'll send for Maxwell."

He shakes his head. "I drank the foul-tasting water from the hole in the ground. I waded into the bitter sea every morning. You see the results of the good doctor's orders. It's you and I who need to talk."

"But first a dish of tea after your long ride," she says, pressing on the settee to get to her feet.

He lays his hand on hers. "I can stomach nothing, just some water."

The cup shakes as he raises it to his lips. "I've had much time to think. My death is sure to rouse a lot of noise. Some will want to blacken my name for wounds I've inflicted in my verses. Every scrap of my writing will be revived against me to the injury of my reputation."

His words come out slowly as if he's searching to find each one. "My papers are in great disorder. I've not the strength to sort through all the half-finished verses. And the letters," he sighs, "written with unguarded freedom. The vultures will be circling, waiting to tear into them."

His eyes turn to glass up as he looks into hers. "But that's the least of my fears. Tis now I envy people of fortune. Gracious God! What will become of my little flock?"

He clasps her arm. "Forgive me, Jean." Then the corners of his mouth turn up in a little smile. "My refrain these past ten years. Hardly worthy of a song, is it?"

Jean can't speak for the lump lodged in her throat. She presses her lips to his hand, so cold and thin, and blinks hard to stop the tears pressing behind her eyes.

"I wrote to Gibby," he says, "entrusting you and the children to his care. He owes me two-hundred pounds, a loan many years ago."

"Your brother has more than enough family to care for," Jean says. Still providing for his mother and two sisters, Gilbert now has a wife, three children and another baby on the way.

"You'll have the widow's pension. And the scraps of verses in my desk might be worth something." He reaches into the pocket of his jacket. "Coila still hovers at my elbow. I scratched out one more. The tune's Rothiemurchie. The measure's difficult. Hard to infuse much genius into the lines. Could you sing it for me?"

Dabbing her eyes, she unfolds the paper and tries to make out the faint, squiggly script. She hums a few bars to get the key and the rhythm. Rab rests his head against the settee and closes his eyes. Then Jean sings a song about a maid on Devon's bank, his final ode to female beauty:

> *Then come, thou fairest of the fair,*
> *Those wonted smiles, O let me share,*
> *And by thou beauteous self I swear*
> *No love but thine my heart shall know.*

At the end of the third verse, he remains still, only the wheeze of his sleeping breath.

The front door bangs open, and many little feet patter in the entryway. They bound into the parlour—Frankie, Willie and

Betty. Jessy follows with Jamie slung upon her hip. Seeing their father slumped on the settee, so grey and dishevelled, the children stop short in front of him. "Tyta?"

His eyelids slowly open and flutter several times, as if he's trying to remember where he is and who these shining faces are before him. "My bonnie bairns," he smiles. Willie and Betty clamber onto his lap; Frankie kneels at his feet. He pats their heads and strokes their arms, saying how much he missed them.

"What was it like at the seaside?"

"Was the water cold?"

"Did you see any sharks?"

Rab chuckles then begins coughing. Turning his head, he wipes his mouth, the handkerchief stained with rusty-red blotches.

"Daddy needs to rest after his long ride," Jean says. "He'll tell you all about it tomorrow."

She and Jessy grip Rab's arms and pull him onto his feet. The children gape as their father limps up the stairs on their mother's arm. Jean leads him to the room across from their bedroom, which she has readied for her lying in—sheets, blankets and nappies stacked and waiting. Helping him into a nightshirt, she restrains a cry at the sight of his skeletal frame. She heaps the quilts over him, but he keeps shivering. After lighting a lump of coal in the hearth, she sits on the edge of the bed.

"Sing for me, Jean," he murmurs.

She croons an old Scots tune he lately wrote some verses for:

> *Ca' the yowes to the knowes,*
> *Ca' them where the heather grows,*
> *Ca' them where the burnie rowes*
>   *My bonie dearie.*

His lips mime the words while his lids droop, and he slides toward sleep.

That night, not a wisp of wind cools the thick air. Jean can find no comfortable position for her heavy belly. Across the passage, Rab coughs and groans fitfully. Birth and death lie on either side of her, like hungry twins vying for her attention, while she wrestles with the question that murders sleep. *What will become of us?*

When Dr. Maxwell steps into Rab's bedroom the next morning, his face turns as ashen as his patient's. His leather satchel thuds to the floor where he stands, shaking his head. He moves to the bed and lifts Rab's eyelids, one by one, then presses his fingers against his wrist.

"I'm an old crow not worth the picking," Rab says, "not even enough feathers to carry me to my grave." He asks Jean to fetch a wooden box from the top drawer of the linen chest. "Something there for Maxwell," he says.

The doctor lifts the lid and takes out a set of duelling pistols. "Bequeathed to me by Lord Glencairn," Rab says. "Couldna leave them in better hands."

Maxwell nods and meets Rab's eyes, acknowledging his friend's intention—payment for the doctor bills.

The news spreads like the plague around Dumfries. Their bard is dying. By the afternoon, people are gathering outside 24 Mill Hole Brae, looking up to the second-storey window. Friends come—rich and poor, cultured and unlearned—to bide a while at Rab's bedside. Their voices trickle into Jean's bedroom, along with occasional chuckling.

"John, dinna let the squad fire over my grave," Rab says to one of the Dumfries Volunteers. "God knows who could end up in there with me."

Descending the stairs, someone says in a hushed voice, "Who will be our poet now?"

Late the next afternoon, the children circle their father's bed, bouquets of gowans, harebells, foxgloves and dog-roses clutched in their hands. They've just returned from a walk along the river with Jessy, who will take them across the street to stay with her family so that the house will be quiet. On the chair next to the bed, Jean holds Jamie squirming in her arms. Rab scrutinizes their sad faces as if trying to recognize them. Then he holds out a shaky hand to Bobbie. "Gibby," he cries, "have you come?"

Their eyes moist and fearful, the children bend in turn to kiss their father's grizzled cheek. His lips turn up as his eyelids sag, and he drifts back to that place in between.

In the evening, Jean sits at Rab's desk. His white quill, *old stumpie*, waits in its stand beside the inkpot. On the wall above hangs a sketch of his poem "The Cotter's Saturday Night," a gift from one of his admirers. Her eyes move to the small window facing the street—*Robert Burns* etched in his bold, even script. She scans the books on his shelves—the millions of words he's read and knows by heart. Many tattered volumes, musty with the odour of dried grass, he inherited from his father.

The surface of the desk is a riot of papers scribbled with half-finished songs and fragments of verses, some written on the back of advertising flyers. Letters fill the top drawer. Jean finds the small packet tied with a red ribbon—the half-dozen letters she's written to him—and tucks it into her apron pocket. The middle drawer contains a massive bundle of letters in the cramped handwriting of Mrs. Dunlop. Beside it, another collection of envelopes has the golden seal of Woodley Park—Maria Riddell's. Good fuel for the fire, Jean decides, and tosses them onto the floor.

She yanks on the brass handle of the heavy bottom drawer: stacks of envelopes addressed in the feathery script of Nancy McLehose. Removing one of the packets, she holds it for several seconds, her hands sweaty with apprehension. Then she unties the yarn, and the letters spill onto the desk, a white waterfall of words. She skims a few of them, addressed to *Dear Sylvander—My situation is a delicate one… I am a strict Calvinist. Religion, the only refuge of the unfortunate, has been my balm in every woe… Oh cruel Fate! I am bound in an iron chain—*and signed, *Your Clarinda.* Long rambling letters with verses the lady had composed for him, pages of high-flown phrases and unfamiliar words. A married woman torn between her love and her religion.

What to do with them? She expects Mrs. McLehose will be asking for them back, and that the lady's own hoard of letters will be locked away in some secret place, perhaps the bottom of her sewing box. Black ink on white paper is all this woman owned of him. Jean reties the bundles and shoves them back into the drawer.

"Get a good night's rest," Dr. Maxwell says, shooing Jean off to her bedroom. "Your hour could come anytime now."

A silvery light beams through the open window onto Jean's face. The moon is full, round and ripe, a time of opening. She prays the pangs will soon be on her, that Rab can meet this child pressing down between her legs. Inhaling the honeysuckle breeze, she closes her eyes and recalls that moonlit night when they first walked out together, the old castle bathed in ethereal light. Then she envisions the orange harvest moon sailing over the river in Ellisland.

The wind howls up from the river with a terrifying birr, ripping the thatch from the roof of the farmhouse. Shutters bang, windows shake, the walls groan. They sit bolt upright in bed, watching the trees bend and sway. Branches snap, fly off and crash against the house. A crack like a gunshot pulls Rab onto his feet. The tree has split, he yells, racing to the door. It's falling on the house!

Too heavy with child, she cannot move. Through the window, she sees him beneath the towering hawthorn, his thin arms outstretched. A cold blast batters his naked body. A cascade of limbs and leaves topple him as he wails.

A cry wrenches Jean back into the half-light of early morning—*Rab*.

Maxwell is kneeling beside the bed, his ear pressed to Rab's chest. Even before the doctor turns and speaks the words, she knows. A void has already filled the room, sucked out all the air. Gasping for a breath, Jean withers onto the bed.

"He spent a peaceful night," Maxwell says. "But as day was breaking, he got agitated, started clawing at the sheets, thrashing about. Tried to get out of bed. He cried out then fell back, still as…" The doctor's eyes blink rapidly several times then he puts an arm around Jean's shoulder. "I'll leave you with him for a spell."

She looks into her husband's empty eyes then gently closes his lids. She holds his limp hand against the bulges stirring in her belly: that once-strong hand that steered the plow; those fine, long fingers that raced the quill over the page, the hand that caressed every part of her. Staring at his rigid face, she half-expects one eye to open and wink at her, for his pale lips to part and flash a wide grin.

His wasted body leaves ample space in the bed for her bulk. She lies down and draws his head against her bosom, always his favourite pillow. Sliding her fingers through his thick hair, she tries to sing him one last song:

We twa ha'e run about the braes,
And pu't the gowans fine;
But we've wadered mony a weary foot
Sin auld lang syne.

Her voice too clotted and choking to continue, she holds him while the sun bleeds into the sky, and the bells of St. Michael's toll six times.

PART IV

Widow Burns

1796–1832

We twa hae paidl'd in the burn
Frae morning sun till dine,
But seas between us braid ha'e roared
Sin auld lang syne.

A YOUNG MAN IN A WHITE DRESS SHIRT AND RED TARTAN
tie pokes his head into the room. "The museum will be closing
in fifteen minutes, ma'am."

Sitting on the box-bed with my notebook and pen, I look up,
confused, and glance at my watch. How long have I been here?
Ten minutes? Ten months? I'm reluctant to leave this bedroom
where death still lingers, in the air and in my mind.

Downstairs, the parlour has been converted into a reception
area. The curator's desk, long display cases and souvenir items
abruptly shatter any illusion of the past. But some artifacts beneath the glass cases give me a thrill of proximity to Jean, items
her hands touched over and over again in daily life: her gold

wedding band, worn thin; a small leather-bound Bible open to the title page—so torn and ragged it would surely crumble to the touch—signed in faded, black ink, *Jean Burns*; her tattered cookbook, *The Art of Cookery Made Plain and Easy*, open to a sepia-toned page, "To make Potato Cakes." Could those brown smudges have been left by her doughy fingers?

As I make my way towards St. Michael's Church, the reddish-brown clock tower and spire jutting into the cerulean sky make it easy to spot in the distance. By the time I reach the end of Burns Street, I'm completely back in the present with the rush of cars and the stink of diesel. But there, unexpectedly, on a grassy square in the middle of the busy, honking intersection, Jean stands bronzed on a granite pedestal.

It's like seeing a photo of someone you haven't seen for years, knowing she would have aged, but startled by the changes: her face rounder, her hair tucked up in a bun; her figure fuller, matronly. In one hand, she holds a small book against her chest. A Bible? Rab's poems? Her other arm is down at her side, and a young boy in knee breeches grips her hand with both of his. Thus has she been cast, Widow Burns, a thirty-one-year old mother of five young children. She stands, halfway between her home and the kirkyard—rock-solid—while streaming traffic swirls around her.

Resting on the edge of Jean's pedestal, I continue my notes, our ongoing conversation: *Your husband lying in his coffin in one room, and you lying in the room next door about to give birth*. I study her face—lips frozen in a half-smile, unseeing eyes looking off into the distance. Her sad voice quavers inside my head: *Ay, my life story these past ten years—birthing and burying.*

In the grey hour of the gloaming, they come to take his body away. The men creep in, quiet as death itself. Not a sound on the stone stairs, only a faint creak of the door and whisperings as they manoeuvre his bier through the narrow passage and down the stairs. Then, the click of the closing door.

Jean rolls onto her side, eases her belly to the edge of the bed, pushes with her arms to sit up. She can just reach the window to part the lace curtains. His coffin juts out from the back of the carriage as it rumbles down the cobbles and turns the corner onto High Street. The slow clomping of hooves fades into the dusk. Her eyes stay dry. Three days after his death, no tears are left; the last of them trickled out that afternoon when she said goodbye.

The room smelled of honeysuckle, their cream and orange blossoms blanketing the bed around his plain coffin. He lay in the blue-and-white uniform of the Royal Dumfries Fusiliers, looking well beyond his thirty-seven years; his body shrunk like a wizened apple, his black hair threaded with silver. She drew back the linen sheet from his face; it looked serene, as if he'd finally escaped. Snipping a curl from the nape of his neck and tucking it into her bodice, she leaned in and kissed his cheek, cold like no other cold.

Tonight he will lie in the Midsteeple. At noon tomorrow, the town will honour their bard with a grand military funeral. Jean wonders if she'll be there to bury her husband. Early that morning she felt the first tightenings clench her belly, and the pressure of a wee head moving into place.

"Any time now," Dr. Maxwell said that afternoon. "Keep to your bed, and dinna fash yourself." But worry clings to her like a shroud: *Six bairns to raise alone.*

"Mrs. Burns?" A tap on the door, and Jessy comes in with a dish of tea and oatcakes. "Thought you might be needing a bite. You've not had much, only a bowl of brose this morning."

"I've little appetite. But I should eat something for the wean." Taking the teacup, Jean looks into the young woman's face, blotchy from crying. "You're an angel sent from heaven, Jessy. What we would have done without you these past months?"

"A privilege to serve such a great man," she says, dropping into the wooden armchair beside the bed. "Canna believe he's gone."

"You served him well," Jean says, taking her hand. "He always needed a bonnie lass to fire his quill."

Jessy's lips turn up, her eyes shiny with memories. "Even through the pain of his last days, he was still joking with me, teasing me about which of my admirers I'd end up marrying. Bob Spalding wouldn't do, he said, the man had not as much brains as a midge could lean its elbow on." She laughs. "He said the lucky lad was sure to be James Thomson."

Of course, Jean smiles, Thomson is a writer, a man after Rab's own heart.

Jessy stares at her freckled hands folded in her lap then looks up into Jean's eyes. "I've been wanting to ask you, Mrs. Burns. What would you be advising about marrying a writer?"

Jean sips her tea and bites into an oatcake, unsure how to answer this young lass, the same age as Jean was when she fell in with Rab and her life went all agley. Jean glances up at the picture next to her bed: the Holy Mother in her blue robes, arms crossed over her chest, a golden light circling her head, silent and forebearing.

"It's nae joke being married to a poet," Jean says, as the bells from the Midsteeple commence their ten o'clock clanging. With each ring that ripples through the murky streets, the past ten years flood before her. Waves of memory pull her back—to a dance floor, a bleaching green, and a black-and-white collie named Luath.

In the dim early light, Jean clinches her cramping belly and counts the chimes drifting up from the parlour—one… two…

three... four... five. Old Clockie Broon, Rab's eight-day clock, wound by his own hand. He brought it from Mossgiel to adorn the mantle in Ellisland. It moved with them to the spence of the Wee Vennel then here to Mill Hole Brae, sounding the hours and the days and the years of their lives.

Rain splats against the window, leaving rivulets of tears running down the glass. She's as fearful as she was giving birth for the first time without Rab. Nobody's wife. *Widow Burns*. She wonders who she is without him, the compass of her life this past decade.

Thank the good Lord for John Syme and Gilbert, she thinks, overseeing the funeral arrangements and composing the announcement letters for Bobbie to sign. Her head is too befuddled with numbers: two pounds in her pocketbook, a widow's annuity of twelve pounds, eight pounds a year for rent; five—or six, God willing—children to feed and clothe. And the funeral expenses: the digging of the grave, the ringing of the bells, the mort cloth, a stone marker. *What will become of us? Will Bobbie have to leave school? Will they try to take my children away?*

Nae, Jean, Rab's lilting voice echoes in her head. *Dinna fash yourself.*

A vise squeeze of a contraction tears at her flesh and pulls her back to the present—time to summon Jessy and Dr. Maxwell.

Six... seven... eight... the bells peal over the cloudy skies of Dumfries... nine... ten... eleven... twelve. Bagpipes drone low in the distance then swell to a skirling as the procession winds down High Street and turns onto Mill Hole Brae. People line both sides of the street all along the route to St. Michael's Kirk, Jessy says, looking from Jean's bedroom window. "Hundreds. I've never seen such a funeral." The two regiments stationed here—

the Cinque Ports Calvary and the Angushire Fencibles—are giving Robert Burns full military honours.

Jean snuggles her infant, mewling at her breast. After an hour of fierce pangs and a few strong pushes, her son had slid into Dr. Maxwell's hands, scrawny and whimpering. He's been fussing ever since, nursing then squawking as if in pain. Jean worries her milk has gone sour with sorrow. The joy of his birth, the elation of them both surviving, eclipsed by the advancing dirge, Handel's *Dead March*: muted drums, solemn and beautiful, and trumpets and flutes soaring into the clearing sky.

Jean asks Jessy to help her out of bed. "Are you sure, Mrs. Burns?" Jessy turns from the window, dabbing her eyes. "The doctor said not to stir."

"Just for a moment." Jean passes her swaddled infant to Jessy and totters to the window. The sun bursts through the clouds as the Royal Dumfries Fusiliers march by, black bands on their swinging arms. The town sergeants follow with their halberds draped in black crepe. Then the coffin—Rab's furry Fusilier hat resting on top—shouldered by six men, faces grim as stone. As they pass beneath her window, one bearer lifts his head and his wet eyes meet Jean's: Dr. Maxwell, carrying the body of the man whose son he pulled into life but three hours ago.

Jean leans into Jessy and takes the baby into her arms, knowing now what he must be called. *Maxwell*, she whispers into his pink ear, *James Maxwell*. The name Rab himself would surely have chosen, his final tribute.

The bier vanishes around the corner, an endless procession trudging behind it. Bobbie, staring down at his feet, shuffles between his uncles, Gilbert and Adam. A member from each family as is the custom. Jean thinks of Rab's mother, so present in her absence. What would she be feeling about this grand display for her son? Too worldly in her eyes, yet still her boy, her firstborn. Jean knows too well the wretched place his mother now inhabits: that foreign, unnatural territory of surviving your child.

Behind the family tramp city magistrates, gentlemen in black top hats, ministers in black robes and Freemasons in full regalia, the gold figures on their collars and leather aprons gleaming in the sunlight. Throngs of people follow, black weepers tied on their sleeves. Jean witnesses the old midwife's prophecy on that wild January night, thirty-seven-and-a-half years ago, manifest in the streets of Dumfries:

> *He'll hae misfortune great an' sma'*
> *But ay a heart aboon them a'.*
> *He'll be a credit to us a':*
> *We'll a' be proud of Robin!*

She watches until her legs grow weak, then Jessy helps her back into bed and tucks Maxwell into his cradle. Jean lies facing the window, picturing the kirkyard, the northeast corner where the earth gapes. All is quiet now, and she imagines his body beneath a pile of dirt, silent and still. But his voice is so alive in her head, in every verse and song he penned.

Gunshots split the air: the Dumfries Volunteers firing three ragged volleys over his grave. Jean can see the grin lighting up Rab's face, his black eyes flashing. She laughs, and she cries. And this, she realizes, is the sum of their years together: heartache and rapture. An unceasing love song—at times sung sorely out of tune and at times in soulful harmony.

Jean gazes at the young woman slouched in the armchair. She reaches for her hand and says, "Marry him." Jessy's green eyes widen in a question. "Your Mr. Thompson, marry him. There's much to forebear in being the wife of a writer. But there's much to bear in marrying any man. *A man's a man for a' that.*"

Jessy twirls a strand of her auburn hair, and a smile brightens her face.

Jean lies alone in the hush of the night, but for Maxwell dozing in the crook of her arm. The air is warm and humid, but her bed feels cold. Will it ever be otherwise? *You've made your bed, now you have to lie in it*, her father would say. Touching the empty pillow beside her, she can't imagine another head there. Her children are in need of a father. But who would want a woman with six bairns? Too much for even her gallant weaver to take on. Thinking of Robin—married now and living back in Mauchline—she wonders how the years have changed him, until finally she slips into sleep.

Rab is scrambling up the brae, purple with heather. Four willowy lasses, dark curls glossy in brilliant sunlight, and a black-and-white dog gambol beside him. At the crest of the hill, they turn and wave, then link arms and disappear to the other side. Only the glaring sun remains, blinding her eyes.

A brilliant light startles Jean awake. A luminous figure stands beside the bed, his bright dark eyes full on her and Maxwell. "I had to see him," Rab says. "They let me come back just to see him. Fash nae mair, Jean. I'll take care of you." Then he fades, slowly, into the dark.

* * *

St. Michael's churchyard is a jungle of tombstones—tall red pillars, massive rectangular slabs, wide stone tables with fat legs—competing for space and grandeur. I wander through the labyrinth of sculptured stone commemorating ministers, provosts, lawyers, writers... On many headstones, the inscription is unreadable, effaced by islands of grey lichen and spongy moss. Some stones have sunk so deeply into the earth, they've almost vanished.

In a far corner behind the eighteenth-century stone church, a square plot is fenced off with cement blocks and a spiked iron railing, the original burial site of Robert Burns, now the grave of Mrs. Frances Dunlop's daughter. Six-foot high tombstones border the grave on both sides. But when Burns was buried here, the plot lay secluded in this back corner, without even a slab of stone to mark it for many years. It's that isolated mound of earth that I envision while sitting on the cold ledge of the grave, traffic whooshing in the background.

As soon as she was able to leave her bed, Jean would have come here, five children at her side and baby Max enfolded in her shawl. I imagine them huddled around a heap of clay, the little ones crying into the folds of her gown, Jean holding back her tears, trying to stay strong for her children.

She often visits his grave alone in the evening when the gloaming is sifting down and everything is still. Then she can talk to him, hear him speaking inside her head. There's no one else she can talk to, no one else she can trust. They all claim to have her best interests at heart. And the children's of course. *Think what's best for your bairns.* It's the lever they use to try to move her to their will. First it was James Burness, Rab's cousin in Montrose, whose letter arrived but four days after Rab was in the ground. His proposal—*to relieve you of the maintenance and education of your eldest boy*—tugged at her deep-rooted fear.

She did not dwell on that offer; she would not be parting with Bobbie again. Though she knows Rab lives in each one of the children, at ten years old Bobbie is Rab wrought in miniature. She clings to him, depends on him. Maybe, expects too much of him. *Bobbie, should I have let you go? Would your story have a better ending?*

During those blurry days in the aftermath of birthing and burying, she cannot see beyond her own need to keep her children close, like a fortress around her. She wrote to James Burness, thanking him, but declining his very obliging offer.

Jean drifts from room to room in a fog of fatigue, feeling her way in the new life she's been given: *Widow Burns.* Rab is everywhere: sitting at his desk, rocking Jamie to sleep, lying in bed beside her. His dark eyes stare out at them from his portrait above the hearth, presiding still over their lives. Despite Jessy's hovering presence and the children's sweet voices, the house feels empty. Jean knows this terrain, knows the only way to survive is to keep busy, not dwell on what cannot be changed. *Six bairns to feed and clothe and school*, she reminds herself, as she awakens, reluctantly, to the blank pillow beside her.

Late one afternoon, Jean is pacing around the parlour with Max skirling his colicky cry in her arms. One month old, he's gained little weight, naps for only a few hours at a stretch and cries for many more. She pats his back, crooning, "*Sing balaloo my lammie, sing balaloo my dear, Does the wee lammie ken that his daddy's no here?*" Jessy has taken the children for a romp along the river, so the sound of footsteps tromping overhead alarms her. Then she remembers: John Syme is here, as he is most days with Dr. Maxwell. Executors of Rab's will, they spend hours at his desk, rifling through his papers, searching for poems to publish and raise money for a trust fund for the poet's family.

Max finally gives in to sleep, and Jean settles him into his cradle. Releasing a long sigh, she collapses into the rocking chair and ponders all that needs to be done in the next hour before the baby stirs and the children return. The parlour door squeaks open. John steps in with a large bundle of envelopes under his arm. Jean wonders if it's just the dimness of this overcast day casting a pall over everything, but his thinning hair seems to have turned grey all at once. Or maybe she's just noticing now as her eyes begin to look outward again.

"Sorry to disturb you, Jean, but…" He shifts nervously from one foot to the other then clears his throat. "I came upon this packet," he says in a low voice, "of very private letters."

He coughs then adds, "Letters of considerable feeling, if you know what I mean."

"From Mrs. Nancy McLehose?"

"Ay." His face reddens as he looks down at the bundle. "Not sure what to do with them."

"Do as you see fit, but she'll surely be asking for them back."

Jean has already met one such request. Decked out in her finery, Maria Riddell came to offer her condolences. Her lace handkerchief dabbing her eyes, she talked of Rab, circled about for several minutes, asking Jean how she was managing and how the children were faring. Then she brought up her letters, slipped them in as if an afterthought. Jean looked at her in bewilderment, said that Syme and Maxwell had gone through all Rab's correspondence, but found nothing from her.

Maria's doe-like eyes widened as she wound her handkerchief through her fingers.

"So many letters in such a short life," Jean said, shaking her head. "Suppose he'd not room to keep them all."

Maria rose with a rustle, smoothed the creases in her grey silk gown. "Well, we did fall out for a while near the end."

Jean nodded, her cheeks glowing with the memory of Maria's packet of words bursting into flames.

The early September sun lights up the faces of the children crowded around the kitchen table crunching on oatcakes while Jean stirs a pot of crowdie, baby Max snuggled close in her shawl. It's her first day without Jessy's help, so she's not pleased to hear a knock on the door. The house needs fixing up; her hair is all a-tangle, her gown mottled with stains. Strangers have started coming to the door at all hours of the day asking questions: *Is this the poet's house? Can they see the room where he died? The desk where he wrote his verses?* Many have travelled from away, like pilgrims seeking a shrine. When they ask for mementos, Jean never has the heart to refuse them and finds some little object—a quill, an ink horn, or Rab's signature on a scrap of paper. Bobbie often guides the visitors to the kirkyard to show them the gravesite, and there he'll recite one of his father's poems.

When Bobbie shows John Syme and Dr. Maxwell into the kitchen, Jean is relieved. Both men seem in unusually good cheer. She hasn't seen either of them smile since Rab's death. They sorely miss their friend, and guilt burdens them: *Should have done more... Could have done more...* Now they're trying to atone, do whatever they can to assist Rab's family and advance his legacy as Scotland's bard.

As Jean ladles out the porridge into five wooden bowls, John asks if they can have a word with her. Leaving the children to sprinkle sugar on their steaming oats, they step across the hall into the spence. John pulls an envelope from the pocket of his waistcoat. "Good news, Jean. This arrived yestreen from James Fergusson, Esquire. You may have heard of him, a wealthy estate owner in Ayrshire."

"Naw."

John passes her the letter. "Well the gentleman has certainly heard of Robert Burns. He's offering to educate all your boys at the Academy in Ayr."

"Gratis!" Dr. Maxwell adds. Both men grin widely as if they've just presented her with a gift she's always wanted.

Jean scans the letter, her heart fluttering like a trapped bird. "But it's on the coast, a good sixty miles from here."

"You'd have to move to Ayr, or somewhere nearby," Maxwell says. "Back home, Jean. Back to your family, and Rab's."

She does not return their smiles. The thought of going back to Ayrshire leaves her cold. Scooping Max from her shawl and settling him against her shoulder, she pats his back to still his fussing and looks up to Rab's portrait above the hearth. She contemplates it daily, the loveliest ornament of her little parlour, peers into his eyes probing for answers to the many questions that have sprung up, like so many weeds in a garden she doesn't have the strength to tend. Depending on the time of day and the play of light flickering on his face, she reads different expressions but always feels a response.

Following her eyes, John says, "Rab would surely be laughing at this handsome offer."

The scraping of spoons on bowls and faint giggles resound from the kitchen, then a chorus of high voices singing, *Once crowdie, twice crowdie, three times crowdie in a day.*

"This is our home. The children have just lost their father. They'll not be losing their home as well."

Glances dart between the two men then Maxwell's thin lips quiver in a small smile. "But the children would have board at the academy as well. You've no family here in Dumfries. The children could have a new home with their Uncle Gilbert in Mossgiel."

Gilbert's pale, drawn face flashes before her. Stooped at her bedside the day after the funeral, turning the rim of his black hat in his hands, he stumbled for words. His red-rimmed eyes blinked, restraining tears, as he explained about seeing to the funeral costs and doing whatever necessary to come good on that loan from Rab of many years ago, even relinquish his farm to raise the two hundred pounds. She told him not to worry about that now.

Jean looks hard at the two men in their fine wool suits. "You mean add seven more bodies to the eight already living in that but and ben?"

John shrugs. "Well, then, you could move back home to Mauchline. Your bairns would have their grandparents to dote on them."

Jean closes her eyes, stifling the urge to shriek—*Live again under the steely fist of James Armour?* "That wouldn't work," she says.

"Will you not think more on it, Jean?" Maxwell pleads. "We believe it's the best course for the children, and for you. Your financial worries would be over."

But Jean isn't so worried about money now. Her widow's pension is only twelve pounds a year, but she's already witnessing Rab's ghostly promise coming true. The trust fund his friends set up raised seventy guineas within a few days, and the contributions continue to mount. Since Rab had been made an honorary burgess in Dumfries, the children's fees are being waived at the grammar school. The most mysterious manifestation of his promise to take care of them came the day she sent Bobbie to their landlord to settle the rent. He returned with the money and a letter stating the rent will be paid *in perpetuity* by a benefactor who wished to remain anonymous.

John stops his pacing in front of the hearth and folds his arms over his chest. "I've already replied to Fergusson saying his offer would surely be gratefully accepted. Told him you could be moved when necessary."

The baby launches into a full gale of crying. "Feeding time," Jean says, rising. "Write back to Mr. Fergusson. Tell him I'm much obliged to him for his generous offer. But we will not be moved."

Up in her bedroom, the rocker pendulums back and forth, creaking the floor boards. With Max tugging at her breast, Jean is pulled in opposing directions. Will she live to regret her decision? Do these learned men know what's best for her and the children? She's followed the lead of men all her life. Trusting her own judgment will take time.

But Jean soon comes to realize that their lives would have been vastly different if she'd accepted that offer. For staying in Dumfries affects the children in ways she could never have imagined. With the flood of visitors, the prying eyes, the publicity, it is not a normal existence. Rab is as present in death as he was in life. For every person who wants to put him on a pedestal, twice as many want to knock him into the mud. Just as he'd predicted: the vultures are circling, dying to tear into his legacy. He was barely cold in the earth before the gossip mongers and the newspapers commenced their slandering: *a hard-drinking fornicator, a useless father and provider who drank himself to death.* Even Maria Riddell's sketch in the *Dumfries Journal* was full of snide innuendoes: *imprudencies that sullied brighter qualifications … a penchant for the joy-inspiring bowl.* Jean can stop her ears to the slurs, the meanness and absurdity of them. But she cannot shield her children from the poisoned arrows.

One day, the front door opens and books thud on the slate floor—Bobbie, back from school earlier than usual. As Jean descends the stairs, he looks up at her, his eye black-and-blue, his cheek grazed raw, the knee of his breeches ripped.

"Gracious, laddie, what's happened?"

"Why do they say those awful things about Tyta?" he cries.

"Because they didn't know him," she says, taking her son into her arms. "But you did." She holds Bobbie's bruised face between her hands. "You know how kind and loving he was."

In the parlour, they sit on the settee staring up at Rab's portrait. "For sure, your father had his failings," Jean says, "but they came from a loose tongue, not the contents of a bottle. He spoke too direct at times and made some enemies."

"I miss him so," Bobbie says. His head resting on her shoulder, Jean feels his heaving sobs against her chest. She has always kept herself from breaking down in front of the children, but now her tears cannot be stayed as Jean realizes she can never take Bobbie's hurt away.

So when the prospect of the book comes up, Jean is hopeful. Something to set the record about Rab's life straight and collect all his verses. They all convince her—John Syme, Dr. Maxwell and Gilbert—that they've found just the man to write and edit the publication. Dr. James Currie of Liverpool met Rab only once, but he's a great admirer of his poetry. He's offering his services at no charge so that all the proceeds will go to the family's trust fund. Currie will be relying on Rab's family and acquaintances to get the facts about his life, so Jean expects he'll be calling on her for a lengthy interview.

Syme and Maxwell clean out Rab's desk, pack all his notebooks, manuscripts, letters, accounts, every scrap of paper into a large wooden box. Currie needs to see everything, and promises all will be returned once the book is finished. Jean and the children watch them lug the heavy chest down the stairs and out the door, feeling the loss. Where is he to be found if not in all the words he wrote on those reams of paper? And Jean senses a deeper loss; they are losing him to the wide world. She wonders if it will turn him into a man they can still recognize.

Jean does not read the book when it's first published four years later. She cannot read anything.

The spring before, Max was sniffling and sneezing one day; the next, he was coughing up greenish phlegm. Dr. Maxwell held his namesake's thin body, afire with fever then shaking with chills. Jean followed the doctor's orders, spooning a mixture of whisky and water into her son's mouth every two hours. On the third day, his lips and fingertips turned purplish-blue, then his faint puff of a breath ceased altogether. He was not yet three years old.

It was April 25, the first primroses budding yellow in the window boxes. Jean could not help but ponder the strange coincidence of dates: Rab, born on January 25, buried on July 25; she, herself, born on February 25. She waited for signs, grasping for clues that Rab was still around, speaking to her in whatever way he could. So when Max's coffin dropped into the earth beside his father's, Jean could shut her eyes and see Rab embracing the son he never knew, and her four daughters, a circle of light surrounding their brother. Only then could she stand up, fold her empty arms across her chest and walk home.

A year later, she opens the first of the four leather-bound volumes, *The Works of Robert Burns: With an Account of His Life and a Criticism of His Writing*. She doesn't have to read too far into the Biographical Sketch before understanding John's reluctance to meet her eyes when he handed her the books. The author hadn't consulted him, John said, or Maxwell or Gilbert, before the books went to press. And, Jean reminded him, James Currie had never talked nor written to her.

Currie's sketch dishes out the same slander, only cloaked in loftier language. *Addicted to excess … Perpetually stimulated by alcohol in one or another of its various forms … He who suffers the pollution of inebriation, how shall he escape other pollution? But let us refrain from the mention of errors over which delicacy and humanity draw the veil.* Jean rereads those sentences a few times then realizes what the author is insinuating. She slams the book shut, wants to heave it into the fire. Or hide it at the bottom of her press to keep it from the children's eyes. But she knows they will come upon it sometime, somewhere, this distorted portrayal of their father. She cannot protect them from the world.

That evening, Jean gathers her five children around the hearth. Holding the books on her lap, she explains that the author has done a great service by collecting all their father's poems and songs together. "I'm obliged to him for that," she says, "and for the considerable money these books have contributed to our trust fund. We want for nothing." Glancing up at Ràb's portrait, she can almost hear him chuckling: *Worth more dead than alive.* The books earned sixty pounds in the first year alone. But the price they exact in return is too high.

"You must remember," Jean continues, "Mr. Currie did not know your father. So he did not get everything right."

The children sit quietly, eying the books then looking up at their mother. She can see memories of their father flitting behind their sad eyes. "I 'member when I was sick," Betty says, "Tyta rocking me on his knee and singing, *She's my bonnie blue-eyed lassie, with an air so sweet and tender.*" Her lips turn up in a reflective smile. Gazing into her teary eyes, Jean knows she'll soon have to tell Betty about her mother Anna, the source of those lovely cornflower eyes.

Leaning against the mantel, Bobbie says, "Remember, just because something's printed in a book does not make it true."

Jean meets her son's glassy brown eyes and realizes he's already read it. At sixteen, he's as tall as she, his face framed by a patchier version of the dark sideburns his father wears in the picture above Bobbie's head. Completing his final year at Dumfries Academy, Bobbie shines in all his lessons and is writing some verses too. In the fall, he'll be attending Glasgow University, thanks to a generous patron who told him, "You'll do justice to the genius of your father."

On that crisp September morning when the stagecoach for Glasgow pulls into the stop at the Whitesands Inn, Jean hugs her oldest son and says, "Your father always said you'd be a scholar, or maybe a poet; *another Burns, with future rhymes, to emulate his sire.*" Then she fidgets with his collar, regretting her words, fearing such remarks only increase the weight of expectation heaped upon his young shoulders. Bobbie smiles and says he'll do his best to make Tyta proud. He stows his grip in the boot and steps aboard.

Jean can't see him through the narrow window, but she waves as the coach lurches down the cobbles and vanishes around the bend. She knows her son's name and his looks will open doors for him. But when he crosses those thresholds will Robert Burns, Jr. ever be seen for himself?

Jean watches her children disappear, in different ways, like so many fledglings taking wing.

A year later, it's Frankie. He jabbers about crossing the big ocean on a sailing ship the following spring. Sir James Shaw, the Mayor of London and a devotee of Robert Burns, has secured a place for Frankie as a cadet in the East India Company. But Jean has always felt that her second son is not quite of this world. She wonders if his infant brush with death during the smallpox epidemic left him vulnerable, a foot on either side. Lean and pale and dreamy, he often misses school due to one illness or another and struggles with his lessons. When the consumption seizes him, Frankie descends into a long, feverish sleep and never awakens.

It's a humid day in July of 1803 when Jean buries her sixth child. Before the casket is nailed shut, she gazes at his freckled face, pitted with smallpox scars. Fourteen years of Frankie to keep in her vault of memory, too many memories to hold, yet not nearly enough. She snips a curl of his auburn hair, then slips his copybook into the coffin, all the stories he wrote about a land of elephants, turbans and loincloths. They can go with him. She cannot read them again.

Her remaining sons disappear through portals opened by men in high places, men of good intention, wanting to do something for the sons of Scotland's bard. Jamie stands at the top of his class, so Mr. Shaw gains a place for him at Christ's Hospital, an excellent boarding school in London. Jean feels riven in two. Her youngest son, blessed with his father's love of song and her talent for singing them. A voice inside her cries, *Too young to leave home at ten years old.* But another voice cries louder: *He'll escape Dumfries, the noxious air and the eyes that stalk the sons of Robert Burns.*

As Jean packs his trunk that September morning in 1804, the clothes she's folding are a blur through her wet eyes. Her only comfort is that Jamie's big brother will be close by. Bobbie is now working as a clerk in the London Stamp Office, Mr. Shaw's patronage once again. After completing two years at Glasgow University and winning the Classics medal, Bobbie moved on to the university in Edinburgh. He stayed for only one session, and left without graduating. He's never come home to visit. Jean can only guess at what might have happened by reading between the lines of his occasional letters. His handwriting so resembles his father's that she wonders if he practises to make it so.

Soon as they hear my name, they slap me on the back, want to stand me a drink. Think they know me. "So like your father." They shake their heads and greet into their pints. Sometimes they ask for a verse, and I'll recite one of mine. But it's his they want. At the end of the night we all stagger home, sad. They get the flavour of him, but not the real thing. And the face I see reflected in the dark window will forever be a weak imitation.

Just as Jean has feared, Robert Burns casts too bright a light. Living in his father's shadow, Bobbie cannot see himself. His letters from Edinburgh always ended with the same request: Could she send a few pounds to tide him over until the end of the month? She did, of course, believing his bursary was insufficient for living in the city. But when the same pleas continue after he's employed at the Stamp Office, Jean has her first suspicions about Bobbie's secret life.

Four years after Jamie's departure, the rooms at 24 Mill Hole Brae echo with her children's absence. Willie packed his satchel for London to join a ship as the captain's clerk. Betty married and moved to Berwick-on-Tweed where her husband's regiment is stationed.

Jean questions if she was mistaken in not encouraging the advances of a couple of well-to-do gentlemen. But at the time she couldn't conceive of another man controlling her and her children, or imagine sharing a bed and all that would entail. She's had enough of birthing, enough of burying.

The voyage to India takes six to nine months. In her mind, Jean follows Willie drifting over the vast Atlantic, rounding the Horn of Africa, sailing up the Indian Ocean to a country she has trouble picturing—a land shaped like a teardrop, shimmering with heat and drenched with monsoons. Willie had assured her the ship was renowned for its seaworthiness, and its captain had the highest reputation. But she's heard the stories: raging seas and ships getting lost, never heard of again. Passengers sickening and dying, their bodies tossed into the brine. In her dreams, ships heave and rock on endless, churning waves, white sails ballooning, thick ropes creaking, timber masts cracking, ships and men being swallowed by the ocean.

Eighteen months later, she holds a smudged, wrinkled envelope stamped with so many postmarks she can hardly read the address. As her fingers trace Willie's sprawling script, Jean can feel him on the page, his excitement as he describes the strings that were pulled to gain him a cadetship in the Madras Army, then a posting to an infantry regiment of the East India Company. *Just like Tyta*, he writes. *I'm twenty-one and five foot nine, and now I be a sodger: Second-Lieutenant William Burns.*

A few years later Jamie, sixteen years old, follows in his brother's wake. Granted a commission in the Bengal Regiment of the East India Company, he boards the *Lord Castlereagh* and sails to Calcutta. Though the great oceans swallow neither of Jean's sons, they are devoured by the country itself. They rise in their military careers and distinguish themselves as officers: Colonel William Nicol Burns and Lieutenant-Colonel James Glencairn Burns. Jean knows their wives, Catherine and Sarah—and their children, Jean and Robert—only as names in letters, two-dimensional cutouts that hardly seem real.

"Maus-o-leum." John Syme repeats the word slowly as he tells Jean about plans to erect a memorial for Rab's gravesite. On this November day, gloomy with leaden clouds, they're standing in the kirkyard beside the sandstone slab carved with *Burns*. Sodden brown leaves blanket the grave, and the earth smells of damp decay.

"It'll be a stately, magnificent monument," John explains, pulling a diagram from his pocket. "Donations are pouring in from peasants and royalty alike. Even Sir Walter Scott is behind the campaign."

Jean examines the sketch of a small circular building with pillars and a rounded top. She's never seen such a memorial in any kirkyard. "It would never fit in this plot," she says.

John rubs his hand against his pointed chin. "It would have to be built on the other side of the kirk, in the far corner. Come, I'll show you." He takes her arm, but Jean digs her boot heels into the soggy ground.

The wind comes up, scattering the leaves, and light rain drizzles over the brown headstone. Jean pulls her shawl up to cover her hair. "It wouldn't be over his grave?"

John lowers his head, and the breeze catches the strands of grey barely concealing his balding crown. He leans on his cane, and his jowls quiver. "Rab's coffin would have to be moved, and your boys' as well. To a new grave, a tomb large enough for the whole family."

"Dig up their graves and move their bodies?"

"Ay."

Jean shakes her head. "Nae, you'll not be disturbing my dead."

He pauses, wiping his rheumy eyes. "Rab belongs to all of Scotland. He did as much for this country as Wallace or Bruce. He saved Scottish literature." He speaks with such feeling that Jean sees it's not only the rain wetting his cheeks.

"Rab wouldn't want such a showy memorial," she says. "*A man's a man for a' that, their tinsel show and a' that.*"

"Robert Burns needs a monument fitting of his stature," John says, jabbing his cane into the stubble with each word. "When William Wordsworth and his sister came to pay homage to Scotland's bard, they couldn't even find the grave. And every year more visitors are flocking here to see it."

Jean nods. Her fifty-year-old joints stiff with rheumatism, she has grown weary of traipsing to the door and putting on a smiling face.

As if reading her mind, John adds, "People would stop pestering you so much."

They tramp across the wet ground, navigating through the headstones, and around the stone church to the far southeast corner of the kirkyard. They stand for a long time surveying the wide, grassy plot. Shivering in the wind and rain, Jean stares at a gnarled hawthorn in the centre, its naked limbs reaching up into the sullen sky.

Two years later, a moonless September night in 1815, Jean sits on the edge of her settee. Clockie Broon chimes twelve times. In the candlelight, she cannot see his face above the mantle, just a gleam from the gilt of the frame. "Rab, you may have been mine," she whispers, "but Robert Burns now belongs to something much larger." She can almost feel the vibrations disturbing the kirkyard: spades gouging into the earth, striking wood; mounds of dirt slithering with stones; the prying and wrenching out of coffins, Rab's and Frankie's hoisted onto men's shoulders, Max's small one cradled in someone's arms. She imagines the lantern-lit procession glowing across the grey mist of the kirkyard and stopping at a white marble vault.

Shuddering, she tightens her red plaid around her chest; though moth-eaten and threadbare, her wedding shawl still warms her like Rab's arms. Then, drowning out the clamour in her head of digging and heaving and trudging, comes his reassuring chuckle: *Dinna fash yourself o'er a pile o' bones, Jean. Here or there, we are with you always.*

*   *   *

Its white dome stark against the fading blue of the sky, the Burns mausoleum dominates the cemetery, towering above the morass of headstones surrounding it. The octagonal structure, with carved pillars and a cupola roof, resembles a mini-temple from ancient Greece and looks completely out of place in this Scottish kirkyard. Inside the wrought-iron railing, a white marble mural shows Burns at his plow gazing up at a hovering female figure, Coila, spreading her mantle of inspiration.

I scan the words carved into the red sandstone beneath the mural: *In memory of Robert Burns, James Maxwell Burns, Francis Wallace Burns...* along with dates of birth and death. The next lines startle me:

Also the Remains of
JEAN ARMOUR
Relict of the Poet
born Feb 1765
died 26 March 1834

I knew Jean was buried here, but she's still so alive in my mind, I'm not ready for this premature ending. Her story is not over yet.

I find a seat on a low, tabular tombstone. The inscribed name no longer discernible, I don't know whose skeleton I'm sitting over. But I imagine the bones and dust of Jean Armour buried so close to me, and reflect on what she has yet to tell me about the last eighteen years of her life. Behind the white dome, the setting sun spreads a trail of pink and mauve banners across the sky. *The gloamin' comin' down*, her voice lilts inside my head.

Her husband's grave is no longer an intimate place for communing, but a very public site of pilgrimage. Would she feel as if her own grave has been dug and is waiting for her? Does old age stretch before her like an ever darkening plain? During this period, Jean wrote in a letter that her "heart is filled with the fever for want of seeing [her children]." And she would have lived with the disappointment of not knowing her grandchildren, except through the letters she tucks into the drawers of Rab's desk. A few years ago, she thrilled at meeting her first grandchild—Betty's little black-haired Robert—when Betty's family was on route to a new home in Glasgow. In his occasional letters, Bobbie promises he'll soon bring his daughter Elizabeth home to visit. But he's never come. Jean often sends little gifts and encloses money in her letters—*to buy something special for the wee one.*

Jamie's long letters are her sustenance. She reads them over and over again. He now has a daughter and a son—Jean and Robert. *Wee Jeanie, like her gran, loves to sing and toddles about the house trilling, "Green grow the rushes, O."* He also relays the latest news about Willie, too active in military campaigns to write his mother or yet find a wife. Though oceans rise between them, she feels closest to Jamie. While Bobbie, only a hundred miles south in London, seems furthest away. Jean reassures herself that he's fine—he has a family to care for, to keep him steady—until that bleak November day in 1820.

The first skiff of snow dusts the streets, and a bitter wind tears the remaining leaves from the trees. The cold has settled into Jean's bones, and she asks her maid-servant to heat some water and fill the bathing tub. A hot soak is what she needs to soothe her aching joints.

Immersed in the steaming water, she watches the vapour rise and fog up the scullery windows, remembering Rab soaking his rheumatic legs in this rusting iron tub, a gift from Mrs. Dunlop. The dear lady died a few years ago at age eighty-five.

Her eldest daughter now lives in Dumfries, and Jean dines with her every Sunday after the service at St. Michael's, sipping their tea and reflecting on the remarkable friendship forged in letters between a young poet and an elderly woman. What pleasure did Rab take in breaking the red seal of Mrs. Dunlop's envelopes, she told Agnes. All those letters and all his papers, never returned, sucked up in some unknown vortex, she reflects as her fingers swirl the water into whirlpools.

A knock on the front door, then Mary calls from the kitchen, "A letter for you Mrs. Burns. Should I bring it in?"

Cheered by the expectation of news from one of her children, Jean dries her hands and examines the envelope. She recognizes the small script to be that of her youngest brother, now a merchant in London. It's been ages since she's seen or heard from Robbie. Their parents died a decade ago, so they seldom return to Mauchline. Even Jean's yearly visits to her daughters' graves have waned since her legs and feet complain with any exertion.

The opening lines burn into her eyes. Robbie regrets to inform her, but feels he must let his sister know about an article in the *London Times: Robert Burns, Jr. imprudently engaged in speculations which have brought him into embarrassed circumstances ... unpaid debts of 200 pounds ... creditors clamouring ... in danger of being imprisoned ... losing his position at the Stamp Office.*

Her heart pounds against her ribs. Unable to speak, she does not call on Mary, but bears down with her arms and pushes herself up and out of the tub. Her thoughts churn with questions as she dries her flabby pink skin; the same ones that have always consumed her when her children's lives have been threatened: *What can I do? How can I save him?*

Wrapped in her red plaid, she slumps in the armchair by the hearth. The fire spits and hisses. She wonders if Bobbie, at thirty-three, still has his father's good looks, those dark eyes that still flicker with life in Rab's portrait. Seventeen years since Jean has seen her firstborn, too ashamed to write and ask his mother for help. She's living comfortably enough. Jamie has provided her with an annuity of 150 pounds a year since his promotion to captain. But she has little by way of savings. The half-smile on Rab's face speaks to her: *I'll take care of you, Jean.* And what needs to be done gradually becomes clear. She lumbers up the stairs to Rab's desk and pulls a sheet of paper from the top drawer. *Old stumpie* dips into the inkpot and scratches the words across the page.

Sitting across from her on the settee, Gilbert looks like a prosperous gentleman, his silver-grey hair glinting in the late afternoon sun. Dressed in a brown tweed topcoat and fine leather boots, he's still trim at sixty years old. Only his stooping shoulders reveal his years as a poor tenant farmer. Those years are long past. Now the estate manager for Lady Balantyre of East Lothian, Gilbert is controlling accounts instead of a plow. All eleven of their children married, he and his wife live in a fine home at Grant's Braes.

"Now Mammie's gone too," he says, removing his wire-rimmed glasses and wiping them with his handkerchief, "and poor Bess before her."

"Ay, a sad story," Jean says, picturing seven young bairns left motherless when Bess died in childbirth a few years ago. "But your mother, she had a good long life," Jean says, pouring tea into his cup.

"Eighty-eight years, more than enough," he chuckles.

"A pity she didn't get to see the new books," Jean says, eyeing the leather-bound volumes stacked on the table, the revised edition of *The Works of Robert Burns* that Gilbert was commissioned to produce, published a month after his mother died.

"Just as well," he says, stirring his tea briskly. "Tis not the work it should have been."

Jean nods. He took on the project to correct the slanders Currie had heaped upon Rab's character. Gilbert added some letters, wrote a few comments about his brother's habits and inserted some favourable testimonies from Rab's bosses at the Excise. But the timid rebuttal did little to restore his brother's reputation.

"They took out everything. Anything that spoke against what Currie had written." Head bowed, Gilbert cannot look at Jean, nor up at his brother's portrait. "My hands were tied."

"At least they paid you well for your efforts?"

He glances up, and Jean can see in the movement of his brown eyes that he's realizing why she asked him to come.

As she explains about Bobbie's circumstances, Gilbert's eyes narrow. He rises and begins pacing in front of the hearth. "What happened? The lad showed all the promise of…"

"Ay, too heavy a name to carry."

"I've a notion of that weight," Gilbert sighs. "The inevitable comparison… the inevitable disappointment."

"My other lads escaped it. I lament the oceans between us, but they're better off." Her lips turn up slightly as she says, "You're lucky to have your bairns and granbairns close by."

Seconds of silence pass as Gilbert's eyes linger on the four books. In all the years since Rab's funeral, they've never talked about the 200 pounds Rab had loaned Gilbert to rescue the Mossgiel farm. "The 250 pounds those books earned me couldn't be put to better use," he says.

As Gilbert shakes her hand, Jean notices he's standing taller than when he walked in the door; his shoulders not so hunched, as if a burden has been lifted. His eyes settle on his brother's face, and he nods with a slight smile.

For the next couple of years, Jean's life flows on in its established course. She plays hostess to an endless stream of Burns enthusiasts—writers, scholars, aristocrats and common folk like her—answering their prying questions with as much patience and good humour as she can muster. It's a more public life than she'd like, always having to be mindful of her appearance and her housekeeping. She lives for news from her children, and worries—especially about Bobbie now that he's living apart from his wife and daughter.

At fifty-seven, Jean doesn't expect any more surprises will appear around the next bend in the river; she'll drift into old age with her maid-servant Mary and her aching joints as her constant companions. Then another one of those letters arrives, the kind that marks a turning point in your life: before and after a day in June of 1822.

Jamie's handwriting on the envelope sets her heart galloping. His third child was expected nine months ago. Jean is desperate to know if his wife has been safely delivered, and whether it's a grandson or granddaughter she's longing to cuddle. Ripping open the envelope at the door, she cries out as the words strike her eyes: *On Nov. 2 Sarah died giving birth to a daughter. A month later, Robert, eighteen months, succumbed to scarlet fever.* Their ayah is caring for three-year-old Jean and the new baby, Sarah Elizabeth. *Mammie,* Jamie writes, *I wish you were here.*

Jean's arms ache with the anguish of not being there to hold and comfort her son. That night she tosses sleepless in her bed, brooding over her motherless granddaughters. When she finally realizes what she must do, sleep pulls her under like a wave.

In the sailing months of autumn and winter, the letter won't reach Jamie for six or seven months at the earliest, and it will take that long again before a response arrives. She waits while the oceans roar between them.

May Day, 1823. Jean cranks open the parlour window to touch the golden heads of the first primroses poking through the soil in her flower boxes. A faint peeping comes from the eaves above, a nest of baby swallows. The scent of greening grass, the sun warming her face, she absorbs the resurgence of spring. The flounder are running again in the Solway Firth, and Mary has gone to the market for the catch of the day. Jean is heading to the kitchen to peel potatoes for chowder when a rapping sounds on the door. It's almost noon, the usual time for the post. She hurries back to answer it.

Jean lifts a hand to her brow to block the glare of the sun and discern what seems like a vision on her front step. A young woman, face brown as milky tea, clutches a grip in one hand; in her other arm, she carries a child, a wee lass, tendrils of dark curls ringing her bonnet. The years fall away. "Jeanie?"

The woman shakes her head and wipes a tear from her cheek. Then, smiling at the child, she says, "This is her sister Sarah, and I'm her ayah." She speaks with an accent, somewhat English but more musical.

"Sarah?" Jean says. The child's wide brown eyes stare intently from her sallow face as she sucks hard on her thumb.

"You are Mrs. Burns, Captain James Burns's mother?"

Jean nods, and it hits her like thunder clapping in her heart—*Sarah. Jamie's baby Sarah.*

"I've a letter for you." The ayah sighs, setting down her case and shifting the child to her other arm. "We've had a long, long journey."

"To be sure," Jean says. "Come in."

The woman bends to pick up the grip. "Please… let me…" Jean says, opening her arms. "Come to your gran," she whispers and slings the child onto her hip in the old familiar way. Sarah begins to whimper, turning to her ayah, and Jean begins to sing: *Baloo, baloo my wee wee thing, For thou are doubly dear to me.* And they cross the threshold, awash in the light of the noonday sun.

*   *   *

July 1831. She wakes to the first twittering of sparrows. The chimes from old Clockie Broon drift up from the spence. Only six, and already the room is warm and dappled with sunlight. She'll not be returning to sleep. Today is the day. A small smile comes to her lips as she looks over at the child snuggled beside her. Most mornings Jean opens her eyes to this tangle of dark brown curls on the pillow, Sarah having slipped into bed with her sometime during the night. And every morning Jean marvels at this gift that washed up around the last bend in the river eight years ago.

After she stepped into her parlour that day with her eighteen-month-old granddaughter, pale and sickly in her arms, the ayah told her about Sarah's four-year-old sister who had set out from India with them. She was to deliver Jeanie to her maternal grandparents in England. Six weeks into the voyage, somewhere in the middle of the Indian Ocean, Jeanie took ill. After a week of fever, stomach pains and vomiting, she died. Two days later, her small mahogany coffin was lowered from the cabin window and slowly dropped into the sea.

The ayah stayed on with Jean for a month, helping to nurse Sarah back to good health. Then, once more, Jean's days were filled with tending to the needs of a young child. But such a delight with only one bairn to nurture. Like a rare plant you can pour all your love into and watch it thrive. And such a bright little lass, learning to read even before starting school. She was determined to read her father's letters and her grandfather's verses by herself. Now Sarah reads to Jean every evening from the Bible or her book of fairy tales. She picks out songs from her grandfather's book, and Jean teaches her the tunes. Her favourite—since Jean told her the story about her grandfather's proposal—Sarah sings over and over again, her high sweet voice echoing through the house: *O my luve's like a red, red rose, That's newly sprung in June.*

These past eight years have elapsed like a dream Jean doesn't want to end. But today, she and Sarah are waking to a new day, one they've been anticipating for months. This afternoon a man will walk through the door and fill a void of longing in each of them—the son Jean hasn't seen for twenty years, the father Sarah has yet to know. And with Jamie will come his new wife and baby daughter, the family with whom Sarah will be returning to India.

Jean lifts the quilt and inches to the edge of the bed, trying not to disturb her granddaughter. The lass needs her rest, so excited this past week she's had trouble sleeping. She's been busy sewing little nappies and tying them on her doll, practising to help with her ten-month-old sister, and rehearsing songs to sing for her father.

Jean pours water into the bowl and splashes it over her face. Staring into the glass as the brush smooths her iron-grey hair, she wonders if her son will recognize the old face reflected there—plump and lined with wrinkles, her chin sagging in folds. Only her dark chestnut eyes remain unchanged. At the same time, she wonders about this man who has replaced the gangly sixteen-year-old she kissed goodbye two decades ago, his fuzzy cheeks grazing her lips. Thirty-seven years old now, the same age as Rab when he died.

Jean is rolling out the dough for oatcakes as paper thin as possible, so they'll be crispy, the way Jamie likes them. "Gran, Gran," Sarah calls from the parlour, "they're here." Jean wipes her hands on her apron as her granddaughter bounds into the kitchen dressed in her new gown, pale blue with short puffed sleeves, a blue velvet ribbon tying back her hair.

Jean's heart flutters. Grasping Sarah's hand, she floats to the door.

Jamie is helping his wife down from the carriage and swings around as the front door opens. Jean descends one step and clutches the railing at the sunlit sight of him: tall and broad-chested, dark curly hair closely cropped, wire-rimmed glasses over brown eyes, a dimpled chin, and a smile that lights up his entire face. *Rab.* Then he has Sarah and her both bound up in his big arms, hugging as if he will never let them go.

He turns at the sound of the baby crying. "This is Mary," he says, opening his arm to a beautiful woman with upswept, auburn hair and a ridge of freckles across her nose. "And wee Annie," he says, "nae pleased with the long ride."

"Teething pains," Mary says, smiling and jostling the baby on her hip as she extends her other hand to Jean and Sarah.

"Let me," Jean says, taking her granddaughter into her arms. She meets the dark blue eyes peering from beneath the lace bonnet. "Gran's got just the thing for a lassie's sore gums." Slow-ly mounting the steps, she sings, *Hee and ba-burdie, and hee and ba-lamb; and hee and ba-burdie, My bonnie wee lamb.* Behind her, Jamie and Sarah follow hand in hand.

Many evenings, Jean and Jamie stay up chatting into the wee hours over glasses of port. One balmy August night, they take a couple of chairs out to the back garden, luminous with moon-light and fireflies blinking through the gorse bushes. "How I miss the sweet smell of thistle," Jamie says, taking a long breath. "And the chirping of crickets, the sound of home." Gazing up at the moon, he begins to sing, softly: "*It was upon a Lammas night, When corn rigs are bonie, Beneath the moon's unclouded light…*"

"*Corn rigs, an' barley rigs, An' corn rigs are bonie,*" Jean joins in. "*I'll ne're forget that happy night…*"

"I've been reading Father's works very carefully lately," Jamie says. "Do you ken the several names which are left blank in some of his poems?"

"Ay, some I can tell you," Jean says.

"I really like his letters, even better than his poetry. With what power of expression are they written."

"You may be finding out more than you want to know," Jean laughs.

"Nae," Jamie says. "I feel as if I'm getting to know him. His words have such fire in them. That letter to Mr. Graham? What a noble defence of his conduct. And expressed in all the honest warmth of a Scot."

"He sorely needed all his powers of expression to quell that tempest." Jean shakes her head and smiles, remembering Rab writing to the commissioner of the Excise to justify why he remained seated in the theatre during the singing of the national anthem.

"What would I give to have a fraction of his abilities," Jamie says, looking up into the star-filled sky.

"So much of him lives in you." She's amazed at the same good humour, the grin that lights up a room, the love of poetry and song, the tender heart. "And he would've killed for your manly baritone."

They laugh, then Jamie's face clouds over as he talks about living in the shadow of Robert Burns, which casts itself across oceans and continents. "I'm honoured to sing his songs for some occasions," Jamie says, "always *Auld Lang Syne* for Hogmanay. But the jokes and snide remarks…" He shakes his head. "I've had to raise my fists more than once. Damn arrogant English blokes. I can't imagine what Bobbie endures." Jamie had visited his brother after disembarking in England. He'd met Bobbie's new family, his common-law wife and three young children, living in a small London flat. "He's still the same gentle soul," Jamie says. "But weighed down with money problems. And sad about never coming home to see you. Too many memories of Tyta here, he said, too many reminders of how he's failed him."

As the gloaming greys the sky, the smell of woodsmoke drifts in from the St. John's Day bonfires lighting up the braes. On this sultry June evening, Jean sits in her shift by the open parlour window, a light breeze cooling her clammy skin. The house feels eerily quiet, only the sound of Clockie Broon ticking on the mantle. Jamie and his family are away for a week. An invitation arrived from Sir Walter Scott to visit him at Abbotsford House, his country estate on the River Tweed. Jean declined; the seventy-mile carriage ride over the rough country roads would torment her stiff, arthritic hips. She was glad Sarah would have this time alone with her family, and gradually grow accustomed to a new mother. And Jean could grow accustomed to the sound of silence again. These past months the walls have been ringing with laughter and singing and a baby's squealing cries. A week after their return, they'll be setting out for Liverpool to board the ship for India.

"Ah, Rab," Jean sighs, putting on her glasses to peer at his candlelit face above the mantle. Then she smiles as her eyes move to the picture hanging beside it. For years, she had resisted sitting for her portrait. Then last year she relented—on one condition. Within the elegant gilt frame, Sarah stands by her side, a slender arm around Jean's shoulders. Now she can forever gaze at her granddaughter's sweet, elfin face. *Tho'twere ten thousand mile.*

Jean surveys the folded gowns and petticoats piled on Sarah's bed. The small trunk is half-full already, and so much left to pack. "Don't forget about your books in the press downstairs," she says. "You'll soon be reading *Mother Goose* to Annie."

Standing at the window, staring out at the red glow of the setting sun, Sarah does not respond. She's not been herself these past few days—more subdued and serious. As they all have been—the dark cloud of their impending goodbye looming over the household. Only little Annie gurgles and babbles with her usual delight at every flower that blooms. *The present only toucheth thee,* Jean thought as her granddaughter toddled around the back garden today. *An forward tho' I canna see, I guess an fear.*

Sarah turns, tears dribbling down her cheeks. "Gran," she cries, "I want to stay with you."

Climbing up on Jean's knee, she wraps her arms around her grandmother's neck, tight as a chain.

Jamie appears in the doorway, a stack of nappies in his arms. "Wondered if these would fit in your trunk, Sarah." She lifts her red-mottled face towards him. "What is it lass?" he says, dropping down onto the bed beside them.

"Tyta, I do want to go with you," she sobs, "but I need to stay with Gran. Maybe I could come when I'm bigger."

Jean watches her son's face collapse as if the air has been knocked out of him. "I'll leave the two of you to talk," she says, squeezing his hand.

Early the next morning, Jean stands on the bottom step in the misty rain. The last thing she can see down the foggy street is the rope-bound trunk jutting out of the boot of the carriage. It rumbles down the cobbles and rounds the corner, the clip-clop of hooves growing fainter and fainter. The sharp pangs in her heart course through her body, numbing her arms and legs, blurring her vision. A small, warm hand clutches her cold fingers and leads her up the stairs. A soothing voice says, "Come Gran, I'll make us a nice dish of tea."

Epilogue

May 21, 2013

THE TRAIN SPEEDS FORWARD, GLIDING WITH A WHISPER along the steel rails. An eternally pastoral landscape slides by the window. Black-face sheep and frisking lambs speckle the hill-sides, vibrant green with the spring rains and crisscrossed with stone dykes. Small towns slip by—Sanquahar... Kirconnel... New Cummnock... timeless with their narrow streets, soot-stained buildings and ancient stone kirks. I sit facing backward, moving forward in time and space while looking back on the last years of Jean's life.

The year after Jamie left, Jean suffered a series of minor strokes. Sarah cared for her grandmother during the last year of her life after a severe stroke paralyzed her right side and left her unable to walk. Jean could no longer speak nor hear on that March night in 1834, a month after her sixty-ninth birthday. But in the candlelight, her milky eyes could see her grand-daughter sitting at her bedside and a portly man with silver grey curls, Bobbie, holding her hand as the flame sputtered and died.

The green braes morph into the rolling fairways of a golf course. *Next stop Kilmarnock* lights up the overhead sign: the city where it all began for Robert Burns with the publication of his first book. It's now a busy commercial centre; old stone buildings and churches vie for space with grey blocks of high rises. Burns—tone-deaf according to his first teacher—may never have produced his immense collection of songs without Jean, a natural soprano and the stabilizing force in the poet's turbulent existence. Not merely a background detail in the tableau of Robert Burns's life, Jean stands in the forefront—a strong, resilient woman, inspiring in her own right.

The sun beams in, heating up the car. A passenger across the aisle pulls down the window; a warm wind brushes my face as I think about my own poet, wondering where he is and how the years have changed him. The concrete towers of Glasgow loom in the distant blue skyline. The train slows to a crawl as it approaches Central Station. We move through a dark tunnel then into the light of today.

Acknowledgements

Should Auld Acquaintance is informed by the many biographies on Robert Burns as well as Burns's letters, poems and songs. As literary non-fiction, the book is based on a framework of facts about the lives of Jean Armour and Robert Burns. A key fact is missing about the cause of the death of their first daughter, Jeanie. In a letter, Burns alludes to her death as "careless, murdering mischance." So in this instance, I have followed the advice of Petrarch: "If true facts are lacking, add imaginary ones. Invention in the service of the truth is not lying."

I wish to thank Okanagan College for granting me financial assistance and release time to work on this book, as well as college librarians Eva Engman and Claudia Valencia-Dobson for their assistance with research sources.

I am grateful to Camilla Gibb, my mentor at the Humber School of Creative Writing, for her insightful commentary and encouragement; to Amber McMillan at Nightwood Editions for her enthusiasm about the book; to my editor Silas White for his close scrutiny of the manuscript and sound editorial suggestions; to Francie Greenslade and Alix Hawley for their writerly advice and support; to Terry Kilshaw for helping with Scottish terms and dialect; and to Mary Ellen Holland for her steadfast encouragement during the many years I've worked on the project.

Many thanks to my niece Mica Francis for relating her experiences of being pregnant with twins as well as birthing and caring for them; to my Burns Night group for being appreciative listeners to the first readings from the manuscript; and to my son Damian for chauffeuring me to Mauchline where it all began.

In the book I quote from Ethel Wilson, *Swamp Angel* (McClelland and Stewart, 1962); Leonard Cohen, *The Spice Box of Earth* (McClelland and Stewart, 1961); and Dōgen Zenji, quoted in Ruth Ozeki, *A Tale for the Time Being* (Penguin, 2013).

About the Author

Melanie Murray is a professor of literature, composition and creative writing at Okanagan College in Kelowna, BC. She holds a BA, BEd and MA in English, and a Graduate Certificate in Creative Writing. Her previous book *For Your Tomorrow: The Way of an Unlikely Soldier* was published by Random House in 2011.

PHOTO CREDIT: DAVID GRIFFIN WHYTE

7/ח